HEALTHY FOOD

KETO SLOW COOKER COOKBOOK

COOKBOOK

500+ EASY LOW-CARB RECIPES FOR BUSY OR
LAZY FOOD LOVERS WHO WANT TO SAVE TIME,
COOK FOOD SLOWLY, AND BURN FAT FAST

CAREN COOPER

The Table of
CONTENTS

Introduction

When it comes to dieting, some cooking methods are more suitable than others, e.g., grilling against frying. However, since Keto cooking is mostly about fats and then protein, you ideally want to try a convenient method that lets you preserve your meals' nutritional goodness and, of course, the necessary fats. And this where slow cooking can come to the rescue. In particular, slow cooking has the following advantages when being on Keto, and you better try this out.

It helps you control what goes inside and specifically the number of sugars and carbs. Since you will be the one choosing the ingredients to add, there will be no more guessing or having to read food labels to add low or zero sugar and carb ingredients like the ones listed earlier. It is perhaps the main benefit of using a slow cooker when on Keto. We have made this easier for you in this guide by outlining the basic nutritional info for each recipe, so you know exactly what goes inside.

It maintains all the fats inside. By now, you have already realized that fats should be your main priority when on Keto. The issue with other cooking methods is that they dissolve and sometimes burn and evaporate the fat, e.g., grilling, which gets rid of the extra fat we need for Keto and makes the fat oxidize, which isn't healthy at all. On the contrary, slow cooking is one of the very few cooking methods that help preserve the ingredients' original fat without oxidation, provided that you don't overcook your meals. It lets you prepare low carb yet fully nutritious liquids and sauces. A Slow Cooker can be used to make excellent chicken, beef, fish, and veggie stock, which are nutrient-dense yet contain little to none carbs - and yes, this is what we are looking for when on Keto. You can use any of these stocks afterward as your base to cook healthy and delicious keto meats or veggie meals without having to add carb-heavy sauces on top to add flavor. Slow Cookers work best with a bit of liquid; this kind of stocks and sauces can become your staples.

Provided you use your slow cooker properly - and we'll attempt to outline all the basic steps and some tips and tricks, there is no reason you shouldn't use your slow cooker when being on Keto.

It will be tough to find people who are not in love with home-cooked food. But with the hectic work schedule of these days, it is extremely hard for a working person to find some time for elaborate cooking. It does not mean working people prefer eating out or depending completely on packaged foods. They, too, want to enjoy the richness of homemade foods, but it is their work schedules that stop them from cherishing their desire.

Culinary innovations have always brought boons for the people who are obsessed with cooking. The slow cooker is one such cooking medium that has been able to solve the trouble of the people who remain busy all day and desire to have homemade foods at the end of the day. It is nothing but a specialized electric cooker that has been designed to cook slowly. Precisely, it is the electronic slow cooker. There are several benefits of cooking with a slow cooker like it is extremely economical, the cooked foods are healthy, and it is super easy to cook on the slow cooker. The separate cooking settings enable us to cook different ingredients with specific precision. Most importantly, it is very easy to cook the Ketogenic recipes in the slow cooker. As the pot cooks slowly, it is easy for working people to dump the ingredients while leaving for work, and when they return home, they can enjoy the bliss of warm homemade dishes.

Chapter 1.
Introduction to the Ketogenic Diet

The Health Benefits of the Keto Diet

The Keto diet allows for an optimal intake of carbohydrates, as well as the optimal use of energy, all of which depend on your way of life. People who are not activated nor have a sedentary job are much better off with a low carb intake. Those that are more active, especially people who are in contact with sports on a daily basis, can add some more carbs to their diet because they will burn it all off in that same day, and so there will be no carbs left over to turn into fats. Regardless of your lifestyle, everyone benefits from the Keto diet in the following ways:

Weight Loss

Far more important than the visual aspect of excess weight is its negative influence on your body. Too much weight affects the efficiency of your body's blood flow, which in turn also affects how much oxygen your heart is able to pump to every part of your system. Too much weight also means that there are layers of fat covering your internal organs, which prevents them from working efficiently. It makes it hard to walk because it puts great pressure on your joints, and makes it very difficult to complete even regular daily tasks. A healthy weight allows your body to move freely, and your entire internal system to work at its optimal levels.

Cognitive Focus

In order for your brain to function at its best, it needs to have balanced levels of all nutrients and molecules, because a balance allows it to focus on other things, such as working, studying, or creativity. If you eat carbs, the sudden insulin spike that comes with them will force your brain to stop whatever it was doing and to turn its focus on the correct breakdown of glucose molecules. This is why people often feel sleepy and with a foggy mind after high-carb meals. The Keto diet keeps the balance strong, so that your brain does not have to deal with any sudden surprises.

Blood Sugar Control

If you already have diabetes, or are prone to it, then controlling your blood sugar is obviously of the utmost importance. However, even if you are not battling a type of diabetes at the moment, that doesn't mean that, you are not in danger of developing it in the future. Most people forget that insulin is a finite resource in your body. You are given a certain amount of it, and it is gradually used up throughout your life. The more often you eat carbs, the more often your body needs to use insulin to break down the glucose; and when it reaches critically low levels of this finite resource, diabetes is formed.

Lower Cholesterol and Blood Pressure

Cholesterol and triglyceride levels maintain, or ruin, your arterial health. If your arteries are clogged up with cholesterol, they cannot efficiently transfer blood through your system, which in some cases even results in heart attacks. The Keto diet keeps all of these levels at an optimal level, so that they do not interfere with your body's normal functioning.

Low-Carb Food

Carbs, or rather the lack of them, is the main point of the Keto diet. In order to explain the Keto phenomenon correctly, we will need to rely on a bit of science to do so.

Your body has a few different sources of energy for its everyday tasks, and especially for periods when you place it under high intensity, such as training, stress, or hard work (both physical and mental). By default, your body uses Glucose as its main energy source because it is the easiest molecule to break down for fuel. Acting as an assistant, your body also releases Insulin, which carries the Glucose around the body via your bloodstream. All of us are born with this default setting. The problem with this setting, however, is that most of us don't use up all of the carbs that we would take in through a modern diet, which means that your body never has the need to switch to its alternative source of energy - fats.

Now here's the catch:

Unused carbs turn into fat. Unused fat stays as fat. Eventually, more and fatter piles up around your muscles and your organs, causing weight gain and, in many cases, obesity and a number of illnesses that go with it.

However, if you drastically reduce your daily carb intake, your body burns up glucose very quickly, and then needs an additional energy source in order to continue with the rest of your daily tasks. Because it's out of carbs, it now turns to your fat storage, using it to produce ketones in the liver. A process that is known as ketosis, and is also where the Keto diet gets its name.

How quickly your body turns to ketosis depends on the carb levels that are currently in your system. In general, your body will switch to ketosis in a period of 2 to 3 days, which means that you do not have to wait long for the positive effects of the Keto diet to take effect. How much you should reduce your daily carb intake depends on your age, weight, and current health. Anything below 50gr of carbs per day will eventually lead to ketosis, but those who are healthy enough to speed up the process usually drop their daily carb intake to about 20gr.

Please note carbs that come from healthy, whole food sources are not destructive for your being. However, our unhealthy way of life simply means that most of us take in way more carbs per day than we burn off, usually between 150 and 250 gr. unless you're an Olympic athlete, you do not need that much carb energy!

Chapter 2.
The Ketogenic Kitchen

Your kitchen will now become ketogenic, so that means stocking up on all the great foods that will usher your body into ketosis. Your kitchen will also have a slow cooker, which is your new best friend on this new eating journey.

What to Stock

When you go grocery-shopping, you always want your cart full of proteins, vegetables, good fats, baking supplies (if you're out), full-fat dairy, and some fruit, nuts, and seeds. Here's a list of what should always be in your kitchen:

Proteins
- Ground grass-fed beef
- Organic chicken
- Ground turkey
- Frozen fish fillets
- Canned tuna
- Bone broth

Oils
- Olive oil (cold-pressed)
- High-quality coconut oil

Dairy
- Grass-fed butter
- Heavy cream
- Plain, whole-milk Greek yogurt
- A hard cheese (in block form)
- A soft cheese

Non-dairy
- Unsweetened almond milk (or your favorite nut milk)
- Full-fat coconut milk
- Coconut cream

Fruit
- Blueberries (fresh or frozen)
- Raspberries (fresh or frozen)
- Strawberries (fresh or frozen)
- Avocados

Vegetables
(If you don't like a certain vegetable, just get more of your favorites)
- Dark leafy greens (Swiss chard, kale, and/or spinach)
- Cauliflower
- Celery
- Zucchini
- Cucumbers
- Bell peppers
- Tomatoes
- Garlic
- Onions

Nuts + seeds
- Whole almonds (unsalted)
- Pecans
- Macadamia nuts or Brazil nuts
- Chia seeds
- Unsweetened almond nut butter

Flours
- Coconut flour
- Almond flour
- Flax Meal

Baking supplies
- Aluminum-free baking powder
- Unsweetened dark cocoa powder
- Rodelle pure vanilla extract
- Sukrin Gold (brown sugar substitute)
- Stevia + erythritol (or blend of both)
- Dark baking chocolate
- Cacao nibs or sugar-free chocolate chips
- Unsweetened shredded coconut

Cooking supplies
- Dry herbs
- Spices
- Homemade ketchup
- Homemade yellow mustard

Why Use a Slow Cooker

The slow cooker is defined by its convenience, which is very important when you're changing your diet. There are three other reasons why the slow cooker can help you transition successfully into ketosis, and stay there:

It breaks down even tough meat

The ketogenic diet has you eating a lot of meat, which is one of the best ingredients to make in a slow cooker. Even cheap, tough cuts of meat become tender and juicy in a slow cooker, so every meal is tasty.

It makes a lot of food

Leftovers will become very important on the ketogenic diet, because you don't want to have to make separate meals all the time. The slow cooker was designed to cook a lot of food at once, so you can make big recipes or double batches for dinner and tomorrow's lunch.

It's versatile

As you'll see in the recipes, the slow cooker can make just about everything. That simplifies the whole "healthy cooking" process, and just makes life way easier. You're a busy person with deadlines and commitments, and you don't want to have to use a bunch of different devices to cook different meals. With the slow cooker, you can make everything from eggs to cakes.

A slow cooker belongs in every ketogenic kitchen. Keep reading, and you'll find 100 recipes all written for the slow cooker and all Keto-compliant!

What to Eat On the Ketogenic Diet

If you're worried that you won't get to eat anything on the ketogenic diet, you'll be happy to learn that there are lots of options. Here is a list of the proteins, veggies, fruit, dairy, nuts, seeds, fats, oils, and beverages you'll be able to have:
Proteins

Eggs - Free-range and organic is best.

Fish - Wild-caught and sustainable salmon, halibut, cod, mahi-mahi, tuna, trout, etc. The fattier the fish, the better.

Shellfish - Clams, crab, scallops, lobster, etc.

Beef - Grass-fed steak roasts, stew, and ground beef.

Pork - Ground, pork loin, pork chops, ham, tenderloin, bacon, etc. Be careful of meat with additives.

Poultry - Free-range chicken, duck, turkey, etc.

Organ meat - Heart, kidney, tongue, liver.

Other - Lamb, veal, goat. Lamb is fatty, so it's especially good.

Nut butters - Unsweetened, all-natural almond and macadamia nut butter.

Veggies

Dark and leafy veggies are best, and if it grows above the ground, it's good for the ketogenic diet. You want to buy organic if you can, but any veggie is still better than no veggies at all. Avoid starchy vegetables like peas, corn, beans, yams, squash, and potatoes.

Cauliflower
Spinach
Kale
Lettuce
Cucumber
Celery
Swiss chard
Zucchini
Broccoli
Cabbage
Garlic
Radishes
Sea vegetables
Tomatoes - In moderation
Onion - In moderation
Bell peppers - In moderation

Fruit
Most fruit is high in sugar, so it should be eaten infrequently. You will notice some fruit in the recipes, but only in small amounts.

Avocado - High in fat

Berries - Raspberries, blackberries, blueberries, strawberries, cranberries

Peaches -Best if rarely eaten

Citrus fruit - Lemon, lime, orange

Cherries - Best if rarely eaten

Watermelon - Best if rarely eaten
Dairy

Dairy is one of the best sources of fat on the ketogenic diet, so always go with full-fat. Go with high-quality brands and avoid packaged shreds, which have potato starch. You also can't have cow's milk, because of the sugar content.

Cheddar cheese
Bleu cheese
Mozzarella cheese
Parmesancheese
Swiss cheese
Ricotta cheese
Greek yogurt
Heavy whipping cream
Coconut cream
Cottage cheese

Cream cheese
Mascarpone cheese
Unsweetened coconut milk
Unsweetened macadamia nut milk
Unsweetened almond milk - Watch out for carrageenan

Nuts + seeds
Choose your type of nuts carefully and always eat in moderation. Legumes are too high in carbs, so no peanuts. Cashews and pistachios are also pretty high in carbs, so avoid them.
Almonds - In moderation
Sunflower seeds - In moderation
Pecans - One of the best ketogenic nuts
Macadamia nuts - One of the best ketogenic nuts
Brazil nuts - One of the best ketogenic nuts
Pumpkin seeds
Flax seeds
Chia seeds
Cooking oils + fat
Both saturated and monounsaturated fats belong on a ketogenic diet. Refined fats, Tran's fats, and oils are not good for you, and can even damage your cells.
Coconut oil - Saturated
Grass-fed butter - Saturated
Duck fat - Saturated
Ghee - Saturated
Cocoa butter - Saturated
Coconut butter - Saturated
Olive oil - Cold-pressed is best
Avocado oil - Monounsaturated
Almond oil - Monounsaturated
Avocado - Monounsaturated
Beverages
Pick your beverages carefully, and always get unsweetened tea and nut milks. Sodas and fruit juices are off-limits. So are diet sodas and energy drinks.
Water
Sparkling water + seltzers
Unsweetened coconut water
Nut milks - Unsweetened
Wine - In moderation
Light beer - In moderation
Hard liquors - In moderation
Black coffee
Herbal tea

Sweeteners + baking supplies

All traditional sweeteners and flours are not allowed on the ketogenic diet. This means white sugar, brown sugar, agave, honey, maple syrup, and all grain-based flour. Instead, you'll be choosing pure, natural sweeteners with zero calories. Getting blends can help with the bitter aftertaste that's common.

Almond flour

Coconut flour - Absorbs more liquid than other flours, shouldn't be used interchangeably with almond flour

Psyllium husk - 100% fiber used as a thickener

Dark + natural cocoa powder

Unsweetened coconut flakes - If you're a vegetarian, you can even get coconut bacon, which are basically savory coconut flakes made to replicate pork bacon

Aluminum-free baking powder and soda

Stevia - Comes in liquid and granulated form

Monk fruit - 300x sweeter than sugar with no aftertaste

Erythritol - Used in stevia blends

What You Cannot Eat On the Ketogenic Diet

If you stick to what you can eat, you shouldn't have a problem. However, you should still know what's not allowed on the diet. Here's what you should cut out completely:

Processed meats - Hot dogs, packaged sausages, grain-fed meats, etc.

Starchy veggies - Sweet potatoes, corn, butternut squash, acorn squash, artichokes, potatoes, yams

Most fruits - Bananas, apples, oranges, grapes, mangos, smoothies, fruit syrups, dried fruit

Milk + dairy marked "low fat" - Cow's milk, butter substitutes, fat-free yogurts, low-fat cream cheese, skim milk, margarine, etc.

Beans + legumes - Kidney, chickpeas, lentils, black beans, fava beans, white beans, peas, etc.

Inflammatory oils - Soybean, corn, canola, grape seed, sesame, peanut, sunflower

All grains - Wheat, corn, quinoa, buckwheat, oats, barley, rice, etc.

Condiments - Bottled ketchup, bottled mustard, bottled salad dressings

Most alcohol - Cocktails, flavored liqueurs, flavored beers, beer, etc.

Sweeteners - White sugar, maple syrup, agave, raw sugar, cane sugar, corn syrup

Artificial sweeteners - Splenda, equal, saccharin, sucralose, aspartame

Anything processed + packaged - Fast food, baked goods, ice cream, wheat gluten, MSG, "diet" food

Chapter 3.
How to Use the Slow Cooker, Tips and Tricks

Slow cookers have changed a lot over the years. These days you can purchase models that range from very simple models all the way to ones that look like they should be on a space station. When buying the right model for your needs, you have to consider what you are cooking, how many portions, and if you will be home during the cooking process. All these factors are important when deciding on the size, shape, and features of your slow cooker.

Size and Shape

Slow cookers come in a multitude of sizes and shapes, so it is important to consider your needs and what will work best for the type of food prepared on the keto diet. There are models that range from ½-quart to large 8-quart models and everything in-between. The small slow cookers (½-quart to 2-quart) are usually used for dips or sauces, as well as recipes designed for one person. Medium-sized slow cookers (3-quart to 4-quart) are great for baking or for meals that create food for two to three people. The slow cooker recommended for most of the recipes in this book is the 5-quart to 6-quart model because it is perfect for the large cuts of meat on the keto diet and can prepare food for four people, including leftovers. The enormous 7-quart to 8-quart appliance is meant for very large meals. If you have money in your budget, owning both a 3-quart and 6-quart model would be the best of both worlds.
When it comes to shapes, you will have to decide between round, oval, and rectangular. Round slow cookers are fine for stews and chili but do not work well for large pieces of meat. These should probably not be your choice. Oval and rectangular slow cookers both allow for the ingredients you will use regularly that are large, like roasts, ribs, and chops, and have the added advantage of fitting loaf pans, ramekins, and casserole dishes, as well. Some desserts and breads are best cooked in another container placed in the slow cooker, and you will see several recipes in this book that use that technique.

Features

Now that you know the size and shape of the recommended slow cooker, it is time to consider what you want this appliance to do for you. Depending on your budget, at a minimum you want a slow cooker with temperature controls that cover warm, low, and high, as well as a removable insert. These are the primary features of the bare-bones models that will get the job done. However, if you want to truly experience a set-it-and-forget-it appliance that creates the best meals possible in this cooking environment, you might want to consider the following features:

Digital programmable controls: You can program temperature, when the slow cooker starts, how long it cooks, and when the slow cooker switches to warm.
Glass lid: These are heavier and allow you to look into the slow cooker without removing them, so there is little heat loss. Opt for a lid with clamps, and you can transport your cooked meal easily to parties and gatherings if needed.
Temperature probe: Once you have a slow cooker with this feature, you will wonder how you cooked previously without it. The temperature probe allows you to cook your meat, poultry, and egg dishes to an exact temperature and then switches to warm when completed.

Precooking feature: Some models have a precooking feature that allows you to brown your meat and poultry right in the insert. You will still have to take the time to do this step, but you won't have a skillet to clean afterward.

Tips for Slow-Cooking Success

Slow cookers are simple to use, but you can increase your success with a few tips and techniques. In the following list, some tips are suggestions, and some should be considered more seriously for safety or health reasons. The intent is to provide the best information possible so that your meals are delicious and easy.

Always
Read the user manual and any other literature. You will find an assortment of instructions included in the slow-cooker box, so take the time to sit down and read everything completely before using a new device. You might think you know how everything works, but each model is a little different, and it is best to be informed about all of the things your slow cooker can do.

Grease the insert of the slow cooker before cooking. Cleaning a slow cooker insert can be a challenge, so grease the insert, even for soups and stews. You don't want to scrub the insert with abrasive brushes or scraping bits of cooked-on food off, because you will wreck its nonstick surface.

Add dairy and herbs at the end of the cooking process. As stated elsewhere in this book, dairy and fresh herbs do not hold up well during long cooking times. Dairy splits and creates a grainy, unpleasant texture, and herbs lose their flavor, color, and texture. Always add these ingredients at the end.
Always cut your ingredients into similar-sized pieces. Slow cookers are not meant to be used for staggered cooking recipes such as stir-fries, where the more delicate ingredients are added last to avoid overcooking. Evenly sized pieces mean your ingredients will be ready at the same time, and your meals will be cooked evenly.
Adjust your seasonings. Slow cookers can have an unexpected effect on herbs and spices so it is important to taste and adjust at the end of the process. Some spices, such as curry or cayenne, can get more intense, while the long cooking time can reduce the impact of dried herbs. It is best to hold off on too much salt until the very end as well, because it will get stronger.

Never

Use frozen meats or poultry. The ingredients in slow cookers need to reach 140°F within 4 hours for food safety, so large cuts of meat or poultry should be fully thawed. You can add small frozen items like meatballs to a slow cooker because these can come to temperature within this time range.

Place your insert right from the refrigerator into the slow cooker. When you remove your previously prepared meal from the refrigerator, let the insert sit out at room temperature for 30 minutes or so to avoid cracking it with extreme temperature changes. Also, never remove the hot insert from your slow cooker and place it on a cold surface.
Resume cooking after a power outage of over two hours. Power outages can happen in any season, and for food-safety reasons, you have to err on the side of caution. If an outage lasts for more than two hours, especially during the first few hours of the cooking time, you need to discard the food because the amount of time spent in the food danger zone (40°F to 140°F) will have been too long. If the outage is less than two hours and it occurs after your food has been cooking for at least four hours, then you can resume cooking until the end of the original time or transfer the food to a pot or casserole dish and finish it on the stove or in the oven. When in doubt, throw the food out.

Use the recommended cooking times in high altitudes. As with most other cooking methods, slow cookers need more cooking time if you live above an altitude of 3,000 feet. The liquid in the slow cooker will simmer at a lower temperature, so high-heat settings are recommended, or if you can program the slow cooker, then set it to maintain the food at 200°F or higher. You can also use a temperature probe set to 165°F internal temperature if your slow cooker has this feature.

Chapter 4.
Keto Diet & Slow Cooker Basics

In the simplest of terms, a ketogenic diet is a very low-carb, high-fat diet. It isn't a new diet, either. It was created in the 1920s as a treatment for children who had epilepsy. It is still used today, but there has been more investigation to see if it is a breakthrough treatment for several other diseases and neurological disorders. So, this isn't just some weight loss trend.

The main goal is to place the body into ketosis. The body burns carbs as energy. But if the amount of carbs in the body is restricted, the body will start breaking down the fat stored within the body, and this will create what is known as ketones. These ketones are then used as fuel.

Move from the 1920s; researchers started to find that the keto diet provided benefits other than the control of epilepsy. Many wellness professionals, the world over, are embracing the word ketogenic. Many people have started using this diet to control and prevent diabetes and to lose weight.

Many studies have found that the ketogenic diet and other low-carb diets are perfect for losing weight. They tend to work better than a low-fat or reduced-calorie diet. The ketogenic diet is sometimes easier to follow because ketones can work as an appetite suppressant without consuming many carbohydrates; you aren't faced with sugar crashes or cravings for carbs. You eat plenty of fat to keep you feeling full.
What Are the Benefits?

Below are some of the benefits of ketones:

Weight Loss – The body has to burn fat to make ketones. When this happens, natural ketosis is going to cause weight loss. Some studies suggest ketones can help you lose weight while also curbing your appetite.

Diabetes Control – Many low-carb diets, like the keto diet, have been found to do a great job at lowering blood sugar levels and insulin resistance. Some studies have found that BHB ketone can reduce inflammation, which is another way to control diabetes.
Longevity – If you want to stay healthy and live a long life, occasionally fasting can help you do that. Studies have found that restricting carbs can help to lengthen your life expectancy.
Preventing Cancer – Glucose can increase cancer cells. When you don't let them have their favorite food, it can reduce cancer cells and help prevent and treat cancer. Many who are at risk of developing cancer or being treated for cancer will follow a ketogenic diet.
Resilience – Ketone bodies can provide your body with powerful and constant energy. They can also help to preserve your performance and resilience better than glucose ever could.

Brainpower – The ketogenic diet was initially meant to be an epilepsy treatment, but it has been found as a great way to protect the neurons in the brain. It can improve focus, mental energy, and create a sharper mind.

Slow Cooker Basics

Having a slow cooker is an effortless, fast, and most flexible cooking method at any home. It didn't require you any cooking skills; it saves your time as the slow cooker does all the working time for you, truly safe and can even be used in any places like a hotel room or even student dorm as they possess a kettle like-shape, making it more portable than a stove. So, in the following guides, we will be talking some of the helpful basic ways to guarantee that you get the best out of your slow cooker.

What is it?

The slow cooker appeared in 1970 and was marketed as a bean cooker. But as it was modified, people started to use it to heat food and keep it warm for prolonged periods. And look how far we've come; people are cooking delicious healthy meals in it. It is a perfect small kitchen appliance that consists of a glass lid, porcelain, or a ceramic pot (it is inside of the heating unit) and, of course, a heating element. The modern Slow Cooker could be of an oval or round shape and various sizes, from small to large. All the Slow Cookers have two settings: LOW (it corresponds to the temperature of 200°F mostly) and HIGH (up to 300°F). The WARM selection that is among the majority of the slow cookers' options nowadays allows keeping the prepared dishes warm for a long time. Some of the Slow Cooker models have a timer that will enable you to control cooking time if you are busy.

The Cooking Utensils Needed

First of all, you will need a Slow Cooker. Even though most models make a range of good varieties, you need to make sure you chose the slow cooker that meets your requirement.

You need to have a chopping board and at least three knives: a paring knife, a chef's knife, and a cleaver. Combining these knives will make it easy to prepare your foods, from herbs to full fleshed chickens.

You will also need a few bowls. These are important if you are going to be doing any mixing, preparing your ingredients in advance, or if you will need to take out some food from the cock-pot to make room for more ingredients.

You will also need a blender for smooth soups, a pestle and mortar if you want to crush your fresh herbs and spices, and a whisk for mixing eggs and sauces. Although these are not necessities, they will make the cooking process much more manageable if present. But in cases where you will be doing some batch cooking, consider investing in some good quality, resilient Tupperware. That way, you will make a great batch of food in advance and refrigerate them for future use.

If you intend to cook shorter recipes while you are out and about, you will either need a Slow Cooker or a Crockpot with a timer, or a plug adapter with a timer built into it. In as much as the Slow Cooker are safe, it is inadvisable to leave your food on high pressure for eight to ten hours, as not only will it be an irresponsible act, but will most certainly ruin your food. In other words, timers are essential when cooking in absentia.

Required Cooking Skills

Cooking with a Slow Cooker requires absolutely no advanced cooking skills, as long as you can peel and chop vegetables, mix herbs in oil, put things into a pot, turn a dial, then you are most certainly fit to cook with a Slow Cooker.

The Cooking Precautions

Even though Slow Cooker cooking is incredibly safe, it is recommended that you should always be careful:
•   Do not place the slow cooker close to the pot or its wires as this could cause a hazard.
•   Do not leave the house if your slow cooker is on without setting a safe timer.
•   Do not leave the slow cooker exposed within reach of children or animals.
•   Do not leave the slow cooker on with nothing inside it.
•   Do not place the slow cooker on an unstable surface.
•   Do not leave foods in it when cooked and cooled, as this can be dangerous to your health. Always move the cooked foods to a refrigerator or freezer for storage.
•   And always make sure to follow these safety guidelines.
•   Always make sure your slow cooker is clean.
•   Always make sure your slow cooker is turned off when not in use.
•   Always put your crockpot somewhere safe and steady when not in use.
•   Always follow the manufacturer's directions during usage, cleaning, and storage processes.

What Are the Benefits of Using the Slow Cooker?

What is the most difficult thing for you in the kitchen? You waste too much time in the kitchen when you might go to the cinema with friends? Do you spend too much money on products, and your ideas on what to prepare today are running out? The solution to all your problem? It is the Slow Cooker!

Firstly, it is possible to prepare meals when you are not at home. During those hectic family mornings, throw all the ingredients together following the recipe, switch the machine on, and go work.

Secondly, you don't like washing the dishes? Just clean the Slow Cooker and the plates after delicious meals. That's all! Using the Slow Cooker means having fewer dishes to wash.

Thirdly, the Slow Cooker cooks' delicious meals and saves your money!

These meals taste even better than usual, and also you can keep the leftovers in the refrigerator to eat afterward. How perfect are the spice flavors if you eat the dishes right after cooking! You might taste the cayenne pepper, cumin, ginger, and other favorite spices of yours. Buy simple products and follow the cookbook. It is easy!
The fourth benefit, the Slow Cooker, is the best way to keep your meal tender and always warm.

Fifth, the Slow Cooker reduces calories and fat. No oil (just olive or avocado oil), no frying is necessary.

Six is the step by step preparation.

Step by step preparation facilitates everyday cooking, especially for those who are not great fans of this process. In most recipes, all the ingredients are added at one time to the Slow Cooker.

Seven, it is energy saving. It requires less electricity than the regular oven.

The flexibility of the Slow Cooker is benefit number eight. You can take it on a trip, put it on the kitchen table or somewhere else. It doesn't need that much space.

And finally, benefit number nine is in the large quantities of prepared meals. Most of these recipes make large quantities of the end products, so you may feed an entire family and even freeze for tomorrow to make easy and quick lunches or suppers.

So, are you already looking for some recipes to get started? Check the great Keto Slow Cooker cookbook, and you'll find the best and most delicious dishes here! Cooking Keto recipes in the Slow Cooker will help you fit cooking into your daily schedule and stay healthy. After a long working day, you'll be back home, and a delicious meal will be there waiting for you.

Cherry Tomatoes Thyme Asparagus Frittata

NUTRITION Calories: 370, Fat: 29g, Carbs: 4g, Protein: 24g

INGREDIENTS

- 2 tablespoons unsalted butter, ghee, or extra-virgin olive oil
- 12 large eggs
- ¼ cup heavy (whipping) cream
- 1 tablespoon minced fresh thyme
- ½ teaspoon kosher salt
- ¼ teaspoon freshly ground black pepper
- 1½ cups shredded sharp white Cheddar cheese, divided
- ½ cup grated Parmesan cheese
- 16 cherry tomatoes
- 16 asparagus spears

DIRECTION

- Glaze the inside of the slow cooker with the butter.
- In the slow cooker, beat the eggs, then whisk in the heavy cream, thyme, salt, and pepper.
- Add ¾ cup of Cheddar cheese and the Parmesan cheese and stir to mix.
- Sprinkle the remaining ¾ cup of Cheddar cheese over the top. Scatter the cherry tomatoes over the frittata.
- Arrange the asparagus spears decoratively over the top. Cook within 6 hours on low or 3 hours on soaring. Serve.

PREPARATION	COOKING TIME	SERVINGS
15	6 *hours*	6

Healthy Low Carb Walnut Zucchini Bread

NUTRITION Calories: 174 , Fat: 15.4 g , Carb: 5.8 g , Protein: 5.3 g

INGREDIENTS

- 3 eggs
- 1/2 cup walnuts, chopped
- 2 cups zucchini, shredded
- 2 tsp vanilla
- 1/2 cup pure all-purpose sweetener
- 1/3 cup coconut oil, softened
- 1/2 tsp baking soda
- 1 1/2 Tsp baking powder
- 2 tsp cinnamon
- 1/3 cup coconut flour
- 1 cup almond flour
- 1/2 Tsp salt

DIRECTION

- Mix the almond flour, baking powder, cinnamon, baking soda, coconut flour, and salt in a bowl. Set aside.
- Whisk eggs, vanilla, sweetener, and oil in another bowl.
- Put dry batter to the wet and fold well. Add walnut and zucchini and fold well.
- Pour batter into the silicone bread pan. Place the bread pan into the slow cooker on the rack.
- Cook on high within 3 hours. Cut the bread loaf into the slices and serve.

PREPARATION	COOKING TIME	SERVINGS
15	3 *hours* 10 *mins*	12

Low-Carb Hash Brown Breakfast Casserole

NUTRITION Calories: 523, Fat: 40g, Carbs: 7g, Protein: 33g

INGREDIENTS

- 1 tablespoon unsalted butter, Ghee
- 12 large eggs
- ½ cup heavy cream
- 1 teaspoon kosher salt
- ½ teaspoon ground black pepper
- ½ teaspoon ground mustard
- 1 head cauliflower, shredded or minced
- 1 onion, diced
- 10 ounces cooked sausage links, sliced
- 2 cups shredded Cheddar cheese, divided

DIRECTION

- Grease the slow cooker with the butter.
- Beat the eggs, then whisk in heavy cream, 1 teaspoon of salt, ½ teaspoon of pepper, and the ground mustard in a large bowl.
- Spread about one-third of the cauliflower in an even layer in the bottom of the cooker.
- Layer one-third of the onions over the cauliflower, then one-third of the sausage, and top with ½ cup of Cheddar cheese. Season with salt and pepper. Repeat twice.
- Pour the egg batter evenly over the layered Ingredients, then sprinkle the remaining ½ cup Cheddar cheese on top—Cook within 6 hours on low. Serve hot.

PREPARATION	COOKING TIME	SERVINGS
15	6 *mins*	6

Onion Broccoli Cream Cheese Quiche

NUTRITION Calories 296 , Fat 24.3 g , Carb 3.9 g , Protein 16.4 g

INGREDIENTS

- 9 eggs
- 2 cups cheese, shredded and divided
- 8 oz. cream cheese
- 1/4 Tsp onion powder
- 3 cups broccoli, cut into florets
- 1/4 Tsp pepper
- 3/4 Tsp salt

DIRECTION

- Add broccoli into the boiling water and cook for 3 minutes. Drain well and set aside to cool.
- Add eggs, cream cheese, onion powder, pepper, and salt in mixing bowl and beat until well combined.
- Spray slow cooker from inside using cooking spray.
- Add cooked broccoli into the slow cooker then sprinkle half cup cheese.
- Pour egg mixture over broccoli and cheese mixture.
- Cook on high within 2 hours and 15 minutes.
- Once it is done, then sprinkle the remaining cheese and cover for 10 minutes or until cheese melted. Serve.

PREPARATION	COOKING	SERVINGS
15	2 25 *hours mins*	8

Delicious Thyme Sausage Squash

NUTRITION Calories: 502 , Fat: 38g , Carbs: 12g , Protein: 27g

PREPARATION	COOKING TIME	SERVINGS
15	6 hours	4

DIRECTION

- Combine the olive oil, sausage, broth, onion, butternut squash, bell peppers, thyme, salt, and pepper in the slow cooker. Toss to mix. Cook within 6 hours on low.
- Before serving, sprinkle the Swiss cheese over the top, cover, and cook for about 3 minutes more to melt the cheese.

INGREDIENTS

- 2 tablespoons extra-virgin olive oil
- 14 ounces smoked chicken sausage, thinly sliced
- ¼ cup chicken broth
- 1 onion, halved and sliced
- ½ medium butternut squash, peeled, diced
- 1 small green bell pepper, strips
- ½ small red bell pepper, strips
- ½ small yellow bell pepper, strips
- 2 teaspoons snipped fresh thyme or ½ teaspoon dried thyme, crushed
- ½ teaspoon kosher salt
- ½ teaspoon freshly ground black pepper
- 1 cup shredded Swiss cheese

Mexican Style Breakfast Casserole

NUTRITION Calories: 320, Fat: 24.1 g, Carb: 5.2 g, Protein: 17.9 g

PREPARATION	COOKING TIME	SERVINGS
15	1 hours 40 mins	4

DIRECTION

- Coat the slow cooker with cooking spray. Mix the eggs, salt, pepper, plus milk in a bowl.
- Add garlic powder, cumin, coriander, and sausage and mix well.
- Pour the mixture into the slow cooker. Set the slow cooker on 'Low' within 4-5 hours or on 'High' for 2-3 hours. Place toppings of your choice and serve.

INGREDIENTS

- 5 eggs
- 6 ounces pork sausage, cooked, drained
- ½ cup 1% milk
- ½ teaspoon garlic powder
- 2 jalapeños, deseeded, finely chopped
- ½ teaspoon ground cumin
- ½ teaspoon ground coriander
- 1 ½ cups chunky salsa
- 1 ½ cup pepper Jack cheese, shredded
- Salt to taste
- Pepper to taste
- ¼ cup fresh cilantro

Almond Lemon Blueberry Muffins

NUTRITION Calories: 223, Fat: 21g, Carb: 5g, Protein: 6 g

PREPARATION	COOKING TIME	SERVINGS
15	3 *hours*	3

INGREDIENTS

- 1 cup almond flour
- 1 large egg
- 3 drops stevia
- ¼ cup fresh blueberries
- ¼ teaspoon lemon zest, grated
- ¼ teaspoon pure lemon extract
- ½ cup heavy whipping cream
- 2 tablespoons butter, melted
- ½ teaspoon baking powder

DIRECTION

- Whisk the egg into a bowl. Add the rest of the fixing, and mix.
- Pour batter into lined or greased muffin molds. Pour up to ¾ of the cup.
- Pour 6 ounces of water into the slow cooker. Place an aluminum foil at the bottom, and the muffin molds inside.
- Set the slow cooker on 'High' within 2-3 hours. Let it cool in the cooker for a while.
- Remove from the cooker. Loosen the edges of the muffins. Invert on to a plate and serve.

Healthy Veggie Omelet

NUTRITION Calories: 200 , Fat: 13.9 g , Carb: 5.8 g , Protein 13.4 g

PREPARATION	COOKING TIME	SERVINGS
15	1 *hour* 40 *mins*	4

DIRECTION

- Grease the slow cooker from inside using cooking spray.
- Whisk egg whites, eggs, parsley, garlic powder, almond milk, pepper, and salt in a large bowl.
- Stir in bell peppers, spinach, and onion. Pour egg batter into the slow cooker.
- Cook on high within 90 minutes or until egg sets. Cut into the slices and serve.

INGREDIENTS

- 6 eggs
- 1 tsp parsley, dried
- 1 tsp garlic powder
- 1 bell pepper, diced
- 1/2 cup onion, sliced
- 1 cup spinach
- 1/2 cup almond milk, unsweetened
- 4 egg whites
- Pepper
- Salt

Arugula Cheese Herb Frittata

NUTRITION Calories: 178 , Fat: 12.8 g , Carb: 6 g , Protein: 11.4 g

INGREDIENTS

- 8 eggs
- 3/4 cup goat cheese, crumbled
- 1/2 cup onion, sliced
- 1 1/2 cups red peppers, roasted and chopped
- 4 cups baby arugula
- 1 tsp oregano, dried
- 1/3 cup almond milk
- Pepper
- Salt

DIRECTION

- Grease the slow cooker using a cooking spray. Whisk eggs, oregano, and almond milk in a mixing bowl.
- Put pepper and salt. Arrange red peppers, onion, arugula, and cheese into the slow cooker.
- Pour egg batter into the slow cooker over the vegetables. Cook on low within 3 hours. Serve hot and enjoy.

PREPARATION	COOKING TIME	SERVINGS
15	3 10 *hours* *mins*	6

Yummy Cauliflower Crust Breakfast Pizza

NUTRITION Calories: 178 , Fat: 12.8 g , Carb: 6 g , Protein: 11.4 g

INGREDIENTS

- 2 large eggs
- 3 cups riced cauliflower
- 1 cup grated Parmesan cheese
- 8 ounces goat cheese, divided
- ½ teaspoon kosher salt
- 1 tablespoon extra-virgin olive oil
- Grated zest of 1 lemon

DIRECTION

- Beat the eggs, cauliflower, Parmesan cheese, 2 ounces of goat cheese, and the salt until well mixed in a large bowl.
- Grease the slow cooker using the olive oil. Press the cauliflower batter in an even layer around the cooker's bottom and extend slightly up the sides.
- Stir the remaining 6 ounces of goat cheese and the lemon zest in a small bowl. Dollop spoonsful onto the cauliflower crust, distributing it evenly.
- Set the lid on the slow cooker, but prop it slightly open with a chopstick or wooden spoon. Cook within 6 hours on low or 3 hours on high, until the edges are slightly browned.
- When finished, turn off the cooker but let the pizza sit in it 30 minutes before serving. Serve warm.

PREPARATION	COOKING TIME	SERVINGS
15	5 *hours*	4

Parmesan Zucchini Paprika & Ricotta Frittata

NUTRITION Calories: 234 , Fat: 23g , Carb: 1g , Protein: 7g

INGREDIENTS

- 2 medium zucchinis, shredded
- 1 teaspoon kosher salt, divided
- 1 tablespoon extra-virgin olive oil
- 12 large eggs
- 3 tablespoons heavy (whipping) cream
- 3 tablespoons finely chopped fresh parsley
- 1 tablespoon fresh thyme
- ½ teaspoon paprika
- ½ teaspoon freshly ground black pepper
- 6 ounces ricotta cheese
- 12 cherry tomatoes, halved
- ½ cup grated Parmesan cheese

DIRECTION

- Toss the shredded zucchini with ½ teaspoon of salt in a colander set in the sink. Let the zucchini sit for a few minutes, then squeeze out the excess liquid with your hands.
- Grease the slow cooker with olive oil.
- Beat the eggs, heavy cream, parsley, thyme, paprika, pepper, and the remaining ½ teaspoon of salt in a large bowl.
- Put the zucchini and stir. Transfer the mixture to the prepared insert.
- Using a large spoon, dollop the ricotta cheese into the egg mixture, distributing it evenly.
- Top with the tomatoes and sprinkle the Parmesan cheese over the top. Set to cook within 6 hours on low or 3 hours on high. Serve at room temperature.

PREPARATION	COOKING TIME	SERVINGS
15	6 *hours*	6

Scrambled Eggs with Smoked Salmon

NUTRITION Calories: 263 , Carbs: 0g , Fat: 0g , Protein: 0g

INGREDIENTS

- Smoked salmon ¼ lb.
- eggs12 pcs fresh
- heavy cream½ cup
- almond flour¼ cup
- Salt and black pepper at will
- Butter2 tablespoons
- fresh chives at will

DIRECTION

- Cut the slices of salmon. Set aside for garnish. Chop the rest of the salmon into small pieces.
- Take a medium bowl, whisk the eggs and cream together. Add half of the chopped chives, season eggs with salt and pepper. Add flour.
- Dissolve the butter over medium heat, then pour into the mixture. Grease the Slow Cooker with oil or cooking spray.
- Add salmon pieces to the mixture, pour it into the Slow Cooker. Set to cook on low within 2 hours.
- Garnish the dish with remaining salmon, chives. Serve warm and enjoy!

PREPARATION	COOKING TIME	SERVINGS
15	2 *mins*	6

Garlic-Parmesan Asparagus Crock Pot

NUTRITION Calories: 88 , Carbs: 7g , Fat: 9g , Protein: 7g

INGREDIENTS

- olive oil extra virgin2 table-spoons
- minced garlic2 teaspoons
- egg 1 pcs fresh
- garlic salt1/2 teaspoon
- fresh asparagus12 ounces
- Parmesan cheese1/3 cup
- Pepper at will

DIRECTION

- Peel the garlic and mince it. Wash the asparagus. Shred the Parmesan cheese.
- Take a medium-sized bowl combine oil, garlic, cracked egg, and salt together. Whisk everything well.
- Cover the green beans and coat them well.
- Spread the cooking spray over the Slow Cooker's bottom, put the coated asparagus, season with the shredded cheese. Toss.
- Cook on high within 1 hour. Once the time is over, you may also season with the rest of the cheese. Serve.

PREPARATION	COOKING TIME	SERVINGS
15	1 hour	6

Persian Omelet Crock Pot

NUTRITION Calories: 220 , Carbs: 9g , Fat: 16g , Protein: 12g

INGREDIENTS

- olive oil 2 tablespoons
- butter 1 tablespoons
- red onion 1 large
- green onions 4 pcs
- garlic 2 cloves
- Spinach 2 oz.
- fresh chives ¼ cup
- cilantro leaves ¼ cup
- parsley leaves ¼ cup
- fresh dill 2 tablespoons
- Kosher salt and black pepper at will
- pine nuts ¼ cup
- eggs 9 large
- whole milk ¼ cup
- Greek yogurt 1 cup

DIRECTION

- Take a saucepan to melt the butter. Add red onion, stirring occasionally; it takes about 8-9 minutes.
- Add green onions, garlic, continue cooking for 4 minutes. Put the spinach, chives, parsley, and cilantro, add salt and pepper at will. Remove the skillet, add the pine nuts.
- Take a bowl, crack the eggs, add milk, and a little pepper and whisk. Mix the eggs with veggie mixture.
- Open the Slow Cooker and spread the cooking spray over the bottom and sides. Pour the mix into the Slow Cooker. Cook on low for 3 hours. Serve with Greek yogurt. Bon Appetite!

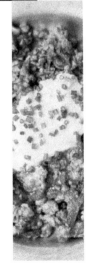

PREPARATION	COOKING TIME	SERVINGS
15	3 hour	14

Broccoli and Cheese Stuffed Squash

NUTRITION Calories: 230 , Carbs: 22g , Fat: 6g , Protein: 21g

INGREDIENTS

- squash 1 pcs, halves
- broccoli florets 2 cups
- garlic 3 pcs
- red pepper flakes 1 teaspoon
- Italian season 1 teaspoon
- mozzarella cheese 1/2 cup
- Parmesan cheese 1/3 cup
- cooking spray
- salt and pepper at will

DIRECTION

- Grease the Slow Cooker. Put the squash halves in the Slow Cooker.
- Add a little bit of water at room temperature to the bottom of the Slow Cooker.
- Put on low within 2 hours, until squash is mild. Take off the squash and let it cool for about 15 minutes.
- Take a medium skillet, add pepper flakes and a little bit oil and cook for 20 seconds, stir it continuously.
- Add broccoli, minced garlic to the skillet, continue to stir thoroughly, until the broccoli is tender.
- Take the squash and using a fork; take off the flesh of the squash. Add it to the medium bowl and con-join with the broccoli mixture.
- Shred the Parmesan cheese carefully, put salt and pepper at will, and add seasoning to the mixture. Mix well and fill the squash.
- Put the filled squash again in the Slow Cooker, dress with mozzarella cheese each squash half.
- Cover and cook on low within 1 hour. Remove the dish and serve.

PREPARATION	COOKING TIME	SERVINGS
15	3 *hours*	7

Garlic Butter Keto Spinach

NUTRITION Calories: 38 , Carbs: 2g , Fat: 3g , Protein: 2g

INGREDIENTS

- salted butter 2 tablespoons
- garlic, minced 4 cloves
- Baby spinach 8 oz.
- Pinch of salt
- lemon juice 1 teaspoons

DIRECTION

- Heat-up a little skillet, add the butter, and melt. Sautee the garlic until a bit tender.
- Spray the cooking spray over the bottom of the Slow Cooker.
- Put the spinach into the Slow Cooker, season with salt and lemon juice, tender garlic, butter.
- Put to cook on low within 1 hour. Garnish with fresh lemon wedges. Serve hot.

PREPARATION	COOKING TIME	SERVINGS
15	1 *hour*	4

Keto Crock Pot Tasty Onions

NUTRITION Calories: 38 , Carbs: 9g , Fat: 0g , Protein: 0g

INGREDIENTS

- Onions 4 (or 5) large pcs, sliced
- Butter or coconut oil 4 table-spoon
- Coconut aminos 1/4 cup
- Splenda (optional)
- Salt and pepper

DIRECTION

- Place the onion slices into the Slow Cooker. Top the onion slices with coconut amino and butter; you might add Splenda at will.
- Cook it on low during 6-7 hours. Serve over the grilled vegetables.

PREPARATION	COOKING TIME	SERVINGS
15	6 *hours*	4

Crock Pot Benedict Casserole

NUTRITION Calories: 286 , Carbs: 16g , Fat: 19g , Protein: 14g

INGREDIENTS

- For the Casserole
- English muffin 1 large, cut into portions
- Canadian bacon1 lb. thick-cut
- eggs 10 large
- milk 1 cup
- salt and pepper
- for garnish
- For the Sauce
- egg 6 yolks
- lemon juice 1 1/2 tablespoon
- unsalted butter, melted1 1/2 sticks
- salt
- pinch of cayenne

DIRECTION

- For the muffin: Using a medium-sized skillet, melt the butter. Add coconut and almond flour, egg, salt, and stir everything well. Add baking soda. Grease the Slow Cooker with cooking spray. Pour the mixture, put on low for 2 hours. Remove once done.
- Grease again the Slow Cooker with cooking spray, cut the muffin into equal pieces, put on the bottom.
- Slice the bacon, sprinkle half of it over top of the muffin pieces.
- Whisk milk, eggs, season with salt and black pepper in a large bowl.
- Pour the egg batter evenly over the muffin pieces and top with the rest of the bacon.
- Cook on low within 2 hours in the slow cooker. Remove, and keep the muffins covered before serving.
- To make the sauce, set up a double boiler, put the egg yolks, squeeze lemon juice in a bowl, and mix.
- Put your bowl over the double boiler, continue whisking carefully; the bowl mustn't get too hot.
- Put in the melted butter while continuing to whisk.
- Season with salt and pepper. You may also add a little bit more lemon juice or cayenne.
- Serve and enjoy.

PREPARATION	COOKING TIME	SERVINGS
15	4 *hours*	7

Crustless Crock Pot Spinach Quiche

NUTRITION Calories: 153 , Carbs: 19g , Fat: 3g , Protein: 9g

INGREDIENTS

- Frozen spinach10 oz. package
- Butter or ghee1 tablespoon
- Red bell pepper1 medium
- Cheddar cheese1 1/2 cups
- Eggs8 pcs
- Homemade sour cream1 cup
- Fresh chives2 tablespoons
- Sea salt1/2 teaspoon
- Ground black pepper1/4 teaspoon
- Ground almond flour 1/2 cup
- Baking soda1/4 teaspoon

DIRECTION

- Let the frozen spinach thaw and drain it well. Chop finely. Wash the pepper and slice it. Remove the seeds.
- Grate the cheddar cheese and set aside. Chop the fresh chives finely.
- Grease the slow cooker with cooking spray.
- Take a little skillet, heat the butter over high heat on the stove, sauté the pepper until tender, for about 6 minutes. Mix the eggs, sour cream, salt, plus pepper in a large bowl.
- Add grated cheese and chives and continue to mix. In another medium-sized bowl, combine almond flour with baking soda.
- Pour into the egg mixture, add peppers to the egg's mixture, and pour gently into the slow cooker.
- Set to cook on high within 2 hours then Serve.

PREPARATION	COOKING TIME	SERVINGS
15	2 hours	1

Broccoli Gratin with Parmesan and Swiss Cheese

NUTRITION Calories: 210 , Carbs: 44g , Fat: 2g , Protein: 5g

INGREDIENTS

- 1 1/2 tablespoons vegetable oil
- 1 cup of water
- ½ cup blackberry jelly
- ½ cup peanut butter
- One teaspoon salt
- One tablespoon white sugar
- 2 cups of bread flour
- 1 cup whole-wheat flour
- 1 1/2 teaspoons active dry yeast

DIRECTION

- Put everything in your bread machine pan.
- Select the basic setting.
- Press the start button.
- Take out the pan when done and set aside for 10 minutes.

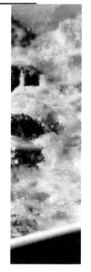

PREPARATION	COOKING TIME	SERVINGS
15	1 hour	7

Crock Pot Cream Cheese French Toast

NUTRITION Calories: 280 , Carbs: 34g , Fat: 8g , Protein: 19g

INGREDIENTS

- cream cheese 1 (8-oz) package
- slivered almonds ¼ cup
- keto bread 1 loaf
- eggs 4 pcs
- almond extract 1 teaspoon
- sweetener 1 tablespoon
- milk 1 cup
- butter 2 tablespoon
- Cheddar cheese ½ cup
- Maple syrup, at will, for dressing

DIRECTION

- Mix cream cheese with almonds in a large bowl. Slice the keto bread into 2-inch slices. Try to make a 1/2-inch slit (horizontal) at the bottom of every piece to make a pocket.
- Fill all the slices with cream mixture. Set aside. In a little bowl, mix eggs, extract the sweetener in milk. Coat the keto slices into the mix.
- Grease with cooking spray the slow cooker over the bottom and sides, then put the coated keto slices on the slow cooker's base. Put on the top of each separate piece additional shredded cheese.
- Cook on low for 2 hours. Serve hot.

PREPARATION	COOKING TIME	SERVINGS
15	2 *mins*	9

Keto Crock Pot Turkey Stuffed Peppers

NUTRITION Calories: 245 , Carbs: 26g , Fat: 7g , Protein: 19g

INGREDIENTS

- olive oil 1 tablespoon
- Ground turkey 1 lb.
- onion 1 pcs
- garlic 1 clove
- green bell peppers 4 pcs
- tomato sauce/pasta sauce (low carb) 24 oz. jar
- water 1/2 cup

DIRECTION

- Peel and cut the small onion, peel the garlic, and press or mince it.
- Wash the bell peppers, cut off the tops and clean them accurately.
- Take a medium bowl, put their ground turkey, cut onion, pressed or minced garlic, and add pasta sauce.
- Separate the compound into four equal parts, place the mixtures into the prepared cleaned peppers.
- Spread the olive oil over the slow cooker bottom, and sides put the peppers inside, and top them with sauce.
- Add a little water into the slow cooker, cook on low for 6-7 hours.
- Serve with remaining sauce and enjoy.

PREPARATION	COOKING TIME	SERVINGS
15	6 *hours*	7

Crock Pot Keto English Muffin

NUTRITION Calories: 188 , Carbs: 3g , Fat: 17g , Protein: 7g

INGREDIENTS

- almond flour3 tablespoons
- coconut flour 1/2 tablespoon
- butter 1 tablespoon
- egg 1 large
- sea salt1 pinch
- baking soda1/2 teaspoons
- salt

DIRECTION

- Take a medium-sized skillet, melt the butter. It usually takes 20-30 seconds.
- Pour coconut and almond flour, egg, salt into the melted butter and stir everything well.
- Remove skillet from the heat and add baking soda.
- Coat the slow cooker with cooking spray. Pour the mixture.
- Put on low for 2 hours. Check the readiness with a fork.
- Remove the baked muffin from the slow cooker and eat with bacon slices, cheese, or other breakfast staples.

PREPARATION	COOKING TIME	SERVINGS
15	40 *mins*	*16 slices*

Cauliflower Casserole with Tomato and Goat Cheese

NUTRITION Calories: 170 , Carbs: 10g , Fat: 13g , Protein: 7g

INGREDIENTS

- cauliflower florets 6 cups
- olive oil 4 teaspoons
- dried oregano 1 teaspoon
- salt 1/2 teaspoon
- ground pepper 1/2 teaspoons
- Goat cheese crumbled 2 oz.
- The Sauce:
- olive oil 1 teaspoon
- garlic 3 cloves
- crushed tomatoes 1 (28 oz.) can
- bay leaves 2 pcs
- salt 1/4 teaspoon
- minced flat-leaf parsley 1/4 cup

DIRECTION

- Grease the slow cooker with cooking spray, put the cauliflower on its bottom, and add olive oil, oregano, and pepper. Salt if desired.
- Cook on the low setting within 2 hours until the cauliflower florets get tender and a little bit brown color.
- For making the sauce: Take a medium-sized skillet, heat the olive oil, add garlic and cook 1 minute, stir it thoroughly all the time.
- Add the crushed tomatoes and bay leaves; let it simmer for some minutes. Remove the bay leaves, dress with pepper and salt.
- Put the sauce over the cauliflower florets in the slow cooker once the time is over.
- Spread the Goat cheese over the dish, cover the slow cooker, and continue cooking for 1 hour on low. Serve warm!

PREPARATION	COOKING TIME	SERVINGS
15	3 *hours*	*12*

Greek Eggs Breakfast Casserole

NUTRITION Calories: 253 , Carbs: 1g , Fat: 17g , Protein: 22g

INGREDIENTS

- eggs (whisked) 12 pcs
- milk ½ cup
- salt ½ teaspoon
- black pepper 1 teaspoon
- Red Onion 1 tablespoon
- Garlic 1 teaspoon
- Sun-dried tomatoes ½ cup
- spinach 2 cups
- Feta Cheese ½ cup crushed
- pepper at will

DIRECTION

- Whisk the eggs in a bowl.
- Add to the mixture milk, pepper, salt, and stir to combine. Add the minced onion and garlic.
- Add dried tomatoes and spinach. Pour all the batter into the slow cooker, add Feta cheese.
- Set to cook on the low setting within 5-6 hours. Serve.

PREPARATION	COOKING TIME	SERVINGS
15	6 *hours*	9

Crock Pot Turkish Breakfast Eggs

NUTRITION Calories: 123 , Carbs: 17g , Fat: 5g , Protein: 1g

INGREDIENTS

- olive oil 1 tablespoon
- onions 2 pcs, chopped
- red bell pepper 1 pcs, sliced
- red chili 1 small
- cherry tomatoes 8 pcs
- keto bread 1 slice
- eggs 4 pcs
- milk 2 tablespoon
- small bunch of parsley, chopped
- natural yogurt 4 tablespoon
- pepper at will

DIRECTION

- Grease the slow cooker using oil.
- Heat-up, the oil, add the onions, pepper, and chili in a large skillet, then stir. Cook until the veggies begin to soften.
- Transfer it in the Slow Cooker, then add the cherry tomatoes and bread, stir everything well.
- Cook on low for 4 hours—season with fresh parsley and yogurt.

PREPARATION	COOKING TIME	SERVINGS
15	4 *mins*	9

Cheesy Garlic Brussels Sprouts

NUTRITION Calories: 159 , Fat: 9.5g , Saturated fat: 5.5g , Carbs: 14.1g , Fiber: 5.4g , Sugars: 3.7 g , Protein: 7.7g , Sodium: 279.8 mg

INGREDIENTS

- 1 tablespoon unsalted butter
- 2½ pounds Brussels sprouts, trimmed and halved
- ¾ cup grated Parmesan cheese
- 2 tablespoons heavy cream
- 1/8 teaspoon freshly grated nutmeg
- 4 cloves garlic, thinly sliced
- 4 ounces cream cheese, cubed
- ½ teaspoon kosher salt
- ¼ teaspoon ground black pepper

DIRECTION

- Coat the insert of a 4- to – 6-quart crockpot with the butter. Add the garlic, cream cheese, Brussels sprouts, pepper, and salt.
- Toss to mix very well—cover and cook on the low, about 2 to 3 hours.
- Turn off the slow cooker. Stir in cream, parmesan, and nutmeg until the cheeses thaw and the Brussels sprouts are coated in a creamy sauce.
- Taste, season with more pepper if required. Serve.

PREPARATION	COOKING TIME	SERVINGS
15	3 _hours_	6

Blueberry Pancake

NUTRITION fdf

INGREDIENTS

- 1½ cups milk
- 2 large eggs
- 1 teaspoon vanilla
- 2 cups all-purpose flour
- 2½ teaspoon baking powder
- 2 tablespoons white sugar
- ¼ cup fresh blueberries

DIRECTION

- Toss the eggs, vanilla, and milk together in a small bowl. Stir flour, sugar, and baking powder together in a large bowl until well-mixed.
- Add the wet fixings to the dry and stir just until mixed.
- Pour the batter into the slow cooker. Add the blueberries.
- Set the timer at 40 minutes on low.
- Check to confirm if the pancake is cooked through by pressing the top. Serve and enjoy with syrup, fruit, or whipped cream.

PREPARATION	COOKING	SERVINGS
15	40 _mins_	8

Sausage and Peppers

NUTRITION Calories: 456 , Fat: 36g , Cholesterol: 86mg , Sodium: 1838mg , Potassium: 746mg , Carbs: 15g , Fiber: 4g , Sugar: 7g , Protein: 19g

INGREDIENTS

- 6 medium cloves garlic
- 2 large yellow onions
- 4 green bell peppers, cleaned and thinly sliced
- 28 ounces canned unsalted crushed tomatoes
- ¼ cup of cold water
- 1 bay leaf
- 2 pounds uncooked Italian Sausage Links, mild or spicy
- 1 tablespoon kosher salt
- 1 teaspoon Italian seasoning
- ¼ teaspoon dried oregano
- ½ teaspoon crushed red pepper flakes

DIRECTION

- Thinly slice the garlic. Peel the onions and halve, then cut.
- Add the chopped garlic and sliced onion into the slow cooker.
- Remember to spray the slow cooker with oil. Cut the bell peppers in half.
- Remove the ribs and any seeds in them. Then slice thinly.
- Add the sliced bell peppers, Italian seasoning, salt, crushed red pepper flakes, dried oregano, 1 can crushed tomatoes, and ¼ cup of water to the slow cooker.
- Toss to coat and liquid is uniformly distributed. Take out almost half of the peppers and the onion mixture to a bowl.
- Immerse the uncooked sausage in the middle and then add the peppers and the onions back to the slow cooker.
- Put the bay leaf, then cover, set to low, and cook for 6 hours. Serve hot.

PREPARATION	COOKING TIME	SERVINGS
15	6 *hours*	8

Breakfast Sausage Casserole

NUTRITION Calories: 77 , Carbs: 2g , Fat: 5g , Protein: 5g

INGREDIENTS

- 1 lb. pork sausage
- ½ cup chopped green bell pepper
- ½ cup chopped red bell pepper
- 1 tablespoon ghee
- 12 large eggs
- ½ cup of coconut milk
- 1 tablespoon nutritional yeast
- 1 teaspoon dry rubbed sage
- 1 teaspoon dried thyme
- ½ teaspoon garlic powder
- ½ teaspoon ground black pepper
- ½ teaspoon salt
- ½ cup sliced red onion

DIRECTION

- Heat-up a medium cast-iron skillet over medium heat for 2 minutes. Add the pork sausage, then break it into small crumbles.
- Cook for 3 minutes. Stir in the black pepper, sea salt, thyme, sage, and garlic powder.
- Cook for an additional 5 minutes. Turn the heat off.
- Stir in the bell peppers and the chopped onion. Coat the bowl of the slow cooker with ghee.
- Add the pork and vegetable mixture into the bottom of the crockpot.
- Whisk the coconut milk, nutritional yeast, and the eggs until the eggs are well incorporated together in a large bowl. Pour it into the crockpot on top of the pork mixture.
- Cook on low for 2 to 3 hours. Chop into 6 servings.

PREPARATION	COOKING TIME	SERVINGS
15	3 *hours*	6

Stuffed Breakfast Peppers

NUTRITION Calories: 180 , Carbs: 3g , Protein: 8g , Fat: 15g , Cholesterol: 205mg , Sodium: 430mg , Fiber: 1g, Sugar: 2g

INGREDIENTS

- 3 bell peppers halved and seeded
- 4 eggs
- ½ cup milk
- ¾ teaspoon salt
- 2 tablespoons chopped green onion
- ¼ cup chopped frozen spinach thawed, squeezed dry
- ¾ cup shredded cheddar cheese divided
- ½ cup finely chopped ham

DIRECTION

- Line slow cooker with tin foil. Arrange the peppers in the slow cooker and fill with the remaining fixings. Cook on low within 3-4 hours. Serve.

PREPARATION	COOKING TIME	SERVINGS
15	45 *mins*	6

Cheese and Sausage Breakfast

NUTRITION Calories: 3 26 ,Carbs: 14g , Protein: 18g , Fat: 22g , Cholesterol: 291mg , Sodium: 650mg, Potassium: 408mg , Fiber: 2g , Sugar: 4g

INGREDIENTS

- 2 tablespoon butter, softened
- 8 oz. breakfast sausage
- 1 lb. sweet potatoes, peeled and cubed
- 12 eggs
- 1 cup milk
- ¾ teaspoon salt
- ¼ teaspoon black pepper
- 4 oz. shredded mild cheddar cheese

DIRECTION

- 2. Coat the slow cooker and inside of the foil collar using softened butter.
- 3. Sauté in a large skillet over medium heat, the breakfast sausage until cooked through and browned, about 5 to 8 minutes.
- 4. Put the sweet potatoes into a microwave-safe bowl. Add 1 tablespoon water and cover bowl with a damp paper towel—microwave on high within 3 to 4 minutes.
- 5. Arrange the sausage and sweet potatoes in the bottom of the slow cooker.
- 6. Toss eggs, black pepper, milk, and salt to combine. Add the cheese; stir to mix very well.
- 7. Pour the egg/cheese mixture over sausage and sweet potatoes.
- 8. Then put 2 layers of paper towels below the slow cooker lid before.
- 9. Cook on high for 2 hours. Slice and serve.

PREPARATION	COOKING TIME	SERVINGS
15	2 *hours*	8

Mushrooms, Cauliflower, and Zucchini Toast

NUTRITION 345 , *Total Fat: 21g , Carbs: 4g , Fiber: 1g , Protein: 34g*

INGREDIENTS

- 3-pound boneless beef chuck roast
- 2 cups keto compliant beef broth
- 5-7 radishes, cut into halves
- 1½ cups cauliflower florets
- ½ cup chopped celery
- 1/3 cup zucchini rounds
- ¼ cup chopped orange bell pepper
- 1 teaspoon xanthan gum (optional to thicken the gravy)
- 2 sprigs fresh rosemary
- Fresh parsley (for garnish)
- 1 teaspoon Himalayan sea salt
- ½ teaspoon freshly ground black pepper
- 1 teaspoon garlic powder
- ½ teaspoon dried Italian seasoning
- 1 tablespoon avocado oil or ghee
- 1 small onion chopped
- ½ cup sliced mushrooms
- 1 tablespoon tomato paste
- 1 teaspoon keto compliant Worcestershire sauce
- 2 teaspoons coconut aminos

DIRECTION

- Season the roast with Italian seasoning, black pepper, garlic powder, and salt. Let it stand alone for about 27 to 30 minutes.
- Add oil to a large skillet on medium-high heat. Add the roast; sear until brown, about 4 minutes on all sides.
- Add the diced mushrooms and onions; let them cook for about 1 to 2 minutes until sweet-smelling.
- Transfer the roast and the onions to the bottom of a slow cooker, then pour in the broth; then cook on high for 4 hours or low for 7 hours.
- Add the vegetables: zucchini, celery, turnips, bell peppers, and cauliflower. Set it again for about 1 hour.
- Transfer then shred into chunks with 2 forks.
- Sprinkle with diced parsley if preferred. Serve hot with gravy.

PREPARATION	COOKING TIME	SERVINGS
15	7 *hours*	8

Pesto Scrambled Eggs

NUTRITION Calories: 167, Carbohydrates: 3.3g, Protein: 20.4g, Fat: 41.5g, Sugar: g, Sodium: 721mg, Fiber: 0.7g

INGREDIENTS

- 3 large eggs, beaten
- 1 tablespoon butter
- 1 tablespoon organic green pesto sauce
- 2 tablespoon sour cream, full-fat
- Salt and pepper to taste

DIRECTION

- In a mixing bowl, combine all fixings.
- Cook in the slow cooker on high within 2 hours or on low for 4 hours.
- Halfway before the cooking time, use a fork to break the eggs into small pieces. Continue cooking until eggs are well done. Serve.

PREPARATION	COOKING TIME	SERVINGS
5	4 *hours*	3

Kale and Cheese Omelet

NUTRITION Calories: 372, Carbohydrates: 2.1g, Protein: 24.5g, Fat: 36.2g, Sugar: 0.2g, Sodium: 362mg, Fiber: 1.3g

INGREDIENTS

- 5 eggs, beaten
- 2 tablespoons onion, chopped
- 2 teaspoons olive oil
- 3 ounces kale, chopped
- 1/3 cup white cheese, grated

DIRECTION

- Mix all fixings in a bowl. Put it in the crockpot. Cook on high within 2 hours or on low for 3 hours.

PREPARATION	COOKING TIME	SERVINGS
15	4 hours	2

Egg Casserole with Italian Cheeses, Sun-Dried Tomatoes, and Herbs

NUTRITION Calories: 140, Carbohydrates: 3.87g, Protein: 10.93g, Fat: 8.89g, Sugar: 1.27g, Sodium: 309mg, Fiber: 0.3g

INGREDIENTS

- 10 eggs
- 2 tablespoons milk
- 3 tablespoons sun-dried tomatoes, chopped
- 2 tablespoons onion, minced
- 2 tablespoons basil, chopped
- 1 tablespoon thyme leaves
- Salt and pepper to taste
- 1 cup mixed Italian cheeses, grated

DIRECTION

- Mix all items in a bowl. Put it inside your slow cooker, and set to cook on high for 2 hours or low for 3 hours.

PREPARATION	COOKING TIME	SERVINGS
5	4 hours	8

Kale, Mushrooms, and Caramelized Onions

NUTRITION Calories: 223, Carbohydrates: 4.6g, Protein: 32.1g, Fat: 36.3g, Sugar: 0.8g, Sodium: 471mg, Fiber: 2.1g

INGREDIENTS

- 2 teaspoons olive oil
- ½ tablespoon onion, caramelized
- 1 red bell pepper, diced
- 1 cup mushrooms, sliced
- 2 cups kale, chopped
- 1 teaspoon dried thyme
- 10 large eggs, beaten
- ¼ cup milk
- 2 cups cheese, shredded
- Salt and pepper to taste

DIRECTION

- Place all fixings in the slow cooker.
- Cook on high within 3 hours or on low for 4 hours.

PREPARATION	COOKING TIME	SERVINGS
10	4 *hours*	6

Egg and Cheese Casserole with Chayote Squash

NUTRITION Calories: 209, Carbohydrates: 6.3g, Protein: 35.2g, Fat: 33.6g, Sugar: 1.5g, Sodium: 362mg, Fiber: 3.2g

INGREDIENTS

- 1 teaspoon olive oil
- 1 red onion, diced
- 2 small chayote squash, grated
- ½ small red bell pepper, diced
- 10 large eggs, beaten
- ¼ cup low-fat cottage cheese
- 2 tablespoons milk
- ½ teaspoon ground cumin
- 2 cups grated cheesed
- Salt and pepper to taste

DIRECTION

- Combine all fixings in a mixing bowl. Pour into the slow cooker.
- Cook on high within 3 hours or on low for 4 hours.

PREPARATION	COOKING TIME	SERVINGS
5	4 *hours*	4

Sausage and Kale Strata

NUTRITION Calories: 231, Carbohydrates: 4.5g, Protein: 32.3g, Fat: 37.4g, Sugar: 0.6g, Sodium: 525mg, Fiber: 3.2g

INGREDIENTS

- 12 eggs, beaten
- 2 ½ cups milk
- Salt and pepper to taste
- 2 tablespoons fresh oregano, minced
- 2 pounds breakfast sausages, sliced
- 1 bunch kale, torn into pieces
- 16 ounces white mushrooms, sliced
- 2 ½ cups Monterey Jack cheese, grated

DIRECTION

- Mix all fixings in a large mixing bowl until well combined.
- Pour into the slow cooker and close the lid. Set to cook on high within 3 hours or low for 4 hours.

PREPARATION	COOKING TIME	SERVINGS
5	4 *hours*	12

Egg Cake Recipe with Peppers, Kale, and Cheddar

NUTRITION Calories: 527, Carbohydrates: 3.1g, Protein: 42.3g, Fat: 45.6g, Sugar: 0.5g, Sodium: 425mg, Fiber: 2.4g

INGREDIENTS

- 1 dozen eggs, beaten
- ¼ cup milk
- ¼ cup almond flour
- 1 clove of garlic, minced
- Salt and pepper to taste
- 1 cup kale, chopped
- 1 red bell pepper, chopped
- ¾ cup mozzarella cheese, grated
- 1 green onion, chopped

DIRECTION

- Directions:
- In a mixing bowl, combine all fixings.
- Pour into the slow cooker. Cook on high within 4 hours or on high for 6 hours. Serve.

PREPARATION	COOKING TIME	SERVINGS
10	4 *mins*	6

Feta Cheese and Kale Breakfast Casserole

NUTRITION Calories: 397, Carbohydrates: 4g, Protein: 32.2g, Fat: 29.4g, Sugar: 0.6g, Sodium: 425mg, Fiber: 3.2g

PREPARATION COOKING TIME SERVINGS

5   4   6
     hours

INGREDIENTS

- 10 ounces kale, chopped
- 2 teaspoons olive oil
- ¾ cup feta cheese, crumbled
- 12 eggs, beaten
- Salt and pepper to taste

DIRECTION

- Mix all fixings in a large mixing bowl until well combined.
- Put the batter inside the slow cooker, then cook on high for 3 hours or low for 4 hours.

Cauliflower and Ham Casserole

NUTRITION Calories: 418, Carbohydrates: 5.2g, Protein: 28.1g, Fat: 42.4g, Sugar: 0.5g, Sodium: 831mg, Fiber: 2.1g

PREPARATION COOKING TIME SERVINGS

5   4   6
     hours

DIRECTION

- Combine the olive oil, sausage, broth, onion, butternut squash, bell peppers, thyme, salt, and pepper in the slow cooker. Toss to mix. Cook within 6 hours on low.
- Before serving, sprinkle the Swiss cheese over the top, cover, and cook for about 3 minutes more to melt the cheese.

INGREDIENTS

- Mix all fixings in a bowl. Pour into the slow cooker.
- Cook on high within 3 hours or on low for 4 hours.

Sausage-Stuffed Eggplants

NUTRITION Calories: 471, Carbohydrates: 6.3g, Protein: 16.83g, Fat: 38.9g, Sugar: 0.4g, Sodium: 1107mg, Fiber: 3.8g

PREPARATION	COOKING TIME	SERVINGS
10	6 *hours*	6

INGREDIENTS

- 12 ounces sausage links, chopped
- 2 cloves of garlic, minced
- 2 tablespoons rosemary, fresh
- Salt and pepper to taste
- 3 small eggplants, sliced
- 6 slices mozzarella cheese

DIRECTION

- Mix all items in a bowl. Line a foil at the bottom of the slow cooker.
- Grease with cooking spray. Pour into the slow cooker and cook on low for 6 hours or on high for 4 hours.

Zucchini Sausage Breakfast "Bake"

NUTRITION Calories: 344, Carbohydrates: 6.3g, Protein: 21g, Fat: 27g, Sugar: 0.4g, Sodium: 736mg, Fiber: 4g

PREPARATION	COOKING TIME	SERVINGS
5	4 *hours*	12

DIRECTION

- Mix all fixings in a bowl. Set in the slow cooker; cook within 3 hours on high or on low for 4 hours.

INGREDIENTS

- 1-pound Italian sausages, chopped
- ½ cup coconut flour
- 2 teaspoons baking powder
- 1 teaspoon salt
- ½ teaspoon pepper
- 8 ounces cream cheese
- 10 large eggs
- 2 small zucchinis, grated and excess water squeezed
- 4 cloves of garlic, minced
- 1 cup cheese, shredded

Cheddar Jalapeno Breakfast Sausages

NUTRITION Calories: 472, Carbohydrates: 1.2g, Protein: 32.6g, Fat: 42.4g, Sugar: 0g, Sodium: 731mg, Fiber: 0.4g

PREPARATION	COOKING TIME	SERVINGS
5	6 *hours*	12

DIRECTION

- Mix all items in a bowl, then put it into the slow cooker.
- Set to cook on low for 6 hours or on high for 4 hours.
- Garnish with parsley on top.

INGREDIENTS

- 12 medium-sized breakfast sausages
- 1 jalapeno pepper, chopped
- ½ cup cheddar cheese, grated
- ¼ cup heavy cream
- Salt and pepper to taste

Chocolate Peanut Butter Breakfast Bars

NUTRITION Calories: 170, Carbohydrates: 4.4g, Protein: 8.1g, Fat: 20.5g, Sugar: 1.2g, Sodium: 732mg, Fiber: 1.7g

PREPARATION	COOKING TIME	SERVINGS
15	6 *hours*	12

DIRECTION

- Mix the cream cheese, egg, almond flour, peanut butter, heavy cream, stevia, vanilla extract, and chocolate chips in a large mixing bowl using a hand mixer.
- Put the bottom of the slow cooker with foil and grease with cooking spray.
- Pour the batter inside the slow cooker and cook for 5 hours or on low or 3 hours on high.

INGREDIENTS

- 4 ounces cream cheese, softened
- 1 large egg, beaten
- 2 cups almond flour
- ½ cup chunky peanut butter
- ½ cup heavy cream
- 3 tablespoons stevia sweetener
- 1 teaspoon vanilla extract
- ½ cup dark chocolate chips

Chapter 6.
Lunch

Lunch Chicken Wraps

NUTRITION Calories 376, Fat 18.5, Fiber 3, Carbs 29.43, Protein 23

PREPARATION	COOKING TIME	SERVINGS
18	6 *hours*	6

DIRECTION

- Put the chicken breast in the slow cooker.
- Sprinkle the meat with the bay leaf, salt, ground pepper, and coriander.
- Add water and cook the chicken breast for 6 hours on LOW.
- Then remove the cooked chicken from the slow cooker and shred it with a fork.
- Chop the lettuce roughly.
- Then chop Feta cheese. Combine the chopped Ingredients: together and add the shredded chicken breast and Caesar dressing.
- Mix everything together well. After this, spread the tortillas with the shredded chicken mixture and wrap them. Enjoy!

INGREDIENTS

- 6 tortillas
- 3 tablespoon Caesar dressing
- 1-pound chicken breast
- ½ cup lettuce
- 1 cup water
- 1 oz. bay leaf
- 1 teaspoon salt
- 1 teaspoon ground pepper
- 1 teaspoon coriander
- 4 oz. Feta cheese

Nutritious Lunch Wraps

NUTRITION Calories 318, Fat 7, Fiber 2, Carbs 3.76, Protein 26

PREPARATION	COOKING TIME	SERVINGS
20	4 hours	5

INGREDIENTS

- 7 oz. ground pork
- 5 tortillas
- 1 tablespoon tomato paste
- ½ cup onion, chopped
- ½ cup lettuce
- 1 teaspoon ground black pepper
- 1 teaspoon salt
- 1 teaspoon sour cream
- 5 tablespoons water
- 4 oz. Parmesan, shredded
- 2 tomatoes

DIRECTION

- Combine the ground pork with the tomato paste, ground black pepper, salt, and sour cream. Transfer the meat mixture to the slow cooker and cook on HIGH for 4 hours.
- Meanwhile, chop the lettuce roughly. Slice the tomatoes.
- Place the sliced tomatoes in the tortillas and add the chopped lettuce and shredded Parmesan. When the ground pork is cooked, chill to room temperature.
- Add the ground pork in the tortillas and wrap them. Enjoy!

Butternut Squash Soup

NUTRITION Calories 129, Fat 2.7, Fiber 2, Carbs 20.85, Protein 7

PREPARATION	COOKING TIME	SERVINGS
10	8 hours	9

INGREDIENTS

- 2-pound butternut squash
- 4 teaspoon minced garlic
- ½ cup onion, chopped
- 1 teaspoon salt
- ¼ teaspoon ground nutmeg
- 1 teaspoon ground black pepper
- 8 cups chicken stock
- 1 tablespoon fresh parsley

DIRECTION

- Peel the butternut squash and cut it into the chunks.
- Toss the butternut squash in the slow cooker.
- Add chopped onion, minced garlic, and chicken stock.
- Close the slow cooker lid and cook the soup for 8 hours on LOW.
- Meanwhile, combine the ground black pepper, ground nutmeg, and salt together.
- Chop the fresh parsley.
- When the time is done, remove the soup from the slow cooker and blend it with a blender until you get a creamy soup.
- Sprinkle the soup with the spice mixture and add chopped parsley. Serve the soup warm. Enjoy!

Eggplant Bacon Wraps

NUTRITION *Calories 131, Fat 9.4, Fiber 2, Carbs 7.25, Protein 6*

PREPARATION | COOKING TIME | SERVINGS

17 | 5 *hours* | 6

INGREDIENTS

- 10 oz. eggplant, sliced into rounds
- 5 oz. halloumi cheese
- 1 teaspoon minced garlic
- 3 oz. bacon, chopped
- ½ teaspoon ground black pepper
- 1 teaspoon salt
- 1 teaspoon paprika
- 1 tomato

DIRECTION

- Rub the eggplant slices with the ground black pepper, salt, and paprika.
- Slice halloumi cheese and tomato.
- Combine the chopped bacon and minced garlic together.
- Place the sliced eggplants in the slow cooker. Cook the eggplant on HIGH for 1 hour.
- Chill the eggplant. Place the sliced tomato and cheese on the eggplant slices.
- Add the chopped bacon mixture and roll up tightly.
- Secure the eggplants with the toothpicks and return the eggplant wraps back into the slow cooker. Cook the dish on HIGH for 4 hours more.
- When the dish is done, serve it immediately. Enjoy!

Mexican Warm Salad

NUTRITION *Calories 182, Fat 7.8, Fiber 2, Carbs 19.6, Protein 9*

PREPARATION | COOKING TIME | SERVINGS

26 | 10 *mins* | 10

DIRECTION

- Put the chicken fillet, sweet corn, black beans, and chicken stock in the slow cooker.
- Close the slow cooker lid and cook the mixture on LOW for 10 hours.
- When the time is done remove the mixture from the slow cooker.
- Shred the chicken fillet with 2 forks. Chill the mixture until room temperature.
- Chop the lettuce roughly. Chop the cucumber and tomatoes.
- Place the lettuce, cucumber, and tomatoes on a large serving plate.
- After this, shred Cheddar cheese and chop the chili pepper.
- Add the chili pepper to the serving plate too.
- After this, add the chicken mixture on the top of the salad.
- Sprinkle the salad with the mayonnaise, minced garlic, and shredded cheese. Enjoy the salad immediately.

INGREDIENTS

- 1 cup black beans
- 1 cup sweet corn, frozen
- 3 tomatoes
- ½ cup fresh dill
- 1 chili pepper
- 7 oz. chicken fillet
- 5 oz. Cheddar cheese
- 4 tablespoons mayonnaise
- 1 teaspoon minced garlic
- 1 cup lettuce
- 5 cups chicken stock
- 1 cucumber

Hot Chorizo Salad

NUTRITION Calories 249, Fat 19.8, Fiber 2, Carbs 7.69, Protein 11

PREPARATION	COOKING TIME	SERVINGS
20	4 30	6
	hours *mins*	

DIRECTION

- Chop the chorizo sausages roughly and place them in the slow cooker.
- Cook the sausages for 4 hours on HIGH.
- Meanwhile, combine the cayenne pepper, chili flakes, ground black pepper, and onion powder together in a shallow bowl.
- Chop the tomatoes roughly and add them to the slow cooker after 4 hours. Cook the mixture for 30 minutes more on HIGH.
- Chop the fresh dill and combine it with oregano.
- When the chorizo sausage mixture is cooked, place it in a serving bowl. Tear the lettuce and add it in the bowl too.
- After this, peel the garlic cloves and slice them.
- Add the sliced garlic cloves in the salad bowl too.
- Then sprinkle the salad with the spice mixture, olive oil, fresh dill mixture, and crush cashew. Mix the salad carefully. Enjoy!

INGREDIENTS

- 8 oz. chorizo
- 1 teaspoon olive oil
- 1 teaspoon cayenne pepper
- 1 teaspoon chili flakes
- 1 teaspoon ground black pepper
- 1 teaspoon onion powder
- 2 garlic cloves
- 3 tomatoes
- 1 cup lettuce
- 1 cup fresh dill
- 1 teaspoon oregano
- 3 tablespoons crushed cashews

Stuffed Eggplants

NUTRITION Calories 277, Fat 9.1, Fiber 24, Carbs 51.92, Protein 11

PREPARATION	COOKING TIME	SERVINGS
20	8	4
	hours	

DIRECTION

- Wash the eggplants carefully and remove the flesh from them.
- Then combine the rice with the salt, paprika, and tomato sauce.
- Chop the fresh cilantro and add it to the rice mixture.
- Then fill the prepared eggplants with the rice mixture.
- Pour the chicken stock and olive oil in the slow cooker.
- Add the stuffed eggplants and close the slow cooker lid.
- Cook the dish on LOW for 8 hours. When the eggplants are done, chill them little and serve immediately. Enjoy!

INGREDIENTS

- 4 medium eggplants
- 1 cup rice, half cooked
- ½ cup chicken stock
- 1 teaspoon salt
- 1 teaspoon paprika
- ½ cup fresh cilantro
- 3 tablespoons tomato sauce
- 1 teaspoon olive oil

Light Lunch Quiche

NUTRITION Calories 287, Fat 18.8, Fiber 1, Carbs 17.1, Protein 11

PREPARATION	COOKING TIME	SERVINGS
21	4 25	8
	hours mins	

INGREDIENTS

- 7 oz. pie crust
- ¼ cup broccoli
- 1/3 cup sweet peas
- ¼ cup heavy cream
- 2 tablespoons flour
- 3 eggs
- 4 oz. Romano cheese, shredded
- 1 teaspoon cilantro
- 1 teaspoon salt
- ¼ cup spinach
- 1 tomato

DIRECTION

- Cover the inside of the slow cooker bowl with parchment.
- Put the pie crust inside and flatten it well with your fingertips.
- Chop the broccoli and combine it with sweet peas. Combine the heavy cream, flour, cilantro, and salt together. Stir the liquid until smooth.
- Then beat the eggs into the heavy cream liquid and mix it with a hand mixer. When you get a smooth mix, combine it with the broccoli.
- Chop the spinach and add it to the mix. Chop the tomato and add it to the mix too. Pour the prepared mixture into the pie crust slowly.
- Close the slow cooker lid and cook the quiche for 4 hours on HIGH.
- After 4 hours, sprinkle the quiche surface with the shredded cheese and cook the dish for 25 minutes more. Serve the prepared quiche! Enjoy!

Chicken Open Sandwich

NUTRITION Calories 314, Fat 9.7, Fiber 3, Carbs 45.01, Protein 12

PREPARATION	COOKING TIME	SERVINGS
15	8	4
	hours	

DIRECTION

- Put the chicken fillet in the slow cooker and sprinkle it with the cayenne pepper.
- Add water and chicken gravy. Close the slow cooker lid and cook the chicken for 8 hours on LOW. Then combine the mashed potato with the mayo sauce.
- Spread toasted French bread with the mashed potato mixture.
- When the chicken is cooked, cut it into the strips and combine with the remaining gravy from the slow cooker.
- Place the chicken strips over the mashed potato. Enjoy the open sandwich warm!

INGREDIENTS

- 7 oz. chicken fillet
- 1 teaspoon cayenne pepper
- 5 oz. mashed potato, cooked
- 6 tablespoons chicken gravy
- 4 slices French bread, toasted
- 2 teaspoons mayo
- 1 cup water

Onion Lunch Muffins

NUTRITION Calories 180, Fat 11, Fiber 1, Carbs 16.28, Protein 4

PREPARATION 15   COOKING TIME 8 hours   SERVINGS 7

INGREDIENTS

- 1 egg
- 5 tablespoons butter, melted
- 1 cup flour
- ½ cup milk
- 1 teaspoon baking soda
- 1 cup onion, chopped
- 1 teaspoon cilantro
- ½ teaspoon sage
- 1 teaspoon apple cider vinegar
- 2 cup water
- 1 tablespoon chives
- 1 teaspoon olive oil

DIRECTION

- Beat the egg in the bowl and add melted butter.
- Add the flour, baking soda, chopped onion, milk, sage, apple cider vinegar, cilantro, and chives. Knead into a dough.
- After this, spray a muffin form with the olive oil inside. Fill the ½ part of every muffin form and place them in the glass jars.
- After this, pour water in the slow cooker vessel.
- Place the glass jars with muffins in the slow cooker and close the lid.
- Cook the muffins for 8 hours on LOW.
- Check if the muffins are cooked with the help of the toothpick and remove them from the slow cooker. Enjoy the dish warm!

Tuna in Potatoes

NUTRITION Calories 247, Fat 5.9, Fiber 4, Carbs 35.31, Protein 14

PREPARATION 16   COOKING TIME 4 hours   SERVINGS 8

DIRECTION

- Wash the potatoes carefully and cut them into the halves.
- Wrap the potatoes in the foil and place in the slow cooker. Close the slow cooker lid and cook the potatoes on HIGH for 2 hours.
- Meanwhile, peel the garlic clove and mince it. Combine the minced garlic clove with the cream cheese, tuna, salt, ground black pepper, onion powder, and dill.
- Then shred Cheddar cheese and add it to the mixture.
- Mix it carefully until homogenous.
- When the time is over – remove the potatoes from the slow cooker and discard the foil only from the flat surface of the potatoes.
- Then take the fork and mash the flesh of the potato halves gently. Add the tuna mixture in the potato halves and return them back in the slow cooker.
- Cook the potatoes for 2 hours more on HIGH. Enjoy!

INGREDIENTS

- 4 large potatoes
- 8 oz. tuna, canned
- ½ cup cream cheese
- 4 oz. Cheddar cheese
- 1 garlic clove
- 1 teaspoon onion powder
- ½ teaspoon salt
- 1 teaspoon ground black pepper
- 1 teaspoon dried dill

Banana Lunch Sandwiches

NUTRITION Calories 248, Fat 7.5, Fiber 2, Carbs 36.74, Protein 10

PREPARATION	COOKING TIME	SERVINGS
15	2	4
	hours	

INGREDIENTS

- 2 banana
- 8 oz. French toast slices, frozen
- 1 tablespoon peanut butter
- ¼ teaspoon ground cinnamon
- 5 oz. Cheddar cheese, sliced
- ¼ teaspoon turmeric

DIRECTION

- Peel the bananas and slice them.
- Spread the French toast slices with the peanut butter well. Combine the ground cinnamon with the turmeric and stir the mixture. Sprinkle the French toasts with the spice mixture.
- Then make the layer of the sliced bananas on the toasts and add the sliced cheese.
- Cover the toast with the second part of the toast to make the sandwich.
- Place the banana sandwiches in the slow cooker and cook them on HIGH for 2 hours.
- Serve the prepared banana sandwiches hot. Enjoy!

Parmesan Potato with Dill

NUTRITION Calories 235, Fat 3.9, Fiber 2, Carbs 32.26, Protein 1

PREPARATION	COOKING TIME	SERVINGS
17	4	5
	hours	

INGREDIENTS

- 1-pound small potato
- ½ cup fresh dill
- 7 oz. Parmesan
- 1 teaspoon rosemary
- 1 teaspoon thyme
- 1 cup water
- ¼ teaspoon chili flakes
- 3 tablespoon cream
- 1 teaspoon salt

DIRECTION

- Peel the potatoes and put them in the slow cooker.
- Add water, salt, thyme, rosemary, and chili flakes.
- Close the slow cooker lid and cook the potato for 2 hours on HIGH.
- Meanwhile, shred Parmesan cheese and chop the fresh dill. When the time is done, sprinkle the potato with the cream and fresh dill. Stir it carefully.
- Add shredded Parmesan cheese and close the slow cooker lid. Cook the potato on HIGH for 2 hours more.
- Then open the slow cooker lid and do not stir the potato anymore. Gently transfer the dish to the serving plates. Enjoy!

Light Taco Soup

NUTRITION *Calories 328, Fat 9.6, Fiber 10, Carbs 45.19, Protein 18*

PREPARATION	COOKING TIME	SERVINGS
24	7 *hours*	5

INGREDIENTS

- 7 oz. ground chicken
- ½ teaspoon sesame oil
- 3 cup vegetable stock
- 3 oz. yellow onion
- 1 cup tomato, canned
- 3 tomatoes
- 5 oz. corn kernels
- 1 jalapeno pepper, sliced
- ½ cup white beans, drained
- 3 tablespoon taco seasoning
- ¼ teaspoon salt
- 3 oz. black olives, sliced
- 5 corn tortillas, for serving

DIRECTION

- Peel the onion and dice it. Chop the fresh and canned tomatoes.
- Place the ground chicken, sesame oil, vegetable stock, diced onion, chopped tomatoes, sliced black olives, sliced jalapeno pepper, and corn in the slow cooker.
- Add the white beans, taco seasoning, and salt.
- Stir the soup mixture gently and close the slow cooker lid.
- Cook the soup for 7 hours on LOW. Meanwhile, cut the corn tortillas into the strips and bake them in the preheated to 365 F oven for 10 minutes.
- When the soup is cooked, ladle it into the serving bowls and sprinkle with the baked corn tortilla strips. Enjoy!

Slow Cooker Risotto

NUTRITION *Calories 268, Fat 3, Fiber 4, Carbs 53.34, Protein 7*

PREPARATION	COOKING TIME	SERVINGS
20	3 *hours* 30 *mins*	6

DIRECTION

- Spray a skillet with olive oil.
- Add the chopped onion and carrot and roast the vegetables for 3 minutes on the medium heat. Then put the seared vegetables in the slow cooker. Toss the long grain rice in the remaining oil and sauté for 1 minute on the high heat.
- Add the roasted long grain rice and sliced garlic in the slow cooker.
- Add green peas, dry wine, salt, ground black pepper, and beef broth. After this, add the chicken broth and stir the mixture gently. Close the slow cooker lid and cook the risotto for 3 hours.
- Then stir the risotto gently.
- Shred Parmigiano-Reggiano and sprinkle over the risotto. Close the slow cooker lid and cook the dish for 30 minutes more. Enjoy the prepared risotto immediately!

INGREDIENTS

- 7 oz. Parmigiano-Reggiano
- 2 cup chicken broth
- 1 teaspoon olive oil
- 1 onion, chopped
- ½ cup green peas
- 1 garlic clove, peeled and sliced
- 2 cups long grain rice
- ¼ cup dry wine
- 1 teaspoon salt
- 1 teaspoon ground black pepper
- 1 carrot, chopped
- 1 cup beef broth

Lemon Orzo

NUTRITION Calories 152, Fat 4, Fiber 3, Carbs 24.79, Protein 7

PREPARATION	COOKING TIME	SERVINGS
20	2 30	5
	hours mins	

INGREDIENTS

- 4 oz. shallot
- 7 oz. orzo
- 2 cup chicken stock
- 1 teaspoon paprika
- 1 teaspoon ground black pepper
- 1 teaspoon salt
- 1 lemon
- ¼ cup cream
- 2 yellow sweet pepper
- 1 cup baby spinach

DIRECTION

- Chop the shallot and place it in the slow cooker.
- Add the chicken stock and paprika. Sprinkle the mixture with the ground black pepper and salt. Stir it gently and cook on HIGH for 30 minutes.
- Meanwhile, grate the zest from the lemon and squeeze the juice. Add the lemon zest and juice in the slow cooker and stir it. After this, chop the baby spinach.
- Add it into the slow cooker. Remove the seeds from the yellow sweet peppers and chop into tiny pieces. Add the chopped peppers to the slow cooker.
- Add orzo and heavy cream. Stir the mass carefully and close the slow cooker lid. Cook the dish for 2 hours on LOW. Mix the dish gently. Enjoy!

Veggie Bean Stew

NUTRITION Calories 207, Fat 3.5, Fiber 8, Carbs 37.67, Protein 8

PREPARATION	COOKING TIME	SERVINGS
20	7	8
	hours	

DIRECTION

- Place barley, black beans, and red beans in the slow cooker vessel.
- Add chopped onion, tomato juice, salt, ground black pepper, and garlic powder. After this, add water and close the slow cooker lid.
- Cook the dish for 4 hours on HIGH.
- Meanwhile, peel the carrots and cut them into the strips. Peel the potatoes and chop.
- Add the carrot strips and chopped potatoes in the slow cooker after 4 hours of cooking.
- Chop the fresh cilantro and add it in the slow cooker too.
- Stir the mix and close the slow cooker lid. Cook the stew for 3 hours more on LOW.
- Serve the prepared dish immediately or keep it in the fridge, not more than 3 days. Enjoy!

INGREDIENTS

- ½ cup barley
- 1 cup black beans
- ¼ cup red beans
- 2 carrots
- 1 cup onion, chopped
- 1 cup tomato juice
- 2 potatoes
- 1 teaspoon salt
- 1 teaspoon ground black pepper
- 4 cups water
- 4 oz. tofu
- 1 teaspoon garlic powder
- 1 cup fresh cilantro

Carrot Soup with Cardamom

NUTRITION Calories 80, Fat 2.7, Fiber 2, Carbs 10.19, Protein 4

PREPARATION	COOKING TIME	SERVINGS
18	12 hours	9

INGREDIENTS

- 1-pound carrot
- 1 teaspoon ground cardamom
- ¼ teaspoon nutmeg
- 1 teaspoon salt
- 3 tablespoons fresh parsley
- 1 teaspoon honey
- 1 teaspoon marjoram
- 5 cups chicken stock
- ½ cup yellow onion, chopped
- 1 teaspoon butter

DIRECTION

- Toss the butter in a pan and add chopped onion.
- Chop the carrot and add it to the pan too.
- Roast the vegetables for 5 minutes on the low heat. After this, place the roasted vegetables in the slow cooker. Add ground cardamom, nutmeg, salt, marjoram, and chicken stock.
- Close the slow cooker lid and cook the soup for 12 hours on LOW.
- Chop the fresh parsley.
- When the time is over, blend the soup with a hand blender until you get a smooth texture. Then ladle the soup into the serving bowls.
- Sprinkle the prepared soup with the chopped fresh parsley and honey. Enjoy the soup immediately!

Cod Chowder

NUTRITION Calories 108, Fat 4.5, Fiber 2, Carbs 8.02, Protein 10

PREPARATION	COOKING TIME	SERVINGS
20	3 hours	6

DIRECTION

- Peel the onion and chop it.
- Put the chopped onion and grated carrot in the slow cooker bowl. Add the sage, almond milk, ground coriander, and water. After this, chop the cod into the 6 pieces.
- Add the fish in the slow cooker bowl too. Then chop the sliced bacon and peel the potatoes.
- Cut the potatoes into the cubes.
- Add the Ingredients: in the slow cooker bowl and close the slow cooker lid.
- Cook the chowder for 3 hours on HIGH. Ladle the prepared cod chowder in the serving bowls.
- Sprinkle the dish with the chopped parsley if desired. Enjoy!

INGREDIENTS

- 1 yellow onion
- 10 oz. cod
- 3 oz. bacon, sliced
- 1 teaspoon sage
- 5 oz. potatoes
- 1 carrot, grated
- 5 cups water
- 1 tablespoon almond milk
- 1 teaspoon ground coriander
- 1 teaspoon salt

Sweet Corn Pilaf

NUTRITION Calories 390, Fat 18.6, Fiber 13, Carbs 54.7, Protein 18

PREPARATION	COOKING TIME	SERVINGS
21	8 *hours*	5

DIRECTION

- Peel the carrot and cut into the small cubes.
- Combine the carrot cubes with the frozen sweet corn and green peas.
- After this, place the vegetable mixture in the slow cooker vessel.
- Add the rice, chicken stock, olive oil, salt, and ground white pepper.
- After this, cut the chicken fillet into the strips and add the meat to the rice mixture.
- Chop all the sweet peppers and add them in the slow cooker too.
- Close the slow cooker lid and cook the pilaf for 8 hours on LOW.
- When the pilaf is cooked, stir it gently and sprinkle with the almonds. Mix the dish carefully again. Serve it immediately. Enjoy!

INGREDIENTS

- 2 cups rice
- 1 cup sweet corn, frozen
- 6 oz. chicken fillet
- 1 sweet red pepper
- 1 yellow sweet pepper
- ½ cup green peas, frozen
- 1 carrot
- 4 cups chicken stock
- 2 tablespoon chopped almonds
- 1 teaspoon olive oil
- 1 teaspoon salt
- 1 teaspoon ground white pepper

Mediterranean Vegetable Mix

NUTRITION Calories 227, Fat 3.9, Fiber 9, Carbs 44.88, Protein 6

PREPARATION	COOKING TIME	SERVINGS
15	40 *mins*	4

DIRECTION

- Combine the olive oil, Mediterranean seasoning, salt, paprika, ground black pepper, and minced garlic together.
- Whisk the mixture well. Wash all the vegetables carefully.
- Cut the zucchini, eggplants, and potatoes into the medium cubes. Cut the asparagus into 2 parts.
- Then peel the onions and cut them into 4 parts. Toss all the vegetables in the slow cooker and sprinkle them with the spice mixture.
- Close the slow cooker lid and cook the vegetable mix for 7 hours on LOW.
- Serve the prepared vegetable mix hot. Enjoy!

INGREDIENTS

- 1 zucchini
- 2 eggplants
- 2 red onion
- 4 potatoes
- 4 oz. asparagus
- 2 tablespoon olive oil
- 1 teaspoon ground black pepper
- 1 teaspoon paprika
- 1 teaspoon salt
- 1 tablespoon Mediterranean seasoning
- 1 teaspoon minced garlic

Spaghetti Cottage Cheese Casserole

NUTRITION Calories: 302g, Fat: 22g, Carbs: 5g, Protein: 34g,

PREPARATION	COOKING TIME	SERVINGS
21	7 hours	8

INGREDIENTS

- 1-pound cottage cheese
- 7 oz. spaghetti, cooked
- 5 eggs
- 1 cup heavy cream
- 5 tablespoons semolina
- 3 tablespoons white sugar
- 1 teaspoon vanilla extract
- 1 teaspoon marjoram
- 1 teaspoon lemon zest
- 1 teaspoon butter

DIRECTION

- Blend the cottage cheese in the blender for 1 minute to fluff.
- Beat the eggs in the cottage mixture and continue to blend it for 3 minutes more on medium speed. Add the heavy cream, semolina, white sugar, vanilla extract, marjoram, lemon zest, and butter. Blend the mixture on the maximum speed for 1 minute.
- Then chopped the cooked spaghetti. Place 3 tablespoon of the cottage cheese mixture in the slow cooker to make the bottom layer.
- After this, make a layer from the chopped cooked spaghetti.
- Repeat the steps till you use all the chopped spaghetti.
- Then spread the last layer of the spaghetti with the cottage cheese mixture and close the slow cooker lid. Cook the casserole for 7 hours on LOW.
- When the casserole is cooked, it will have a light brown color. Serve it warm and enjoy!

Meatballs with Coconut Gravy

NUTRITION Calories: 312g, Fat: 22g, Carbs: 5g, Protein: 34g

PREPARATION	COOKING TIME	SERVINGS
20	7 hours	8

DIRECTION

- Combine the coconut, curry paste, and salt together.
- Add heavy cream and flour.
- Whisk the mixture and pour in the slow cooker. Cook on the LOW for 1 hour.
- Meanwhile, beat the egg in the big bowl and whisk.
- Add the cayenne pepper, ground pork, semolina, chopped onion, kosher salt, bread crumbs, and ground black pepper. Mix well and then make the small balls from the meat mixture and place them in the slow cooker.
- Coat the meatballs with the prepared coconut gravy and close the lid.
- Cook the dish for 7 hours on LOW. When the meatballs are cooked, serve them only with the coconut gravy. Enjoy!

INGREDIENTS

- 3 tablespoons coconut
- 1 tablespoon curry paste
- 1 teaspoon salt
- 1 cup heavy cream
- 1 tablespoon flour
- 1 teaspoon cayenne pepper
- 10 oz. ground pork
- 1 egg
- 1 tablespoon semolina
- ½ cup onion, chopped
- 1 teaspoon kosher salt
- 3 tablespoons bread crumbs
- 1 teaspoon ground black pepper

Fresh Dal

NUTRITION *Calories: 102g, Fat: 22g, Carbs: 5g, Protein: 34g*

PREPARATION	COOKING TIME	SERVINGS
15	5 *hours*	11

INGREDIENTS

- 1 teaspoon cumin
- 1 oz. mustard seeds
- 10 oz. lentils
- 1 teaspoon fennel seeds
- 7 cups water
- 6 oz. tomato, canned
- 4 oz. onion
- ½ teaspoon fresh ginger, grated
- 1 oz. bay leaf
- 1 teaspoon turmeric
- 1 teaspoon salt
- 2 cups rice

DIRECTION

- Peel the onion. Chop the onion and tomatoes and place them in a slow cooker.
- Combine the cumin, mustard seeds, and fennel seeds in a shallow bowl.
- Add the bay leaf and mix. Sprinkle the vegetables in the slow cooker with the spice mixture.
- Add salt, turmeric, and grated fresh ginger. Add rice and mix.
- Add the lentils and water. Stir gently.
- Then close the slow cooker lid and cook Dal for 5 hours on LOW.
- When the dish is done, stir and transfer to serving plates. Enjoy!

Pulled Pork Salad

NUTRITION *Calories: 302g, Fat: 22g, Carbs: 5g, Protein: 34g,*

PREPARATION	COOKING TIME	SERVINGS
15	8 *hours*	4

INGREDIENTS

- 1 avocado, chopped
- 1 tomato, chopped
- 1 cup lettuce, chopped
- 1 tablespoon olive oil
- ½ teaspoon chili flakes
- 7 oz. pork loin
- 1 cup water
- 1 bay leaf
- 1 teaspoon salt
- ¼ teaspoon peppercorns

DIRECTION

- Place the pork loin in the slow cooker.
- Add the water, bay leaf, salt, and peppercorns.
- Add the chili flakes and close the lid.
- Cook the pork loin for 8 hours on Low.
- Meanwhile, mix the chopped avocado, tomato, and lettuce in a large salad bowl.
- When the pork loin is cooked, remove it from the water and place it in a separate bowl.
- Shred the pork loin with two forks.
- Add the shredded pork loin into the salad bowl.
- Stir the salad gently and sprinkle with the olive oil.
- Enjoy!

Garlic Pork Belly

NUTRITION *Calories: 321g, Fat: 22g, Carbs: 5g, Protein: 34g*

PREPARATION
15

COOKING TIME
7
hours

SERVINGS
8

INGREDIENTS

- 1-pound pork belly
- 4 garlic cloves, peeled
- 1 teaspoon peppercorns
- 2 tablespoons mustard
- ½ teaspoon salt
- 1 tablespoon butter
- 1 cup water

DIRECTION

- Dice the garlic cloves and combine them with the peppercorns and mustard.
- Add the salt and butter and stir.
- Rub the pork belly with the prepared mixture well.
- Place the pork belly in the slow cooker.
- Add the water and close the lid.
- Cook the pork belly for 7 hours on Low.
- Slice the cooked pork belly and serve!

Sesame Seed Shrimp

NUTRITION *Calories: 102g, Fat: 22g, Carbs: 5g, Protein: 34g*

PREPARATION
20

COOKING TIME
30
mins

SERVINGS
4

DIRECTION

- Sprinkle the shrimp with the apple cider vinegar.
- Add paprika and stir the shrimp.
- Let the shrimp marinade for 15 minutes.
- Pour water into the slow cooker.
- Add the butter and marinated shrimp.
- Cook the shrimp for 30 minutes on High.
- Transfer the shrimp to a serving bowl.
- Mix together the remaining liquid and sesame seeds.
- Sprinkle the shrimp with the sesame mixture and enjoy!

INGREDIENTS

- 1-pound shrimp, peeled
- 2 tablespoons apple cider vinegar
- 1 teaspoon paprika
- 1 teaspoon sesame seeds
- ¼ cup water
- 3 tablespoons butter

Cod Fillet in Coconut Flakes

NUTRITION Calories 268, Fat 3, Fiber 4, Carbs 53.34, Protein 7

PREPARATION	COOKING TIME	SERVINGS
20	1	4
	hours	

INGREDIENTS

- ¼ cup coconut flakes, unsweetened
- 1 egg, beaten
- ½ teaspoon salt
- 1 teaspoon ground black pepper
- 10 oz. cod fillets
- 1 tablespoon butter
- 3 tablespoons water

DIRECTION

- Whisk the egg, combine it with the salt, and ground black pepper.
- Place the cod fillets in the egg mixture and stir well.
- Coat the egged cod fillets in the coconut flakes.
- Add the butter to the slow cooker.
- Add water and coated cod fillets.
- Close the lid and cook the fish for 1 hour on High.
- Then transfer the cod fillets onto a cutting board and cut them into servings.
- Enjoy the cod fillet warm!

Chicken Liver Pate

NUTRITION Calories 368, Fat 3, Fiber 4, Carbs 53.34, Protein 7

PREPARATION	COOKING TIME	SERVINGS
25	2	6
	hours	

INGREDIENTS

- 1-pound chicken liver
- 1 onion, chopped
- 2 cups water
- 1 teaspoon salt
- ¼ teaspoon ground nutmeg
- 2 tablespoons butter
- 1 bay leaf

DIRECTION

- Place the chicken liver in the slow cooker.
- Add chopped onion, water, salt, ground black pepper, and bay leaf.
- Close the lid and cook the liver for 2 hours on High.
- After this, strain the chicken liver, discarding the liquid, and place it in the blender.
- Add butter and blend the mixture until smooth (approximately for 3 minutes at maximum speed).
- Transfer the cooked pate into a bowl and let it cool in the freezer for 10 minutes.
- Serve with keto bread!

Garlic Duck Breast

NUTRITION Calories 268, Fat 3, Fiber 4,Carbs 53.34, Protein 7

PREPARATION	COOKING TIME	SERVINGS
20	5 *hours*	6

INGREDIENTS

- 11 oz. duck breast, boneless, skinless
- 4 garlic cloves, roughly diced
- 1 teaspoon rosemary
- 1 tablespoon butter
- ½ cup water
- 1 teaspoon chili flakes

DIRECTION

- Make small cuts in the duck breast.
- Sprinkle the duck breast with the rosemary and chili flakes.
- Fill the cuts with the diced garlic.
- Place the duck breast in the slow cooker.
- Add butter and water and close the lid.
- Cook the duck breast for 5 hours on Low.
- When the duck breast is cooked, remove it from the slow cooker and let it rest for 10 minutes.
- Slice the duck breast and serve!

Thyme Lamb Chops

NUTRITION Calories 368, Fat 3, Fiber 4, Carbs 53.34, Protein 7

PREPARATION	COOKING TIME	SERVINGS
20	7 *hours*	2

DIRECTION

- Combine the olive oil, sausage, broth, onion, butternut squash, bell peppers, thyme, salt, and pepper in the slow cooker. Toss to mix. Cook within 6 hours on low.
- Before serving, sprinkle the Swiss cheese over the top, cover, and cook for about 3 minutes more to melt the cheese.

INGREDIENTS

- Mix the liquid stevia, thyme, olive oil, and ground cinnamon.
- Rub the lamb chops with the spice mixture.
- Place the lamb chops in the slow cooker and add chopped onion and water.
- Add the bay leaf and close the lid.
- Cook the lamb chops for 7 hours on Low.
- When the meat is cooked, serve it immediately!

Autumn Pork Stew

NUTRITION Calories 168, Fat 3, Fiber 4, Carbs 53.34, Protein 7

PREPARATION	COOKING TIME	SERVINGS
30	6	5
	hours	

INGREDIENTS

- 1 eggplant, chopped
- 4 oz. white mushrooms, chopped
- 1 white onion, chopped
- 2 cups water
- ½ teaspoon clove
- ½ teaspoon salt
- ½ teaspoon cayenne pepper
- 8 oz. pork tenderloin

DIRECTION

- Place the chopped eggplant, mushrooms, onion, and water in the slow cooker.
- Chop the pork tenderloin roughly and sprinkle it with the cayenne pepper, salt, and clove.
- Stir the meat and place it in the slow cooker too.
- Close the lid and cook the stew for 6 hours on Low.
- When the stew is cooked, let it rest for 20 minutes.
- Enjoy!

Handmade Sausage Stew

NUTRITION Calories 268, Fat 3, Fiber 4, Carbs 53.34, Protein 7

PREPARATION	COOKING TIME	SERVINGS
25	3	3
	hours	

DIRECTION

- Mix the ground pork and yolk. Add salt and ground black pepper.
- Stir the mixture and form small sausages with your hands.
- Place the sausages in the slow cooker.
- Add the chopped broccoli and water.
- Add chopped tomato and butter.
- Close the lid and cook the stew for 3 hours on High.
- Place the cooked stew in bowls and enjoy!

INGREDIENTS

- 7 oz. ground pork
- 1 egg yolk
- ½ teaspoon salt
- ½ teaspoon ground black pepper
- 7 oz. broccoli, chopped
- ½ cup water
- 1 tomato, chopped
- 1 teaspoon butter

Marinated Beef Tenderloin

NUTRITION Calories 68, Fat 3, Fiber 4, Carbs 53.34, Protein 7

PREPARATION	COOKING TIME	SERVINGS
20	6 hours	6

INGREDIENTS

- 2 tablespoons butter
- 1-pound Beef Tenderloin
- 1 teaspoon minced garlic
- ½ teaspoon ground nutmeg
- 1 teaspoon turmeric
- 1 teaspoon paprika
- 1 tablespoon apple cider vinegar
- ½ teaspoon dried oregano
- 1 cup water

DIRECTION

- Melt the butter and mix it up with the minced garlic, ground nutmeg, turmeric, paprika, apple cider vinegar, and dried oregano.
- Whisk the mixture.
- Rub the beef tenderloin with the spice mixture.
- Place the beef tenderloin in the slow cooker and add the remaining spice mixture.
- Add water and close the lid.
- Cook the beef tenderloin for 8 hours on Low.
- Chop the beef tenderloin and serve it!

Chicken Liver Sauté

NUTRITION Calories 168, Fat 3, Fiber 4, Carbs 53.34, Protein 7

PREPARATION	COOKING TIME	SERVINGS
20	5 hours	4

INGREDIENTS

- 10 oz. chicken liver
- 1 onion, chopped
- 2 tablespoons full-fat cream
- 5 oz. white mushrooms, chopped
- 1 cup water
- 1 tablespoon butter
- 1 teaspoon salt
- ½ teaspoon ground black pepper

DIRECTION

- Place the chicken liver, onion, full-fat cream, mushrooms, water, butter, salt, and ground black pepper in the slow cooker and close the lid.
- Cook the mixture for 5 hours on Low.
- When the liver saute is cooked, let it rest for 10 minutes.
- Enjoy!

Chicken in Bacon

NUTRITION Calories 268, Fat 3, Fiber 4, Carbs 53.34, Protein 7

PREPARATION	COOKING TIME	SERVINGS
20	3 *hours*	6

INGREDIENTS

- 1-pound chicken thighs
- 7 oz. bacon, sliced
- 1 tablespoon butter
- ¾ cup water
- ½ teaspoon ground black pepper
- 1 teaspoon chili flakes
- 1 teaspoon paprika

DIRECTION

- Sprinkle the chicken thighs with the ground black pepper, chili flakes, and paprika.
- Wrap the chicken thighs in the sliced bacon and transfer to the slow cooker.
- Add the water and butter and close the lid.
- Cook the chicken for 3 hours on High.
- Serve the cooked meal immediately!

Whole Chicken

NUTRITION Calories 248, Fat 7.5, Fiber 2, Carbs 36.74, Protein 10

PREPARATION	COOKING TIME	SERVINGS
40	10 *hours*	10

INGREDIENTS

- 2-pound whole chicken
- 4 oz. celery stalk, chopped
- 1 onion, chopped
- 3 garlic cloves, peeled
- 1 tablespoon rosemary
- 1 teaspoon dried oregano
- 2 tablespoons butter
- 1 teaspoon salt
- ½ teaspoon ground coriander
- 1 teaspoon turmeric
- 2 cups water

DIRECTION

- Rub the chicken with the rosemary, dried oregano, salt, ground coriander, and turmeric.
- Fill the chicken cavity with the chopped celery, garlic cloves, onion, and butter.
- Place the chicken in the slow cooker and add water.
- Close the lid and cook the chicken for 10 hours on Low.
- When the chicken is cooked, leave it for 20 minutes to rest.
- Serve and enjoy!

Duck Rolls

NUTRITION Calories 248, Fat 7.5, Fiber 2, Carbs 36.74, Protein 10

PREPARATION	COOKING TIME	SERVINGS
25	3 hours	6

INGREDIENTS

- 2-pound duck fillets
- 1 teaspoon minced garlic
- 1 cup spinach, chopped
- ¼ cup water
- 1 teaspoon rosemary
- 1 tablespoon olive oil

DIRECTION

- Beat the duck fillets gently to tenderize and flatten then sprinkle them with the minced garlic, rosemary, and olive oil.
- Place the chopped spinach on each of the duck fillets and roll them up, enclosing the spinach inside the duck.
- Secure the duck rolls with the toothpicks and place them in the slow cooker.
- Add water and close the lid.
- Cook the duck rolls for 3 hours on High.
- Cool the rolls slightly and serve!

Keto Adobo Chicken

NUTRITION Calories 348, Fat 7.5, Fiber 2, Carbs 36.74, Protein 10

PREPARATION	COOKING TIME	SERVINGS
15	2 hours	4

DIRECTION

- Chop the chicken breast roughly and sprinkle it with the soy sauce, olive oil, apple cider vinegar, and minced garlic.
- Mix and then let sit for 20 minutes to marinate.
- Transfer the chicken and all the remaining liquid into the slow cooker.
- Close the lid and cook the meal for 2 hours on High.
- Enjoy!

INGREDIENTS

- 1-pound chicken breast, boneless, skinless
- 1 tablespoon soy sauce
- 1 tablespoon olive oil
- 1 tablespoon apple cider vinegar
- 1 teaspoon minced garlic

Cayenne Pepper Drumsticks

NUTRITION Calories 248, Fat 7.5, Fiber 2, Carbs 36.74, Protein 10

PREPARATION	COOKING TIME	SERVINGS
20	5 *hours*	2

INGREDIENTS

- 10 oz. chicken drumsticks
- 1 teaspoon cayenne pepper
- 1 bell pepper, chopped
- ½ cup water
- 1 tablespoon butter
- 1 teaspoon thyme
- 1 teaspoon cumin
- ½ teaspoon chili pepper

DIRECTION

- Mix the cayenne pepper, chopped bell pepper, butter, thyme, cumin, and chili pepper.
- Stir the mixture until smooth.
- Rub the chicken drumsticks with the spice mixture and place them in the slow cooker.
- Add water and close the lid.
- Cook the drumsticks for 5 hours on Low.
- Transfer the cooked meal onto a platter and serve!

Keto BBQ Chicken Wings

NUTRITION Calories 148, Fat 7.5, Fiber 2, Carbs 36.74, Protein 10

PREPARATION	COOKING TIME	SERVINGS
20	2 *hours*	4

INGREDIENTS

- 1-pound chicken wings
- 1 teaspoon minced garlic
- 1 teaspoon cumin
- 1 teaspoon ground coriander
- 1 teaspoon dried dill
- 1 teaspoon dried parsley
- 1 tablespoon mustard
- 1 teaspoon liquid stevia
- 1 tablespoon tomato paste
- 1 teaspoon salt
- 1 tablespoon apple cider vinegar

DIRECTION

- Mix the minced garlic, cumin, ground coriander, dried dill, dried parsley, mustard, liquid stevia, tomato paste, salt, and apple cider vinegar.
- Stir the mixture until smooth.
- Combine the spice mixture and chicken wings and stir well.
- Transfer the chicken wings and all the remaining spice mixture into the slow cooker.
- Close the lid and cook for 2 hours on High.
- Cool the chicken wings slightly and serve!

Prawn Stew

NUTRITION Calories 278, Fat 7.5, Fiber 2, Carbs 36.74, Protein 10

INGREDIENTS

- 10 oz. prawns, peeled
- 1 onion, sliced
- 4 oz. Parmesan, grated
- 1 garlic clove, peeled
- 1 teaspoon salt
- ½ cup almond milk
- 1 teaspoon butter
- 1 teaspoon chili flakes

DIRECTION

- Place the peeled prawns, sliced onion, garlic clove, salt, almond milk, butter, and chili flakes into the slow cooker.
- Close the lid and cook the stew for 1 hour on High.
- Transfer the cooked stew into serving bowls and sprinkle with the grated cheese.
- Serve it!

PREPARATION	COOKING TIME	SERVINGS
15	1 *hours*	4

Pork-Jalapeno Bowl

NUTRITION Calories 148, Fat 7.5, Fiber 2, Carbs 36.74, Protein 10

INGREDIENTS

- 2 jalapeno peppers, chopped
- 9 oz. pork chops
- 1 onion, grated
- ½ cup water
- 1 teaspoon butter
- ½ teaspoon chili flakes
- 1 teaspoon ground black pepper

DIRECTION

- Sprinkle the pork chops with the chili flakes and ground black pepper.
- Place the pork chops in the slow cooker.
- Add water, grated onion, and butter,
- Add the jalapeno peppers and close the lid.
- Cook the meal for 3 hours on High.
- Stir the cooked meal and transfer it to serving bowls.
- Serve it!

PREPARATION	COOKING TIME	SERVINGS
15	3 *hours*	4

Chicken Marsala

NUTRITION Calories 248, Fat 7.5, Fiber 2, Carbs 36.74, Protein 10

INGREDIENTS

- 1-pound chicken breast, skinless, boneless
- 2 oz. white mushrooms, chopped
- 1 Oz Marsala cooking wine
- 1 teaspoon garlic powder
- 3 tablespoons butter
- 1 teaspoon salt
- 1 teaspoon ground black pepper

DIRECTION

- Chop the chicken breast roughly and sprinkle it with the garlic powder, salt, and ground black pepper.
- Stir the chicken and transfer it to the slow cooker.
- Add butter, Marsala cooking wine, mushrooms, and close the lid.
- Cook chicken Marsala for 7 hours on Low.
- Stir the cooked meal gently.
- Serve it in serving bowls.
- Enjoy!

PREPARATION	COOKING TIME	SERVINGS
15	7 *hours*	4

Chickpeas Soup

NUTRITION Calories: 302g, Fat: 22g, Carbs: 5g, Protein: 34g

INGREDIENTS

- 30 ounces canned chickpeas, drained
- 2 tablespoons mild curry powder
- 1 cup lentils, dry
- 1 sweet potato, cubed
- 15 ounces canned coconut milk
- 1 teaspoon ginger powder
- 1 teaspoon turmeric, ground
- A pinch of salt
- 6 cups veggie stock
- Black pepper to the taste

DIRECTION

- Put chickpeas in your slow cooker.
- Add lentils, sweet potato cubes, curry powder, ginger, turmeric, salt, pepper and stock.
- Stir and then mix with coconut milk.
- Stir again, cover and cook on High for 4 hours.
- Ladle chickpeas soup into bowls and serve.
- Enjoy!

PREPARATION	COOKING TIME	SERVINGS
10	4 *hours*	6

Hot and Delicious Soup

NUTRITION Calories: 102g, Fat: 22g, Carbs: 5g, Protein: 34g

INGREDIENTS

- 8 ounces canned bamboo shoots, drained and chopped
- 10 ounces mushrooms, sliced
- 8 shiitake mushrooms, sliced
- 4 garlic cloves, minced
- 2 tablespoons ginger, grated
- 15 ounces extra firm tofu, pressed and cubed
- 2 tablespoons vegan bouillon
- 4 cups water
- 1 teaspoon sesame oil
- 2 tablespoons coconut aminos
- 1 teaspoon chili paste
- 1 and ½ cups peas
- 2 tablespoons rice wine vinegar

DIRECTION

- Put the water in your slow cooker.
- Add bamboo shoot, mushrooms, shiitake mushrooms, garlic, 1 tablespoon ginger, tofu, vegan bouillon, oil, aminos, chili paste, peas and vinegar.
- Stir, cover and cook on Low for 8 hours.
- Add the rest of the ginger, stir soup again, ladle into bowls and serve right away.
- Enjoy!

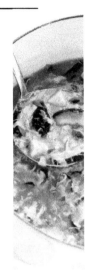

PREPARATION	COOKING TIME	SERVINGS
10	8 *hours*	4

Delicious Eggplant Salad

NUTRITION Calories: 302g, Fat: 22g, Carbs: 5g, Protein: 34g

INGREDIENTS

- 1 big eggplant, cut into quarters and then sliced
- 25 ounces canned plum tomatoes
- 2 red bell peppers, chopped
- 1 red onion, sliced
- 2 teaspoons cumin, ground
- A pinch of sea salt
- Black pepper to the taste
- 1 teaspoon smoked paprika
- Juice of 1 lemon

DIRECTION

- In your slow cooker, mix eggplant pieces with tomatoes, bell peppers, onion, cumin, salt, pepper, paprika and lemon juice, stir, cover and cook on Low for 8 hours.
- Stir again, divide into bowls and serve cold.
- Enjoy!

PREPARATION	COOKING TIME	SERVINGS
10	8 *hours*	4

Tasty Black Beans Soup

NUTRITION Calories: 202g, Fat: 22g, Carbs: 5g, Protein: 34g

INGREDIENTS

- 4 cups veggie stock
- 1 pound black beans, soaked overnight and drained
- 1 yellow onion, chopped
- 2 jalapenos, chopped
- 1 red bell pepper, chopped
- 1 cup tomatoes, chopped
- 4 garlic cloves, minced
- 1 tablespoon chili powder
- Black pepper to the taste
- 2 teaspoons cumin, ground
- A pinch of sea salt
- ½ teaspoon cayenne pepper
- 1 avocado, pitted, peeled and chopped
- ½ teaspoon sweet paprika

DIRECTION

- Put the stock in your slow cooker.
- Add beans, onion, jalapenos, bell pepper, tomatoes, garlic, chili powder, black pepper, salt, cumin, cayenne and paprika.
- Stir, cover and cook on Low for 6 hours.
- Blend soup using an immersion blender, ladle into bowls and serve with chopped avocado on top.
- Enjoy!

PREPARATION	COOKING TIME	SERVINGS
10	6 *hours*	6

Rich Sweet Potato Soup

NUTRITION Calories: 302g, Fat: 22g, Carbs: 5g, Protein: 34g

INGREDIENTS

- 5 cups veggie stock
- 2 celery stalks, chopped
- 3 sweet potatoes, chopped
- 1 cup yellow onion, chopped
- 2 garlic cloves, minced
- 1 cup rice milk
- 1 teaspoon tarragon, dried
- 2 cups baby spinach
- 8 tablespoons almonds, sliced
- A pinch of salt
- Black pepper to the taste

DIRECTION

- Put the stock in your slow cooker.
- Add celery, potatoes, onion, garlic, salt, pepper and tarragon.
- Stir, cover and cook on Low for 8 hours.
- Add rice milk and blend using an immersion blender.
- Add almonds and spinach, stir, cover and leave aside for 20 minutes.
- Ladle into bowls and serve.
- Enjoy!

PREPARATION	COOKING TIME	SERVINGS
10	8 *mins*	5

Pumpkin Chili

NUTRITION Calories: 242g, Fat: 22gCarbs: 5g, Protein: 34g

INGREDIENTS

- *1 cup pumpkin, pureed*
- *45 ounces canned black beans, drained*
- *30 ounces canned tomatoes, chopped*
- *1 yellow bell pepper, chopped*
- *1 yellow onion, chopped*
- *¼ teaspoon nutmeg, ground*
- *1 teaspoon cinnamon powder*
- *1 tablespoon chili powder*
- *1 teaspoon cumin, ground*
- *1/8 teaspoon cloves, ground*
- *A pinch of sea salt*
- *Black pepper to the taste*

DIRECTION

- Put pumpkin puree in your slow cooker.
- Add black beans, tomatoes, onion, bell pepper, cumin, nutmeg, cinnamon, chili powder, cloves, salt and pepper, stir, cover and cook on Low for 8 hours.
- Stir your chili again, divide into bowls and serve.
- Enjoy!

PREPARATION	COOKING TIME	SERVINGS
10	8 *hours*	6

Crazy Cauliflower and Zucchini Surprise

NUTRITION Calories: 302g, Fat: 22g, Carbs: 5g, Protein: 34g

INGREDIENTS

- *1 cauliflower head, florets separated*
- *2 garlic cloves, minced*
- *¾ cup red onion, chopped*
- *1 teaspoon basil, dried*
- *2 teaspoons oregano flakes*
- *28 ounces canned tomatoes, chopped*
- *¼ teaspoon red pepper flakes*
- *½ cup veggie stock*
- *5 zucchinis, cut with a spiralizer*
- *A pinch of salt*
- *Black pepper to the taste*

DIRECTION

- Put cauliflower florets in your slow cooker.
- Add garlic, onion, basil, oregano, tomatoes, stock, pepper flakes, salt and pepper, stir, cover and cook on High for 3 hours and 30 minutes.
- Mash cauliflower mix a bit using a potato masher.
- Divide zucchini noodles in bowls, top each with cauliflower mix and serve.
- Enjoy!

PREPARATION	COOKING TIME	SERVINGS
10	3 *hours* 3 *mins*	4

Quinoa and Veggies

NUTRITION Calories: 302g, Fat: 22g, Carbs: 5g, Protein: 34g

INGREDIENTS

- 1 tablespoon olive oil
- 1 and ½ cups quinoa
- 3 cups veggie stock
- 1 yellow onion, chopped
- 1 carrot, chopped
- 1 sweet red pepper, chopped
- 1 cup green beans, chopped
- 2 garlic cloves, minced
- 1 teaspoon cilantro, chopped
- A pinch of salt
- Black pepper to the taste

DIRECTION

- Put the stock in your slow cooker.
- Add oil, quinoa, onion, carrot, sweet pepper, beans, cloves, salt and pepper, stir, cover and cook on Low for 4 hours.
- Add cilantro, stir again, divide on plates and serve.
- Enjoy!

PREPARATION	COOKING TIME	SERVINGS
10	4 *hours*	4

Spaghetti Squash Bowls

NUTRITION Calories: 102g, Fat: 22g, Carbs: 5g, Protein: 34g

INGREDIENTS

- 5 pounds spaghetti squash, peeled
- 2 cups water
- 2 cups broccoli florets, steamed
- 1 tablespoon sesame seeds
- Chopped peanuts for serving
- ½ batch salad dressing
- For the salad dressing:
- 1 tablespoon palm sugar
- 1 tablespoon ginger, grated
- 3 tablespoons rice wine vinegar
- 3 tablespoons olive oil
- 2 tablespoons peanut butter
- 1 tablespoon soy sauce
- 3 garlic cloves, minced
- 1 teaspoon sesame oil
- ½ teaspoon sesame seeds

DIRECTION

- In your blender, mix ginger with sugar, vinegar, oil, soy sauce, garlic, peanut butter, sesame oil and ½ teaspoon sesame seeds, pulse really well and leave aside.
- Put the squash in your slow cooker, add the water, cover and cook on Low for 8 hours.
- Leave squash to cool down, cut in halves, scrape flesh and transfer into a bowl.
- Add broccoli florets, 1 tablespoon sesame seeds, chopped peanuts and the salad dressing.
- Toss salad well and serve.
- Enjoy!

PREPARATION	COOKING TIME	SERVINGS
10	8 *hours*	4

Amazing Curry

NUTRITION Calories: 302g, Fat: 22g, Carbs: 5g, Protein: 34g

INGREDIENTS

- 3 cups sweet potatoes, cubed
- 2 cups broccoli florets
- 1 cup water
- 1 cup white onion, chopped
- 28 ounces canned tomatoes, chopped
- 15 ounces canned chickpeas, drained
- ¼ cup quinoa
- 29 ounces canned coconut milk
- 1 tablespoon garlic, minced
- 1 tablespoon ginger root, grated
- 1 tablespoon turmeric, ground
- 2 teaspoons vegan tamari sauce
- 1 teaspoon chili flakes

DIRECTION

- Put the water in your slow cooker.
- Add potatoes, broccoli, onion, tomatoes, chickpeas, quinoa, garlic, ginger, turmeric, chili flakes, tamari sauce and coconut milk.
- Stir, cover and cook on High for 4 hours.
- Stir your curry again, divide into bowls and serve.
- Enjoy!

PREPARATION	COOKING TIME	SERVINGS
10	4 hours	6

Lentils and Lemon Soup

NUTRITION Calories: 332g, Fat: 22g, Carbs: 5g, Protein: 34g

INGREDIENTS

- 1 yellow bell pepper, chopped
- 1 yellow onion, chopped
- 6 carrots, chopped
- 4 garlic cloves, minced
- A pinch of cayenne pepper
- 4 cups veggie stock
- 3 cups red lentils, dried
- 3 cups water
- A pinch of sea salt
- 1 tablespoon rosemary, chopped
- Zest and juice from 1 lemon

DIRECTION

- Put the stock and water in your slow cooker.
- Add bell pepper, onion, carrots, garlic, lentils, cayenne and salt.
- Stir, cover and cook on Low for 6 hours.
- Add rosemary, lemon zest and juice, stir, ladle into bowls and serve.
- Enjoy!

PREPARATION	COOKING TIME	SERVINGS
10	6 hours	6

Autumn Veggie Mix

NUTRITION Calories 376, Fat 18.5, Fiber 3, Carbs 29.43, Protein 23

INGREDIENTS

- 2 sweet potatoes, cubed
- 1 yellow onion, chopped
- 1 small cauliflower head, florets separated
- 14 ounces canned coconut milk
- 2 teaspoons Sirach sauce
- 3 tablespoons coconut aminos
- A pinch of salt
- 1 tablespoon palm sugar
- 3 tablespoons red curry paste
- 1 cup green peas
- 8 ounces white mushrooms, roughly chopped
- ½ cup cashews, toasted and chopped
- ¼ cup cilantro, chopped
- A few basil leaves, chopped for serving
- Brown rice for serving

DIRECTION

- Put coconut milk in your slow cooker.
- Add potatoes, onion, cauliflower florets, sriracha sauce, aminos, salt, curry paste and sugar, stir, cover and cook on Low for 4 hours.
- Add mushrooms, peas, cilantro and basil, stir, cover and cook on Low for 30 minutes more.
- Divide into bowls and serve with brown rice on the side and toasted cashews on top.
- Enjoy!

PREPARATION	COOKING TIME	SERVINGS
10	4 30 hours mins	6

Special Veggie Stew

NUTRITION Calories 176, Fat 18.5, Fiber 3, Carbs 29.43, Protein 23

INGREDIENTS

- 1 yellow onion, chopped
- 1 teaspoon olive oil
- 2 red potatoes, chopped
- A pinch of salt and black pepper
- 1 tablespoon stevia
- 1 tablespoon curry powder
- 1 tablespoon ginger, grated
- 3 garlic cloves, minced
- 30 ounces canned chickpeas, drained
- 1 green bell pepper, chopped
- 2 cups veggie stock
- 1 red bell pepper, chopped
- 1 cauliflower head, florets separated
- 28 ounces canned tomatoes, chopped
- 1 cup coconut milk
- 10 ounces baby spinach

DIRECTION

- In your slow cooker, mix oil with onion, potatoes, salt, pepper, stevia, curry powder, ginger, garlic, chickpeas, red and green bell pepper, stock, cauliflower, tomatoes, spinach and milk, stir, cover and cook on High for 4 minutes.
- Stir your stew again, divide into bowls and serve.
- Enjoy!

PREPARATION	COOKING TIME	SERVINGS
10	4 hours	8

Vegan Chickpeas Winter Mix

NUTRITION Calories 176, Fat 18.5, Fiber 3, Carbs 29.43, Protein 23

INGREDIENTS

- 1 yellow onion, chopped
- 1 tablespoon ginger, grated
- 1 tablespoon olive oil
- 4 garlic cloves, minced
- A pinch of salt and black pepper
- 2 red Thai chilies, chopped
- ½ teaspoon turmeric powder
- 2 tablespoons gram masala
- 4 ounces tomato paste
- 2 cups veggie stock
- 6 ounces canned chickpeas, drained
- 2 tablespoons cilantro, chopped

DIRECTION

- Heat up a pan with the oil over medium high heat, add ginger and onions, stir and cook for 4-5 minutes.
- Add garlic, salt, pepper, Thai chilies, garam masala and turmeric, stir, cook for 2 minutes more and transfer everything to your slow cooker.
- Add stock, chickpeas and tomato paste, stir, cover and cook on Low for 4 hours.
- Add cilantro, stir, divide into bowls and serve.
- Enjoy!

PREPARATION	COOKING TIME	SERVINGS
10	4 10 *hours* *mins*	6

Indian Lentils Mix

NUTRITION Calories 376, Fat 18.5, Fiber 3, Carbs 29.43, Protein 23

INGREDIENTS

- 4 garlic cloves, minced
- 4 cups brown lentils
- 2 yellow onions, chopped
- 1 tablespoon ginger, grated
- 4 tablespoons olive oil
- 1 tablespoon garam masala
- 4 tablespoons red curry paste
- 2 teaspoons stevia
- 1 and ½ teaspoons turmeric powder
- A pinch of salt and black pepper
- 45 ounces canned tomato puree
- ½ cup coconut milk
- 1 tablespoon cilantro, chopped

DIRECTION

- In your slow cooker, mix lentils with onions, garlic, ginger, oil, curry paste, garam masala, turmeric, salt, pepper and stevia.
- Also add tomato puree, stir, cover and cook on Low for 7 hour and 20 minutes.
- Add coconut milk and cilantro, stir, cover and cook on Low for 40 minutes.
- Divide into bowls and serve.
- Enjoy!

PREPARATION	COOKING TIME	SERVINGS
10	8 *hours*	16

"Baked" Beans

NUTRITION Calories 576, Fat 18.5, Fiber 3, Carbs 29.43, Protein 23

INGREDIENTS

- 1 pound navy beans, soaked overnight and drained
- 1 cup maple syrup
- 1 cup vegan BBQ sauce
- 4 tablespoons stevia
- 1 cup water
- ¼ cup tomato paste
- ¼ cup mustard
- ¼ cup olive oil
- ¼ cup apple cider vinegar
- 2 tablespoons coconut aminos

DIRECTION

- In your slow cooker, mix beans with maple syrup, BBQ sauce, stevia, water, tomato paste, mustard, oil, vinegar and aminos, stir, cover and cook on Low for 12 hours.
- Divide into bowls and serve hot.
- Enjoy!

PREPARATION	COOKING TIME	SERVINGS
10	12 *hours*	6

Squash Chili

NUTRITION Calories 376, Fat 18.5, Fiber 3, Carbs 29.43, Protein 23

INGREDIENTS

- 2 carrots, chopped
- 1 yellow onion, chopped
- 2 celery stalks, chopped
- 2 green apples, cored, peeled and chopped
- 4 garlic cloves, minced
- 2 cups butternut squash, peeled and cubed
- 6 ounces canned chickpeas, drained
- 6 ounces canned black beans, drained
- 7 ounces canned coconut milk
- 2 teaspoons chili powder
- 1 teaspoon oregano, dried
- 1 tablespoon cumin, ground
- 2 cups veggie stock
- 2 tablespoons tomato paste
- Salt and black pepper to the taste
- 1 tablespoon cilantro, chopped

DIRECTION

- In your slow cooker, mix carrots with onion, celery, apples, garlic, squash, chickpeas, black beans, coconut milk, chili powder, oregano, cumin, stock, tomato paste, salt and pepper, stir, cover and cook on High for 6 hours.
- Add cilantro, stir, divide into bowls and serve.
- Enjoy!

PREPARATION	COOKING TIME	SERVINGS
10	6 *hours*	8

Rich Lentils Soup

NUTRITION Calories 176, Fat 18.5, Fiber 3, Carbs 29.43, Protein 23

INGREDIENTS

- 2 teaspoons garlic, minced
- 1 tablespoon olive oil
- 1 yellow onion, chopped
- 1 teaspoon cumin, ground
- 1 teaspoon coriander seeds
- 1 teaspoon turmeric powder
- 1 teaspoon cinnamon powder
- ½ teaspoon garam masala
- 1 and ½ cups red lentils
- 4 cups veggie stock
- 14 ounces coconut milk
- 4 cups spinach
- Salt and black pepper to the taste

DIRECTION

- In your slow cooker, mix garlic with oil, onion, cumin, coriander, turmeric, cinnamon, garam masala, lentils and stock, stir, cover and cook on High for 2 hours.
- Add coconut, spinach, salt and pepper, stir and cook on High for 30 minutes more.
- Ladle into bowls and serve.
- Enjoy!

PREPARATION	COOKING TIME	SERVINGS
10	2 *hours*	4

Easy Lentils Mix

NUTRITION Calories 176, Fat 18.5, Fiber 3, Carbs 29.43, Protein 23

INGREDIENTS

- 6 cups sweet potatoes, cubed
- 1 yellow onion, chopped
- 3 cups veggie stock
- 2 teaspoons coriander, ground
- 4 garlic cloves, minced
- 2 teaspoons chili powder
- 2 teaspoons garam masala
- 1 and ½ cups red lentils
- 8 ounces canned coconut milk
- 1 cup water
- A pinch of salt and black pepper to the taste

DIRECTION

- In your slow cooker, mix potatoes with onion, stock, coriander, garlic, chili powder, garam masala, salt and pepper, stir, cover and cook on High for 3 hours.
- Add lentils and water, stir, cover and cook on High for 1 hour and 30 minutes more.
- Add coconut milk, more salt and pepper if needed, stir, cover, leave aside for a few minutes, divide between plates and serve.
- Enjoy!

PREPARATION	COOKING TIME	SERVINGS
10	4 30 *hours mins*	6

Quinoaand Beans Chili

NUTRITION Calories 376, , Fat 18.5, Fiber 3, Carbs 29.43, Protein 23

INGREDIENTS

- *15 ounces canned black beans, drained*
- *2 and ¼ cups veggie stock*
- *½ cup quinoa*
- *14 ounces canned tomatoes, chopped*
- *¼ cup red bell pepper, chopped*
- *1 carrot, shredded*
- *¼ cup green bell pepper, chopped*
- *2 garlic cloves, minced*
- *½ chili pepper, chopped*
- *2 teaspoons chili powder*
- *1 small yellow onion, chopped*
- *A pinch of salt and black pepper*
- *1 teaspoon oregano, dried*
- *1 teaspoon cumin, ground*
- *½ cup corn*
- *For the cashew cream:*
- *4 tablespoons water*
- *½ cup cashews, soaked overnight and drained*
- *A pinch of salt and black pepper*
- *A drizzle of white vinegar*
- *1 teaspoon lime juice*

DIRECTION

- In your slow cooker, mix black beans with stock, quinoa, tomatoes, red and green bell pepper, carrot, garlic, chili, chili powder, onion, salt, pepper, oregano, cumin and corn, stir, cover and cook on High for 3 hours.
- Meanwhile, in your blender, mix cashews with water, salt, pepper, vinegar and lime juice and pulse really well.
- Divide chili into bowls, spread cashew cream on top and serve.
- Enjoy!

PREPARATION	COOKING TIME	SERVINGS
5	3 *hours*	4

Potatoes and Spinach Mix

NUTRITION Calories 276, Fat 18.5, Fiber 3, Carbs 29.43, Protein 23

INGREDIENTS

- *1 pound potatoes, cubed*
- *1 small onion, chopped*
- *2 tablespoons water*
- *1 tablespoon olive oil*
- *½ teaspoon cumin, ground*
- *½ teaspoon coriander, ground*
- *½ teaspoon garam masala*
- *½ teaspoon chili powder*
- *½ pound spinach, torn*
- *Black pepper to the taste*

DIRECTION

- In your slow cooker, mix potatoes with onion, water, oil, cumin, coriander, garam masala, chili, spinach and black pepper, stir, cover and cook on High for 3 hours.
- Divide into bowls and serve.
- Enjoy!

PREPARATION	COOKING TIME	SERVINGS
10	3 *hours*	4

Rich White Bean Soup

NUTRITION Calories 376, Fat 18.5, Fiber 3, Carbs 29.43, Protein 23

INGREDIENTS

- 1 pounds navy beans, dried
- 1 yellow onion, chopped
- 2 quarts veggie stock
- Salt and black pepper to the taste
- 2 potatoes, cubed
- 1 pound carrots, sliced
- 1 cup sun-dried tomatoes, chopped
- 2 teaspoons dill, chopped
- 4 tablespoons parsley, chopped

DIRECTION

- In your slow cooker, mix beans with onion, stock, salt, pepper, potatoes, carrots, tomatoes, dill and parsley, stir, cover and cook on High for 4 hours.
- Ladle into bowls and serve.
- Enjoy!

PREPARATION	COOKING TIME	SERVINGS
10	10 *hours*	5

Intense Tofu and Pineapple Mix

NUTRITION Calories 126, Fat 18.5, Fiber 3, Carbs 29.43, Protein 23

INGREDIENTS

- 2 pounds firm tofu, pressed and cut into medium rectangles
- 1 tablespoons sesame oil
- 3 tablespoons coconut aminos
- ½ cup veggie stock
- 1 cup pineapple juice
- ¼ cup rice vinegar
- 2 tablespoons stevia
- 1 tablespoon ginger, grated
- 3 garlic cloves, minced
- 6 pineapple rings

DIRECTION

- In your slow cooker, mix tofu with sesame oil, coconut aminos, stock, pineapple juice, vinegar, stevia, ginger, garlic and pineapple rings, stir, cover and cook on Low for 10 hours.
- Divide into bowls and serve.
- Enjoy!

PREPARATION	COOKING TIME	SERVINGS
5	10 *hours*	5

Vegan Jambalaya

NUTRITION Calories 376, Fat 18.5, Fiber 3, Carbs 29.43, Protein 23

INGREDIENTS

- 1 green bell pepper, chopped
- 1 cup okra
- 1 small yellow onion, chopped
- 2 garlic cloves, minced
- 3 celery ribs, chopped
- 16 ounces canned tomatoes, chopped
- 1 and ½ cups veggie stock
- ½ teaspoon paprika
- A pinch of salt and black pepper

DIRECTION

- In your slow cooker, mix bell pepper with okra, onion, garlic, celery, tomatoes, stock, paprika, salt and pepper, stir, cover and cook on Low for 4 hours.
- Divide into bowls and serve.
- Enjoy!

PREPARATION	COOKING TIME	SERVINGS
10	4 *hours*	6

Chapter 7.Dinner

Pork Chops

NUTRITION Net Carbs: 1g, Calories: 235 , Total Fat: 15g , Saturated Fat: 3g , Protein: 24g , Carbs: 1g , Fiber: 0g, Sugar: 0g

INGREDIENTS

- 2 pounds pasture-raised pork chops
- 1 teaspoon salt
- 1 tablespoon dried thyme
- 1 tablespoon dried rosemary
- 1 tablespoon ground cumin
- 1 tablespoon dried curry powder
- 1 tablespoon chopped fresh chives
- 1 tablespoon fennel seeds
- 1 tablespoons avocado oil

DIRECTION

- Place 2 tablespoons oil in a small bowl, add remaining Ingredients: except for pork, and stir until well mixed.
- Rub this mixture on all sides of pork chops until evenly coated.
- Grease a 6-quart slow cooker with remaining oil, add seasoned pork chops, and shut with lid.
- Plug in the slow cooker and cook pork for 6 hours at a low heat setting or 4 hours at a high heat setting.
- Serve straight away.

PREPARATION	COOKING TIME	SERVINGS
5	6 hours	8

Spicy Pork & Spinach Stew

NUTRITION Net Carbs: 3.3g , Calories: 604 , Total Fat: 38.3g , Saturated Fat: 9g , Protein: 56g , Carbs: 9g , Fiber: 5g; Sugar: 4g

INGREDIENTS

- 1-pound pasture-raised pork butt, fat trimmed and cut into 2-inch pieces
- 4 cups chopped baby spinach
- 4 ounces Rotel tomatoes
- 1 large white onion, peeled and quartered
- cloves of garlic, peeled
- 1 teaspoon dried thyme
- 2 teaspoons Cajun seasoning blend
- 2 tablespoons avocado oil
- ¾ cup heavy whipping cream

DIRECTION

- Place tomatoes, onion, and garlic in a food processor and pulse for 1 to 2 minutes or until blended.
- Pour this mixture into a 6-quart slow cooker, add Cajun seasoning mix, thyme, avocado oil, and pork pieces, and stir well until evenly coated.
- Plug in the slow cooker, then shut with lid and cook for 5 hours at low heat setting or 2 hours at high heat setting.
- When done, stir in cream until combined, add spinach and continue cooking at low heat setting for 20 minutes or more until spinach wilts.
- Serve straight away.

PREPARATION	COOKING TIME	SERVINGS
5	4 hours 20 mins	5

Stuffed Taco Peppers

NUTRITION Net Carbs: 4g , Calories: 270 , Total Fat: 18g , Saturated Fat: 5g , Protein: 21g , Carbs: 6g , Fiber: 2g , Sugar: 3g

INGREDIENTS

- 1 cup cauliflower rice
- 1 small red bell peppers
- 18-ounce minced pork, pasture-raised
- 1 teaspoon garlic powder
- ¾ teaspoon salt
- 1 teaspoon red chili powder
- 1 cup shredded Monterey jack cheese and more for topping
- 2 tablespoons avocado oil
- 1 cup water

DIRECTION

- Remove and discard stem from each pepper and then scoop out seeds.
- Place meat in a large bowl, add garlic, salt, and red chili powder, and stir until combined.
- Then stir in cauliflower rice and oil until just combine and then stir in cheese.
- Stuff this mixture into each pepper and place them in a 4-quart slow cooker.
- Pour water into the bottom of the slow cooker, switch it on, and shut with the lid.
- Cook peppers for 4 hours at high heat setting or 8 hours at low heating setting and top peppers with more cheese in the last 10 minutes of cooking time.
- Serve straight away.

PREPARATION	COOKING TIME	SERVINGS
5	8 *hours*	6

Lamb Barbacoa

NUTRITION Net Carbs: 0.7g , Calories: 477 , Total Fat: 35.8g , Saturated Fat: 14.8g , Protein: 37.5g , Carbs: 1.2g , Fiber: 0.5g , Sugar: 5g

INGREDIENTS

- 2 pounds pasture-raised pork shoulder, fat trimmed
- 2 tablespoons salt
- 1 teaspoon chipotle powder
- 2 tablespoons smoked paprika
- 1 tablespoon ground cumin
- 1 tablespoon dried oregano
- ¼ cup dried mustard
- 1 cup water

DIRECTION

- Stir together salt, chipotle powder, paprika, cumin, oregano, and mustard and rub this mixture generously all over the pork.
- Place seasoned pork into a 6-quart slow cooker, plug it in, then shut with lid and cook for 6 hours at high heat setting.
- When done, shred pork with two forks and stir well until coated well.
- Serve straight away.

PREPARATION	COOKING TIME	SERVINGS
5	8 *hours*	12

Pork Chile Verde

NUTRITION Net Carbs: 4g , Calories : 342 , Total Fat: 22g , Saturated Fat: 12g , Protein: 32g , Carbs: 6g , Fiber: 2g , Sugar: 4g

INGREDIENTS

- 2 pounds pasture-raised pork shoulder, cut into 6 pieces
- 1 teaspoon sea salt
- ½ teaspoon ground black pepper
- 1 ½ tablespoon avocado oil
- 1 ½ cup salsa Verde
- 1 cup chicken broth

DIRECTION

- Season pork with salt and black pepper.
- Place a large skillet pan over medium heat, add oil, and when hot, add seasoned pork pieces.
- Cook pork for 3 to 4 minutes per side or until browned and then transfer to a 6-quart slow cooker.
- Whisk together salsa and chicken broth and pour over pork pieces.
- Plug in the slow cooker, then shut with lid and cook for 6 to 7 hours at low heat setting or until pork is very tender.
- When done, shred pork with two forks and stir until combined.

PREPARATION	COOKING TIME	SERVINGS
5	7 hours 5 mins	6

Ham Soup

NUTRITION Net Carbs: 3g , Calories : 349 , Total Fat: 23g , Saturated Fat: 10g , Protein: 34g , Carbs: 5g , Fiber: 2g , Sugar: 2g

INGREDIENTS

- 2 pounds pasture-raised smoked ham hock
- 2 cups cauliflower florets
- 2 bay leaves
- ¼ teaspoon nutmeg
- cups bone broth

DIRECTION

- Place cauliflower florets in a 6-quarts slow cooker, add remaining Ingredients, and pour in water until all the Ingredients are just submerged.
- Plug in the slow cooker, then shut with lid and cook for 4 hours at high heat setting or until cauliflower florets are very tender.
- Transfer ham to a bowl, shred with two forms, and discard bone and fat pieces.
- Puree cauliflower in the slow cooker with a stick blender for 1 to 2 minutes or until smooth, return shredded ham, and stir until well combined.
- Taste soup to adjust seasoning and serve.

PREPARATION	COOKING TIME	SERVINGS
5	4 hours	6

Minced Pork Zucchini Lasagna

NUTRITION Carbohydrates: 10 grams , Protein: 23 grams , Fat: 30 grams , Calories: 398

INGREDIENTS

- medium zucchinis
- 1 diced small onion
- 1 minced clove of garlic
- 2 cups of minced lean ground pork
- 2 cans of Italian diced tomatoes
- 2 tablespoons of olive oil
- 2 cups of shredded Mozzarella cheese
- 1 large egg
- 1 tablespoon of dried basil
- Salt and pepper
- 2 tablespoons of butter

DIRECTION

- Slice the zucchini lengthwise into 6 slices.
- Heat the olive oil in a saucepan, and sauté the garlic and onions for 5 minutes.
- Add the minced meat and cook for a further 5 minutes.
- Add the tomatoes and cook for a further 5 minutes.
- Add the seasoning and mix thoroughly.
- In a small bowl, combine the egg and cheese and whisk together.
- Use the butter to grease the crock pot and then begin to layer the lasagna.
- First, layer with the zucchini slices, add the meat mixture, and then top with the cheese.
- Repeat and finish with the cheese.
- Cover and cook for 8 hours on low.

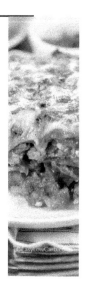

PREPARATION	COOKING TIME	SERVINGS
20	8 *hours*	4

Beef Dijon

NUTRITION Calories: 535 , Net Carbs: 5.0 g , Fat: 40 g , Protein: 39 g

INGREDIENTS

- 6 oz.) small round steaks
- 2 tbsp. of each:
- Steak seasoning - to taste
- Avocado oil
- Peanut oil
- Balsamic vinegar/dry sherry
- tbsp. large chopped green onions/small chopped onions for the garnish - extra
- 1/4 c. whipping cream
- 1 c. fresh crimini mushrooms - sliced
- 1 tbsp. Dijon mustard

DIRECTION

- Warm up the oils using the high heat setting on the stove top. Flavor each of the steaks with pepper and arrange to a skillet.
- Cook two to three minutes per side until done.
- Place into the slow cooker. Pour in the skillet drippings, half of the mushrooms, and the onions.
- Cook on the low setting for four hours.
- When the cooking time is done, scoop out the onions, mushrooms, and steaks to a serving platter.
- In a separate dish - whisk together the mustard, balsamic vinegar, whipping cream, and the steak drippings from the slow cooker.
- Empty the gravy into a gravy server and pour over the steaks.
- Enjoy with some brown rice, riced cauliflower, or potatoes.

PREPARATION	COOKING TIME	SERVINGS
15	5 *hours*	4

Cabbage & Corned Beef

NUTRITION Calories: 583 , Net Carbs: 13 g , Fat: 40 g , Protein: 42 g

INGREDIENTS

- lb. corned beef
- 1 large head of cabbage
- c. water
- 1 celery bunch
- 1 small onion
- 4 carrots
- ½ t. of each:
- Ground mustard
- Ground coriander
- Ground marjoram
- Black pepper
- Salt
- Ground thyme
- Allspice

DIRECTION

- Dice the carrots, onions, and celery and toss them into the cooker. Pour in the water.
- Combine the spices, rub the beef, and arrange in the cooker. Secure the lid and cook on low for seven hours.
- Remove the top layer of cabbage. Wash and cut it into quarters it until ready to cook. When the beef is done, add the cabbage, and cook for one hour on the low setting.
- Serve and enjoy.

PREPARATION	COOKING TIME	SERVINGS
10	8 *hours*	10

Chipotle Barbacoa

NUTRITION Calories: 242 , Net Carbs: 2 g , Fat: 11 g , Protein: 32 g

INGREDIENTS

- ½ c. beef/chicken broth
- 2 med. chilies in adobo (with the sauce, it's about 4 teaspoons)
- lb. chuck roast/beef brisket
- minced garlic cloves
- 2 tbsp. of each:
- Lime juice
- Apple cider vinegar
- 2 t. of each:
- Sea salt
- Cumin
- 1 tbsp. dried oregano
- 1 t. black pepper
- 2 whole bay leaves
- Optional: ½ t. ground cloves

DIRECTION

- Mix the chilies in the sauce, and add the broth, garlic, ground cloves, pepper, cumin, salt, vinegar, and lime juice in a blender, mixing until smooth.
- Chop the beef into two-inch chunks and toss it in the slow cooker. Empty the puree on top. Toss in the two bay leaves.
- Cook four to six hrs. On the high setting or eight to ten using the low setting.
- Dispose of the bay leaves when the meat is done.
- Shred and stir into the juices to simmer for five to ten minutes.

PREPARATION	COOKING TIME	SERVINGS
20	4 *hours*	9

Corned Beef Cabbage Rolls

NUTRITION Calories: 481.4 , Net Carbs: 4.2 g , Protéine: 34.87 g , Fat: 25.38 g

INGREDIENTS

- ½ lb. corned beef
- large savoy cabbage leaves

¼ c. of each:
- White wine
- Coffee
- 1 large lemon
- 1 med. sliced onion

1 tbsp. of each:
- Rendered bacon fat
- Erythritol
- Yellow mustard

2 t. of each:
- Kosher salt
- Worcestershire sauce

¼ t. of each:
- Cloves
- Allspice
- 1 large bay leaf

1 t. of each:
- Mustard seeds
- Whole peppercorns
- ½ t. red pepper flakes

DIRECTION

- Add the liquids, spices, and corned beef into the cooker. Cook six hours on the low setting.
- Prepare a pot of boiling water.
- When the time is up, add the leaves along with the sliced onion to the water for two to three minutes.
- Transfer the leaves to a cold-water bath - blanching them for three to four minutes. Continue boiling the onion.
- Use a paper towel to dry the leaves. Add the onions and beef. Roll up the cabbage leaves.
- Drizzle with freshly squeezed lemon juice.

PREPARATION	COOKING TIME	SERVINGS
25	6 *hours*	5

Cube Steak

NUTRITION Calories : 154 , Net Carbs: 4 g , Protein: 23.5 g , Fat: 5.5 g

INGREDIENTS

- Cubed steaks (28 oz.)
- 1 ¾ t. adobo seasoning/garlic salt
- 1 can (8 oz.) tomato sauce
- 1 c. water
- Black pepper to taste
- ½ med. onion
- 1 small red pepper
- 1/3 c. green pitted olives (+) 2 tbsp. brine

DIRECTION

- Slice the peppers and onions into ¼-inch strips.
- Sprinkle the steaks with the pepper and garlic salt as needed and place them in the cooker.
- Fold in the peppers and onion along with the water, sauce, and olives (with the liquid/brine from the jar).
- Close the lid. Prepare using the low-temperature setting for eight hours.

PREPARATION	COOKING TIME	SERVINGS
15	8 *hours*	8

Ragu

NUTRITION Calories: 224 , Net Carbs: 6 g , Protein: 27 g , Fat: 9 g

PREPARATION	COOKING TIME	SERVINGS
10	8 hours	2

DIRECTION

- Place the prepared celery, garlic, onion, and carrots into the slow cooker.
- Trim away the fat and add the meat to the slow cooker. Sprinkle with the salt and pepper
- Stir in the rest of the Ingredient.
- Prepare on the low setting for six to eight hours. Enjoy any way you choose.

INGREDIENTS

¼ of each - diced:
- 4 Carrot
- Rib of celery
- 1 Onion
- 1 minced garlic clove
- ½ lb. top-round lean beef

(3 oz.) Of each:
- Diced tomatoes
- Crushed tomatoes
- 2 ½ t. beef broth (+) ¼ c.

1 ¼ t. of each:
- Chopped fresh thyme
- Minced fresh rosemary
- 1 bay leaf
- Pepper & Salt to taste

Rope Vieja

NUTRITION Calories: 257 , Net Carbs: 7 g , Fat: 10 g , Protein: 35 g

PREPARATION	COOKING TIME	SERVINGS
15	8 hours	6

DIRECTION

- Prepare the crockpot with the spray or use a liner and combine all of the fixings.
- Stir everything together and prepare using low for eight hours.
- Top it off with your chosen garnishes.

INGREDIENTS

- 2 lb. flank steak – remove fat

1 of each:
- Yellow pepper
- Thinly sliced onion
- Green pepper
- Bay leaf
- ¼ t. salt

¾ t. of each:
- Oregano
- Non-fat beef broth
- Tomato paste
- Cooking spray

Spinach Soup

NUTRITION Calories 322 , Fats 28.2g , Net carbs 10.1g , Protein 12.2g

PREPARATION	COOKING TIME	SERVINGS
15	6-8 *hours*	4

INGREDIENTS

- 2 pounds spinach
- ¼ cup cream cheese
- 1 onion, diced
- 2 cups heavy cream
- 1 garlic clove, minced
- 2 cups water
- salt, pepper, to taste

DIRECTION

- Pour water into the slow cooker. Add spinach, salt, and pepper.
- Add cream cheese, onion, garlic, and heavy cream.
- Close the lid and cook on Low for 6-8 hours.
- Puree soup with blender and serve.

Mashed Cauliflower with Herbs

NUTRITION Calories 115 , Fats 12g , Net carbs 4.7g , Protein 6.2g

PREPARATION	COOKING TIME	SERVINGS
15	3-6 *hours*	4

DIRECTION

- Pour broth into the slow cooker, add cauliflower florets.
- Add water, it should cover the cauliflower.
- Close the lid and cook on Low for 6 hours or on High for 3 hours.
- Once cooked, drain water from the slow cooker.
- Add herbs, salt, and pepper, and ghee, puree with a blender.

INGREDIENTS

- 1 cauliflower head, cut into florets
- garlic cloves, peeled
- ½ teaspoon fresh rosemary, chopped
- ½ teaspoon fresh thyme, chopped
- ½ teaspoon fresh sage, chopped
- ½ teaspoon fresh parsley, chopped
- 1 cup vegetable broth
- 2 cups water
- 1 tablespoons ghee
- Salt, pepper, to taste

Kale Quiche

NUTRITION Calories 273 , Fats 24.4g , Net carbs 5.8g , Protein 10.5g

PREPARATION	COOKING TIME	SERVINGS
15	3-5 hours	3

INGREDIENTS

- 1 cup almond milk
- 4 eggs
- 1 cup Carbquick Baking Mix
- 2 cups spinach, chopped
- ½ bell pepper, chopped
- cups fresh baby kale, chopped
- 1 teaspoon garlic, chopped
- 1/3 cup fresh basil, chopped
- salt, pepper, to taste
- 1 tablespoon olive oil

DIRECTION

- Add oil to a slow cooker or use a cooking spray.
- Beat eggs into a slow cooker; add almond milk and Baking Mix, mix to combine.
- Add spinach, bell pepper, garlic, and basil, stir to combine.
- Close the lid and cook on Low for 5 hours or on High for 3 hours.
- Make sure the quiche is done, check the center with a toothpick, it should be dry.

Spinach Stuffed Portobello

NUTRITION Calories 310g , Fats 21 , Net carbs 3g , Protein 12g

PREPARATION	COOKING TIME	SERVINGS
15	3 hours	8

DIRECTION

- Heat oil in a medium pan over high heat. Add onion, cook until translucent, stirring steadily. Add spinach and thyme, cook for 1-2 minutes until spinach is wilted.
- Brush each mushroom with olive oil.
- Put 1 tablespoon of onion and spinach stuffing into each mushroom.
- Pour chicken broth into a slow cooker. Put stuffed mushrooms on the bottom.
- Close the lid and cook on High for 3 hours.
- Once cooked, sprinkle mushrooms with parmesan cheese and serve.

INGREDIENTS

- oz. medium-sized Portobello mushrooms, stems removed
- 1 tablespoons olive oil
- ½ onion, chopped
- 2 cups fresh spinach, rinsed and chopped
- garlic cloves, minced
- 1 cup chicken broth
- tablespoons parmesan cheese, grated
- 1/3 teaspoon dried thyme
- salt, pepper, to taste

Poached Salmon

NUTRITION Calories 273 , Fats 21g , Net carbs 4.2g , Protein 35g

PREPARATION	COOKING TIME	SERVINGS
15	1 *hours*	4

INGREDIENTS

- medium salmon fillets
- water
- 2 tablespoons dry white wine
- 1 yellow onion, sliced
- ½ lemon, sliced
- ½ teaspoon salt
- ¼ teaspoon garlic powder
- ¼ teaspoon dried basil

DIRECTION

- Pour water and wine into a slow cooker. Heat on High for 30 minutes with the lid open.
- Season salmon fillets with salt, garlic powder, and basil.
- Put salmon into a slow cooker. Add onion and lemon onto salmon fillets.
- Close the lid and cook on High for 20-30 minutes.

Cod and Vegetables

NUTRITION Calories 150 , Fats 11.6g , Net carbs 6.2g , Protein 26.9g

PREPARATION	COOKING TIME	SERVINGS
15	1-3 *hours*	4

DIRECTION

- Season cod fillets with salt and pepper.
- Pour broth into a slow cooker, add garlic, rosemary, bell pepper, onion, and zucchini into the slow cooker.
- Put fish into your crockpot, add lemon slices on top.
- Close the lid and cook on Low for 2-3 hours or on High for 1 hour.

INGREDIENTS

- (5-6 oz.) cod fillets
- 1 bell pepper, sliced or chopped
- 1 onion, sliced
- ½ fresh lemon, sliced
- 1 zucchini, sliced
- garlic cloves, minced
- ¼ cup low-sodium broth
- 1 teaspoon rosemary
- ¼ teaspoon red pepper flakes
- Salt, pepper, to taste

Balsamic Beef Pot Roast

NUTRITION Calories : 393 , Net Carbs: 3 g , Protein: 30 g

PREPARATION	COOKING TIME	SERVINGS
15	10 hours	4

DIRECTION

- Season the chuck roast with garlic powder, pepper, and salt over the entire surface.
- Use a large skillet to sear the roast until browned.
- Deglaze the bottom of the pot using balsamic vinegar. Cook one minute. Add to the slow cooker.
- Mix in the onion and add the water. Once it starts to boil, secure the lid, and continue cooking on low for three to four hours.
- Take the meat out of the slow cooker, and place it in a large bowl where you will break it up carefully into large chunks.
- Remove all fat and anything else that may not be healthy such as too much fat.
- Whisk the xanthan gum into the broth, and add it back to the slow cooker.
- Serve and enjoy with a smile!

INGREDIENTS

- 1 boneless (3 lb.) chuck roast
- 1 tbsp. of each:
- Kosher salt
- Black ground pepper
- Garlic powder
- ¼ c. balsamic vinegar
- ½ c. chopped onion
- 2 c. water
- ¼ t. xanthan gum
- For the Garnish: Fresh parsley

Moist and Spicy Pulled Chicken Breast

NUTRITION Calories: 42 , Carbs: 1g , Fat: 1g , Protein: 9g

PREPARATION	COOKING TIME	SERVINGS
15	6 hours	8

DIRECTION

- Mix dry seasoning, sprinkle half on the bottom of crockpot.
- Place the chicken breasts over it, sprinkle the rest of the spices.
- Pour the salsa over the chicken. Cover, cook on low for 6 hours.

INGREDIENTS

- 1 teaspoon dry oregano
- 1 teaspoon dry thyme
- 1 teaspoon dried rosemary
- 1 teaspoon garlic powder
- 1 teaspoon sweet paprika
- ½ teaspoon chili powder
- Salt and pepper to taste
- tablespoons butter
- pounds of chicken breasts
- 1 ½ cups ready-made tomato salsa
- 2 Tablespoons of olive oil

Whole Roasted Chicken

Calories: 120 , Carbs: 1g , Fat: 6g , Protein: 17g

PREPARATION	COOKING TIME	SERVINGS
15	8 *hours*	6

DIRECTION

- Mix all dry Ingredients: well.
- Stuff the chicken belly with garlic and onions.
- On the bottom of the crockpot, place four balls of aluminum foil.
- Set the chicken on top of the balls. Rub it generously with olive oil.
- Cover the chicken with seasoning, drop in butter pieces. Cover, cook on low for 8 hours.

INGREDIENTS

- 1 whole chicken (approximately 5.5 pounds)
- garlic cloves
- small onions
- 1 Tablespoon olive oil, for rubbing
- 2 teaspoons salt
- 2 teaspoons sweet paprika
- 1 teaspoon Cayenne pepper
- 1 teaspoon onion powder
- 1 teaspoon ground thyme
- 2 teaspoons fresh ground black pepper
- Tablespoons butter, cut into cubes

Pot Roast Beef Brisket

Calories: 280 , Carbs: 4g , Fat: 20g , Protein: 20g

PREPARATION	COOKING TIME	SERVINGS
15	12 *hours*	10

DIRECTION

- In a bowl, mix dry seasoning, add olive oil, apple cider vinegar.
- Place the meat in the crockpot, generously coat with seasoning mix.
- Cover, cook on low for 12 hours.
- Remove the brisket, place it on a pan. Sear it under the broiler for 2-4 minutes, observe it, so the meat doesn't burn.
- Wrap it using a foil, then let it rest for 1 hour. Slice and serve.

INGREDIENTS

- pounds beef brisket, whole
- 2 Tablespoons olive oil
- 2 Tablespoons apple cider vinegar
- 1 teaspoon dry oregano
- 1 teaspoon dry thyme
- 1 teaspoon dried rosemary
- 2 Tablespoons paprika
- 1 teaspoon Cayenne pepper
- 1 tablespoon salt
- 1 teaspoon fresh ground black pepper

Seriously Delicious Lamb Roast

NUTRITION *Calories: 206 , Carbs: 4g , Fat: 9g , Protein: 32g*

PREPARATION
15

COOKING TIME
8
hours

SERVINGS
8

INGREDIENTS

- medium radishes, scrubbed, washed, and cut in half
- Salt and pepper to taste
- 1 red onion, diced
- 2 garlic cloves, minced
- 1 lamb joint (approximately 4.5 pounds) at room temperature
- 2 Tablespoons olive oil
- 1 teaspoon dry oregano
- 1 teaspoon dry thyme
- 1 sprig fresh rosemary
- cups heated broth, your choice

DIRECTION

- Place cut radishes along the bottom of the crockpot. Season. Add onion and garlic.
- Blend the herbs plus olive oil in a small bowl until it forms to paste.
- Place the meat on top of the radishes. Knead the paste over the meat.
- Heat the stock, pour it around the meat.
- Cover, cook on low for 8 hours. Let it rest for 20 minutes. Slice and serve.

Lamb Provençal

NUTRITION *Calories: 140 , Carbs: 3g , Fat: 5g , Protein: 21g*

PREPARATION
15

COOKING TIME
8
hours

SERVINGS
4

DIRECTION

- Preheat the crockpot on low.
- In a pan, heat 1 tablespoon olive oil. Brown the meat for 2 minutes per side.
- Mix remaining Ingredients: in a bowl.
- Place the lamb in the crockpot, pour the remaining seasoning over the meat.
- Cover, cook on low for 8 hours.

INGREDIENTS

- 2 racks lamb, approximately 2 pounds
- 1 Tablespoon olive oil
- 2 Tablespoons fresh rosemary, chopped
- 1 Tablespoon fresh thyme, chopped
- garlic cloves, minced
- 1 teaspoon dry oregano
- 1 lemon, the zest
- 1 teaspoon minced fresh ginger
- 1 cup (Good) red wine
- Salt and pepper to taste

Greek Style Lamb Shanks

Calories: 250, Carbs: 3g , Fat: 16g , Protein: 22g

PREPARATION	COOKING TIME	SERVINGS
15	6 *hours*	8

DIRECTION

- Liquify the butter in a pan, then cook the shanks on each side.
- Remove, then add oil, onions, garlic. Cook for 3-4 minutes. Add tomatoes, olives, spices, then stir well. Put the liquids and return the meat. Boil for 1 minute.
- Transfer everything to the slow cooker.
- Cover, cook on medium-high for 6 hours.

INGREDIENTS

- Tablespoons butter
- lamb shanks, approximately 1 pound each
- 2 Tablespoons olive oil
- 8-10 pearl onions
- garlic cloves, minced
- 2 beef tomatoes, cubed
- ¼ cup of green olives
- bay leaves
- 1 sprig fresh rosemary
- 1 teaspoon dry thyme
- 1 teaspoon ground cumin
- 1 cup fresh spinach
- ¾ cup hot water
- ½ cup red wine, Merlot or Cabernet
- Salt and pepper to taste

Homemade Meatballs and Spaghetti Squash

Calories: 235 , Carbs: 12g , Fat: 14g , Protein: 15g

PREPARATION	COOKING TIME	SERVINGS
15	8 *hours*	8

DIRECTION

- Grease the crockpot, place both squash halves open side down in the crockpot.
- Mix meatball Ingredients: in a bowl—form approximately 20 small meatballs.
- In a pan, heat the olive oil. Fry the meatballs within 2-3 minutes per side. Transfer to the crockpot.
- In the small bowl, add the tomatoes, tomato paste, oil, water, onion, and parsley, add ½ teaspoon each of salt and sugar. Mix well.
- Pour the marinara sauce in the crockpot around the squash halves.
- Cover, cook on low for 8 hours.

INGREDIENTS

- 1 medium-sized spaghetti squash, washed, halved
- 1 Tablespoon butter, to grease the crockpot
- pounds lean ground beef
- 2 garlic cloves
- 1 red onion, chopped
- ½ cup almond flour
- 2 Tablespoons of dry Parmesan cheese
- 1 egg, beaten
- 1 teaspoon ground cumin
- Salt and pepper to taste
- cans diced Italian tomatoes
- 1 small can tomato paste, 28 ounces
- 1 cup hot water
- 1 red onion, chopped
- ¼ cup chopped parsley
- ½ teaspoon each, salt and sugar (optional)
- 1 bay leaf

Beef and Cabbage Roast

NUTRITION Calories: 150 , Carbs: 8g , Fat: 3g , Protein: 22g

PREPARATION
15

COOKING TIME
8
hours

SERVINGS
10

INGREDIENTS

- 1 red onion, quartered
- 2 garlic cloves, minced
- 2-3 stocks celery, diced (approximately 1 cup)
- 4-6 dry pimento berries
- 2 bay leaves
- pounds beef brisket (two pieces)
- 1 teaspoon chili powder
- 1 teaspoon ground cumin
- 2 cups broth, beef + 2 cups hot water
- Salt and pepper to taste
- 1 medium cabbage (approximately 2.2 pounds), cut in half, then quartered

DIRECTION

- Add all Ingredients, except cabbage, to the crockpot in order of the list.
- Cover, cook on low for 7 hours.
- Uncover, add the cabbage on top of the stew. Re-cover, cook for 1 additional hour.

Simple Chicken Chili

NUTRITION Calories: 210 , Carbs: 32g , Fat: 4g , Protein: 14g

PREPARATION
15

COOKING TIME
6
hours

SERVINGS
8

INGREDIENTS

- 1 Tablespoon butter
- 1 red onion, sliced
- 1 bell pepper, sliced
- 2 garlic cloves, minced
- pounds boneless chicken thighs
- slices bacon, chopped
- 1 teaspoon chili powder
- Salt and pepper to taste
- 1 cup chicken broth
- ¼ cup of coconut milk
- Tablespoons tomato paste

DIRECTION

- Add all Ingredients: to the crockpot, starting with the butter.
- Cover, cook on low for 6 hours.
- Strip the chicken using a fork in the crockpot. Serve.

Beef Shoulder in BBQ Sauce

NUTRITION *Calories: 140 , Carbs: 5g , Fat: 9g , Protein: 8g*

PREPARATION COOKING TIME SERVINGS

15 10 *hours* *12*

DIRECTION

- In a bowl, mix seasoning. Set aside.
- Liquify the butter in a pan, add the meat. Brown on all sides. Transfer to crockpot.
- Fry the onion within 2-3 minutes in the same pan, then pour over the meat.
- Pour in the seasoning. Cover, cook on low for 10 hours.
- Remove, cover it with foil, and then let it rest for 1 hour.
- Turn the crockpot on high, reduce the remaining liquid by half and serve with the shredded beef.

INGREDIENTS

- pounds beef shoulder, whole
- 1 Tablespoon butter
- 1 yellow onion, diced
- 1 garlic bulb, peeled and minced
- Tablespoons red wine vinegar
- 2 Tablespoons Worcestershire sauce
- Tablespoons Swerve (or a suitable substitute)
- 1 Tablespoon mustard
- 1 teaspoon salt
- 1 teaspoon fresh ground black pepper

Dressed Pork Leg Roast

NUTRITION *Calories: 143 , Carbs: 0g , Fat: 3g , Protein: 28g*

PREPARATION COOKING TIME SERVINGS

15 8 *hours* *14*

DIRECTION

- Butter the crockpot. Slice crisscrosses along the top of the pork leg.
- Arrange onion slices and minced garlic along the bottom of the crockpot.
- Place meat on top of vegetables.
- In a small bowl, mix the herbs. Rub it all over the pork leg.
- Add the water. Cover, cook on high for 8 hours.
- Remove and transfer, cover with foil. Let it rest for 1 hour.
- Shred the meat and serve.

INGREDIENTS

- pounds pork leg
- 1 Tablespoon butter
- 1 yellow onion, sliced
- garlic cloves, peeled and minced
- 2 Tablespoons ground cumin
- 2 Tablespoons ground thyme
- 2 Tablespoons ground chili
- 1 teaspoon salt
- 1 teaspoon fresh ground black pepper
- 1 cup hot water

Rabbit & Mushroom Stew

NUTRITION Calories: 122 , Carbs: 19g , Fat: 1g , Protein: 10g

PREPARATION	COOKING TIME	SERVINGS
15	6 hours	6

INGREDIENTS

- 1 rabbit, in portion size pieces
- 2 cups spicy Spanish sausage, cut into chunks
- 2 Tablespoons butter, divided
- 1 red onion, sliced
- 1 cup button mushrooms, washed and dried
- 1 teaspoon cayenne pepper
- 1 teaspoon sweet paprika
- 1 teaspoon salt
- 1 teaspoon fresh ground black pepper
- 1 cup chicken broth+1 cup hot water

DIRECTION

- Butter the slow cooker.
- In a large pan, melt the butter, add the rabbit pieces, brown on all sides. Transfer to a slow cooker.
- In the same pan, sauté the onions, sausage chunks, and spices for 2-3 minutes. Set the chicken broth, heat on high for 1 minute, then pour the mixture over the rabbit.
- Add the mushrooms. Adjust the seasoning, if needed.
- Add the water. Cover, cook on high for 6 hours. Serve.

Italian Spicy Sausage & Bell Peppers

NUTRITION Calories: 180 , Carbs: 19g , Fat: 6g , Protein: 12g

PREPARATION	COOKING TIME	SERVINGS
15	6 hours	5

DIRECTION

- Grease with butter the slow cooker. Add the sliced onions and peppers. Salt.
- Pour the tomatoes over it, then add seasoning. Mix it in.
- Arrange sausages in the middle of the pepper and onion mixture.
- Add ¼ cup hot water. Cover, cook on low for 6 hours. Serve.

INGREDIENTS

- 2 Tablespoons butter
- 2 red onions, sliced
- bell peppers, sliced
- 2 regular cans Italian tomatoes, diced
- pounds spicy Italian sausage
- 1 teaspoon dry oregano
- 1 teaspoon dry thyme
- 1 teaspoon dry basil
- 1 teaspoon sweet paprika
- 1 teaspoon salt
- 1 teaspoon fresh ground black pepper

Chicken in Salsa Verde

NUTRITION Calories: 145 , Carbs: 5g , Fat: 2g , Protein: 26g

PREPARATION	COOKING TIME	SERVINGS
15	6 *hours*	4

INGREDIENTS

- pounds of chicken breasts
- bunches parsley, chopped
- ¾ cup olive oil
- ¼ cup capers, drained and chopped
- anchovy fillets
- 1 lemon, juice, and zest
- 2 garlic cloves, minced
- 1 teaspoon salt
- 1 teaspoon fresh ground black pepper

DIRECTION

- Place the chicken breasts in the crockpot.
- Blend the rest of the fixing in a blender, then pour over the chicken.
- Cover, cook on low for 6 hours. Shred with a fork and serve.

Salmon Poached in White Wine and Lemon

NUTRITION Calories: 216 , Carbs: 1g , Fat: 12g , Protein: 23g

PREPARATION	COOKING TIME	SERVINGS
15	2 *hours*	4

DIRECTION

- Add all fixings, except salmon and seasoning, to the slow cooker. Cover, cook on low for 1 hour.
- Season the salmon, place in the slow cooker skin-side down.
- Cover, cook on low for another hour. Serve.

INGREDIENTS

- 2 cups of water
- 1 cup cooking wine, white
- 1 lemon, sliced thin
- 1 small mild onion, sliced thin
- 1 bay leaf
- 1 mixed bunch fresh tarragon, dill, and parsley
- pounds salmon fillet, skin on
- 1 teaspoon salt
- 1 teaspoon ground black pepper

Keto Lasagna

NUTRITION Calories 197, Fat 11, Fiber 0.5, Carbs 2.5, protein 22.5

PREPARATION	COOKING TIME	SERVINGS
20	7 hours	6

INGREDIENTS

- oz. ground beef
- 1 tablespoon tomato puree
- 1 zucchini
- oz. Parmesan, grated
- 1 tablespoon butter
- ½ teaspoon salt
- 1 teaspoon paprika
- 1 teaspoon chili flakes
- 1 tablespoon full-fat heavy cream

DIRECTION

- Slice the zucchini lengthwise.
- Mix the ground beef, salt, paprika, and chili flakes.
- Then mix the full-fat cream and tomato puree.
- Chop the butter and put it in the slow cooker.
- Make a layer of the zucchini in the bottom of the slow cooker bowl.
- Put a layer of the ground beef mixture on top of the zucchini layer.
- After this repeat, the same layers until you use all the Ingredients.
- Sprinkle the lasagna with the grated Parmesan and close the lid.
- Cook the lasagna for 7 hours on Low.
- Chill the cooked meal and serve!

Butter Chicken

NUTRITION Calories 208, , Fat 13.9, Fiber 0.7, Carbs 1.6, Protein 18.9

PREPARATION	COOKING TIME	SERVINGS
15	3 hours	4

DIRECTION

- Beat the chicken breasts gently to tenderize and sprinkle it with the salt and paprika.
- Then place the butter and spinach in a blender.
- Add onion powder and blend the mixture for 1 minute at high speed.
- Spread the chicken breast with the butter mixture on each side.
- Place the buttered chicken in the slow cooker and the chicken stock.
- Close the lid and cook the chicken for 3 hours on Low.
- Serve the chicken immediately!

INGREDIENTS

- 1 tablespoons butter
- oz. spinach, chopped
- 1 teaspoon onion powder
- 1 teaspoon paprika
- oz. chicken breast, skinless, boneless
- ½ teaspoon salt
- ¼ cup chicken stock

Tuscan Chicken

NUTRITION *Calories 136, Fat 7.2, Fiber 0.2, Carbs 1.4, protein 16*

PREPARATION	COOKING TIME	SERVINGS
15	7 *hours*	8

INGREDIENTS

- 1-pound chicken breast, skinless, boneless
- 1 tablespoon olive oil
- ½ cup full-fat cream
- 1 oz. spinach, chopped
- oz. Parmesan, grated
- 1 teaspoon chili flakes
- ½ teaspoon paprika
- 1 teaspoon minced garlic
- ½ teaspoon ground black pepper

DIRECTION

- Chop the chicken breast roughly and sprinkle it with the chili flakes, paprika, minced garlic, and ground black pepper.
- Stir the chicken and transfer to the slow cooker.
- Add the full-fat cream and olive oil.
- Add spinach and grated cheese.
- Stir the chicken gently and close the lid.
- Cook the chicken for 7 hours on Low.
- Transfer cooked Tuscan chicken on the serving plates and serve!

Corned Beef

NUTRITION *Calories 178, Fat 13.5, Fiber 0.3, Carbs 1.3, Protein 12.2*

PREPARATION	COOKING TIME	SERVINGS
10	8 *hours*	6

DIRECTION

- Mix the peppercorns, chili flakes, mustard seeds, and salt in the bowl.
- Then rub the corned beef with the spice mixture well.
- Peel the garlic and place it in the slow cooker.
- Add the corned beef.
- Add water, butter, and bay leaf.
- Add the bacon fat and close the lid.
- Cook the corned beef for 8 hours on Low.
- When the corned beef is cooked, discard the bay leaf, then transfer the beef to a plate and cut into servings.
- Enjoy!

INGREDIENTS

- 1-pound corned beef
- 1 teaspoon peppercorns
- 1 teaspoon chili flakes
- 1 teaspoon mustard seeds
- 1 bay leaf
- 1 teaspoon salt
- 1 oz. bacon fat
- garlic cloves
- 1 cup water
- 1 tablespoon butter

Sardine Pate

NUTRITION Calories 170, Fat 12.3, Fiber 0, carbs 0.3, Protein 14.1

PREPARATION	COOKING TIME	SERVINGS
15	3	6
	hours	

INGREDIENTS

- ½ cup water
- 1 tablespoons butter
- 1 teaspoon onion powder
- 1 teaspoon dried parsley
- oz. sardine fillets, chopped

DIRECTION

- Put the chopped sardine fillets, dried parsley, onion powder, and water in the slow cooker.
- Close the lid and cook the fish for 3 hours on Low.
- Strain the sardine fillet and put it in a blender.
- Add butter and blend the mixture for 3 minutes at high speed.
- Transfer the cooked pate into serving bowls and serve!

Spare Ribs

NUTRITION Calories 203, Fat 14.1, fiber 0.6, Carbs 10, Protein 9.8

PREPARATION	COOKING TIME	SERVINGS
10	8	6
	hours	

DIRECTION

- Mix the olive oil, minced garlic, cumin, and chili flakes in a bowl.
- Melt the butter and add to the spice mixture.
- Stir it well and add water. Stir again.
- Then rub the pork ribs with the spice mixture generously and place the ribs in the slow cooker.
- Close the lid and cook the ribs for 8 hours on Low.
- When the ribs are cooked, serve them immediately!

INGREDIENTS

- 1-pound pork loin ribs
- 1 teaspoon olive oil
- 1 teaspoon minced garlic
- ¼ teaspoon cumin
- ¼ teaspoon chili powder
- 1 tablespoon butter
- 1 tablespoons water

Pork Shoulder

NUTRITION Calories 234, Fat 16.4, Fiber 0.7, Carbs 2.8, Protein 18

PREPARATION	COOKING TIME	SERVINGS
25	7 *hours*	6

INGREDIENTS

- 1-pound pork shoulder
- 2 cups water
- 1 onion, peeled
- 2 garlic cloves, peeled
- 1 teaspoon peppercorns
- 1 teaspoon chili flakes
- ½ teaspoon paprika
- 1 teaspoon turmeric
- 1 teaspoon cumin

DIRECTION

- Sprinkle the pork shoulder with the peppercorns, chili flakes, paprika, turmeric, and cumin.
- Stir it well and let it sit for 15 minutes to marinate.
- Transfer the pork shoulder to the slow cooker.
- Add water and peeled the onion.
- Add garlic cloves and close the lid.
- Cook the pork shoulder for 7 hours on Low.
- Remove the pork shoulder from the slow cooker and serve!

Lamb Chops

NUTRITION Calories 290, Fat 12.5, Fiber 0.4, Carbs 2, Protein 40.3

PREPARATION	COOKING TIME	SERVINGS
15	3 *hours*	2

INGREDIENTS

- oz. lamb chops
- 1 tablespoon tomato puree
- ½ teaspoon cumin
- ½ teaspoon ground coriander
- 1 teaspoon garlic powder
- 1 teaspoon butter
- tablespoons water

DIRECTION

- Mix the tomato puree, cumin, ground coriander, garlic powder, and water in the bowl.
- Brush the lamb chops with the tomato puree mixture on each side and let marinate for 20 minutes.
- Toss the butter in the slow cooker.
- Add the lamb chops and close the lid.
- Cook the lamb chops for 3 hours on High.
- Transfer the cooked lamb onto serving plates and enjoy!

Rosemary Leg of Lamb

NUTRITION Calories 225, Fat 8.7, Fiber 0.6, Carbs 2.2, Protein 32.4

PREPARATION	COOKING TIME	SERVINGS
5	7 *hours*	8

INGREDIENTS

- 2-pound leg of lamb
- 1 onion
- 2 cups water
- 1 garlic clove, peeled
- 1 tablespoon mustard seeds
- 1 teaspoon salt
- ½ teaspoon turmeric
- 1 teaspoon ground black pepper

DIRECTION

- Chop the garlic clove and combine it with the mustard seeds, turmeric, black pepper, and salt.
- Peel the onion and grate it.
- Mix the grated onion and spice mixture.
- Rub the leg of lamb with the grated onion mixture.
- Put the leg of lamb in the slow cooker and cook it for 7 hours on Low.
- Serve the cooked meal!

Creamy Chicken Thighs

NUTRITION Calories 224, Fat 14.3, Fiber 1.1, Carbs 4.7, Protein 18.9

PREPARATION	COOKING TIME	SERVINGS
15	6 *hours*	4

INGREDIENTS

- 1-pound chicken thighs, skinless
- ¼ cup almond milk, unsweetened
- 1 tablespoon full-fat cream cheese
- 1 teaspoon salt
- 1 onion, diced
- 1 teaspoon paprika

DIRECTION

- Mix the almond milk and full-fat cream.
- Add salt, diced onion, and paprika.
- Stir the mixture well.
- Place the chicken thighs in the slow cooker.
- Add the almond milk mixture and stir it gently.
- Close the slow cooker lid and cook the chicken thighs for 6 hours on High.
- Transfer the cooked chicken thighs into the serving bowls and serve immediately!

Peppered Steak

NUTRITION Calories 192, Fat 12, Fiber 4, Carbs 1, Protein 12

PREPARATION	COOKING TIME	SERVINGS
15	4 *hours*	4

INGREDIENTS

- oz. Sirloin Steak
- 2 cups water
- 1 tablespoon peppercorns
- 1 teaspoon salt
- ½ teaspoon ground nutmeg
- 2 garlic cloves, peeled
- 1 teaspoon olive oil

DIRECTION

- Make the small cuts in the sirlion and chop the garlic cloves roughly.
- Place the garlic cloves in the sirloin cuts.
- Sprinkle the steak with the salt, ground nutmeg, and peppercorns.
- Transfer the steak to the slow cooker and add water.
- Close the lid and cook the steak for 4 hours on Low.
- Then remove the steak from the slow cooker and slice it.
- Enjoy!

Rabbit Stew

NUTRITION Calories 168, Fat 6.1, Fiber 7.2, Carbs 13.6, Protein 16.1

PREPARATION	COOKING TIME	SERVINGS
15	5 *hours*	6

DIRECTION

- Place the chopped eggplants, zucchini, onion, and rabbit in the slow cooker.
- Add water, butter, salt, and chili flakes.
- Stir the stew gently and close the lid.
- Cook the stew for 5 hours on Low.
- Then let the cooked rabbit stew cool slightly, then serve it!

INGREDIENTS

- 2 eggplants, chopped
- 1 zucchini, chopped
- 1 onion, chopped
- oz. rabbit, chopped
- 2 cups water
- 1 tablespoon butter
- 1 teaspoon salt
- 1 teaspoon chili flakes

Duck Breast

NUTRITION Calories 199, Fat 10.3, Fiber 0.1, Carbs 0.3, Protein 25.1

PREPARATION	COOKING TIME	SERVINGS
10	5 *hours*	4

INGREDIENTS

- 1 teaspoon liquid stevia
- 1-pound duck breast, boneless, skinless
- 1 teaspoon chili pepper
- 2 tablespoons butter
- ½ cup water
- 1 bay leaf

DIRECTION

- Rub the duck breast with the chili pepper and liquid stevia, then transfer it to the slow cooker.
- Add the bay leaf and water.
- Add butter and close the lid.
- Cook the duck breast for 5 hours on Low.
- Let the cooked duck breast rest for 10 minutes, then remove it from the slow cooker.
- Slice it into the servings.
- Enjoy!

Jerk Chicken

NUTRITION Calories 247, Fat 11.5, Fiber 0.5, Carbs 4.9, Protein 33

PREPARATION	COOKING TIME	SERVINGS
25	5 *hours*	4

DIRECTION

- Mix the nutmeg, cinnamon, minced garlic, cloves, and ground coriander.
- Add Erythritol and stir the Ingredients: until well blended.
- Sprinkle the chicken thighs with the spice mixture.
- Let the chicken thighs sit for 10 minutes to marinate, then put the chicken thighs in the slow cooker.
- Add the butter and water.
- Close the lid and cook Jerk chicken for 5 hours on Low.
- Serve Jerk chicken immediately!

INGREDIENTS

- 1 teaspoon nutmeg
- 1 teaspoon cinnamon
- 1 teaspoon minced garlic
- ½ teaspoon cloves
- 1 teaspoon ground coriander
- 1 tablespoon Erythritol
- 1-pound chicken thighs
- ½ cup water
- 1 tablespoon butter

Balsamic Beef

NUTRITION Calories 241, Fat 13.1, Fiber 0.1, Carbs 0.6, Protein 30.5

PREPARATION	COOKING TIME	SERVINGS
20	7 *hours*	4

DIRECTION

- Chop the beef loin roughly and place it in a large bowl, then sprinkle it with the balsamic vinegar.
- Add olive oil, minced garlic, ground coriander, cumin, and dried dill.
- Stir the meat well and let sit for 10 minutes.
- Place the meat in the slow cooker and add water.
- Close the lid and cook the beef for 7 hours on Low.
- When the beef is tender, it is cooked!
- Enjoy!

INGREDIENTS

- 2 tablespoons balsamic vinegar
- 1 tablespoon olive oil
- 1-pound beef loin
- 1 teaspoon minced garlic
- ½ teaspoon ground coriander
- 1 teaspoon cumin
- ½ teaspoon dried dill
- 2 tablespoons water

Onion Beef

NUTRITION 306 calories, 39.6g protein, 1.7g carbohydrates, 14.7g fat, 0.4g fiber, 133mg cholesterol, 301mg sodium, 551mg potassium.

PREPARATION	COOKING TIME	SERVINGS
10	5.5 *hours*	14

DIRECTION

- Mix beef sirloin with salt and ground black pepper and transfer to the slow cooker.
- Add butter, water, onion, and bay leaf.
- Close the lid and cook the meat on High for 5.5 hours.

INGREDIENTS

- 4-pounds beef sirloin, sliced
- 2 cups white onion, chopped
- 2 cups of water
- ½ cup butter
- 1 teaspoon ground black pepper
- 1 teaspoon salt
- 1 bay leaf

Cilantro Beef

NUTRITION 211 calories, 30.4g protein, 0.4g carbohydrates, 9.5g fat, 0.1g fiber, 81mg cholesterol, 66mg sodium, 412mg potassium.

INGREDIENTS

- 1-pound beef loin, roughly chopped
- ¼ cup apple cider vinegar
- 1 tablespoon dried cilantro
- ½ teaspoon dried basil
- 1 cup of water
- 1 teaspoon tomato paste

DIRECTION

- Mix meat with tomato paste, dried cilantro, and basil.
- Then transfer it to the slow cooker.
- Add apple cider vinegar and water.
- Cook the cilantro beef for 4.5 hours on High.

PREPARATION	COOKING TIME	SERVINGS
10	4.5 hours	4

Garlic Sweet Potato

NUTRITION 320 calories, 3.6g protein, 63.5g carbohydrates, 6.2g fat, 9.3g fiber, 15mg cholesterol, 648mg sodium, 1857mg potassium.

INGREDIENTS

- 2-pounds sweet potatoes, chopped
- 1 teaspoon minced garlic
- tablespoons vegan butter
- 1 teaspoon salt
- water

DIRECTION

- Pour water into the slow cooker. Add sweet potatoes.
- Then add salt and close the lid.
- Cook the sweet potato on Low for 6 hours.
- After this, drain the water and transfer the vegetables in the big bowl.
- Add minced garlic and butter. Carefully stir the sweet potatoes until butter is melted.

PREPARATION	COOKING TIME	SERVINGS
10	6 hours	4

Potato Salad

NUTRITION 129 calories, 5.5g protein, 12.4g carbohydrates, 6.7g fat, 2.5g fiber, 12mg cholesterol, 1479mg sodium, 465mg potassium.

INGREDIENTS

- 1 cup potato, chopped
- 1 cup of water
- 1 teaspoon salt
- oz. celery stalk, chopped
- oz. fresh parsley, chopped
- ¼ onion, diced
- 1 tablespoon mayonnaise

DIRECTION

- Put the potatoes in the slow cooker.
- Add water and salt.
- Cook the potatoes on High for 3 hours.
- Then drain water and transfer the potatoes in the salad bowl.
- Add all remaining Ingredients: and carefully mix the salad.

PREPARATION	COOKING TIME	SERVINGS
10	3 *hours*	2

Sautéed Greens

NUTRITION 49 calories, 1.8g protein, 3.2g carbohydrates, 3.7g fat, 1.1g fiber, 11mg cholesterol, 45mg sodium, 117mg potassium

INGREDIENTS

- 1 cup spinach, chopped
- 2 cups collard greens, chopped
- 1 cup Swiss chard, chopped
- water
- ½ cup half and half

DIRECTION

- Put spinach, collard greens, and Swiss chard in the slow cooker.
- Add water and close the lid.
- Cook the greens on High for 1 hour.
- Then drain water and transfer the greens in the bowl.
- Bring the half and half to boil and pour over greens.
- Carefully mix the greens.

PREPARATION	COOKING TIME	SERVINGS
15	1 *hours*	4

Mashed Turnips

NUTRITION 162 calories, 8.6g protein, 15.1g carbohydrates, 8.1g fat, 4.1g fiber, 22mg cholesterol, 475mg sodium, 490mg potassium.

INGREDIENTS

- 3-pounds turnip, chopped
- 2 cup water
- 1 tablespoon vegan butter
- 1 tablespoon chives, chopped
- oz. Parmesan, grated

DIRECTION

- Put turnips in the slow cooker.
- Add water and cook the vegetables on low for 7 hours.
- Then drain water and mash the turnips.
- Add chives, butter, and Parmesan.
- Carefully stir the mixture until butter and Parmesan are melted.
- Then add chives. Mix the mashed turnips again.

PREPARATION	COOKING TIME	SERVINGS
10	8 *hours*	10

Cilantro Meatballs

NUTRITION 178 calories, 24.1g protein, 1.5g carbohydrates, 7.7g fat, 0.1g fiber, 95mg cholesterol, 61mg sodium, 321mg potassium.

INGREDIENTS

- 1-pound minced beef
- 1 teaspoon minced garlic
- 1 egg, beaten
- 1 teaspoon chili flakes
- 2 teaspoons dried cilantro
- 1 tablespoon semolina
- ½ cup of water
- 1 tablespoon sesame oil

DIRECTION

- In the bowl, mix minced beef, garlic, egg, chili flakes, cilantro, and semolina.
- Then make the meatballs.
- After this, heat the sesame oil in the skillet.
- Cook the meatballs in the hot oil on high heat for 1 minute per side.
- Transfer the roasted meatballs to the slow cooker, add water, and close the lid.
- Cook the meatballs on High for 4 hours.

PREPARATION	COOKING TIME	SERVINGS
20	4 *hours*	6

Stuffed Jalapenos

NUTRITION 55 calories, 7.5g protein, 2.3g carbohydrates, 1.9g fat, 0.9g fiber, 0mg cholesterol, 2mg sodium, 71mg potassium.

INGREDIENTS

- jalapenos, deseed
- oz. minced beef
- 1 teaspoon garlic powder
- ½ cup of water

DIRECTION

- Mix the minced beef with garlic powder.
- Then fill the jalapenos with minced meat and arrange it in the slow cooker.
- Add water and cook the jalapenos on High for 4.5 hours.

PREPARATION	COOKING TIME	SERVINGS
25	6 hours	5

BBQ Beef Short Ribs

NUTRITION 266 calories, 32.8g protein, 7.9g carbohydrates, 10.4g fat, 0.3g fiber, 103mg cholesterol, 308mg sodium, 468mg potassium.

INGREDIENTS

- 1-pound beef short ribs
- ¼ cup of water
- 1/3 cup BBQ sauce
- 1 teaspoon chili powder

DIRECTION

- Rub the beef short ribs with chili powder and put in the slow cooker.
- Mix water with BBQ sauce and pour the liquid into the slow cooker.
- Cook the meat on High for 5 hours.

PREPARATION	COOKING TIME	SERVINGS
10	5 hours	4

Spiced Beef

NUTRITION 219 calories, 30.4g protein, 0.6g carbohydrates, 10.7g fat, 0.2g fiber, 81mg cholesterol, 65mg sodium, 395mg potassium.

INGREDIENTS

- 1-pound beef loin
- 1 teaspoon allspice
- 1 teaspoon olive oil
- 1 tablespoon minced onion
- 1 cup of water

DIRECTION

- Rub the beef loin with allspice, olive oil, and minced onion.
- Put the meat in the slow cooker.
- Add water and close the lid.
- Cook the beef on Low for 9 hours.
- When the meat is cooked, slice it into servings.

PREPARATION	COOKING TIME	SERVINGS
10	9 hours	4

Green Peas Chowder

NUTRITION 113 calories, 18.2g protein, 4.1g carbohydrates, 2.2g fat, 1.3g fiber, 49mg cholesterol, 244mg sodium, 359mg potassium.

INGREDIENTS

- 1-pound chicken breast, skinless, boneless, chopped
- 2 cups water
- 1 cup green peas
- ¼ cup Greek Yogurt
- 1 tablespoon dried basil
- 1 teaspoon ground black pepper
- ½ teaspoon salt

DIRECTION

- Mix salt, chicken breast, ground black pepper, and dried basil.
- Transfer the Ingredients: to the slow cooker.
- Add water, green peas, yogurt, and close the lid.
- Cook the chowder on Low for 8 hours.

PREPARATION	COOKING TIME	SERVINGS
10	8 hours	6

Chorizo Soup

NUTRITION 210 calories, 11g protein, 4.3g carbohydrates, 16.4g fat, 0.7g fiber, 37mg cholesterol, 927mg sodium, 326mg potassium.

INGREDIENTS

- oz. chorizo, chopped
- 2 cup water
- 1 cup potato, chopped
- 1 teaspoon minced garlic, chopped
- 1 zucchini, chopped
- ½ cup spinach, chopped
- 1 teaspoon salt

DIRECTION

- Put the chorizo in the skillet and roast it for 2 minutes per side on high heat.
- Then transfer the chorizo to the slow cooker.
- Add water, potato, minced garlic, zucchini, spinach, and salt.
- Close the lid and cook the soup on high for 5 hours.
- Then cool the soup to room temperature.

PREPARATION	COOKING TIME	SERVINGS
10	5 *hours*	6

Chapter 8. Poultry

Aromatic Jalapeno Wings

NUTRITION Calories 246 , Total Fat 7.4 g , Saturated Fat 4.6 g , Cholesterol 105 mg , Total Carbs 9.4 g , Sugar 6.5 g , Fiber 2.7 g , Sodium 353 mg , Potassium 529 mg , Protein 37.2 g

INGREDIENTS

- 1 jalapeño pepper, diced
- ½ cup of fresh cilantro, diced
- 3 tablespoon of coconut oil
- Juice from 1 lime
- 2 garlic cloves, peeled and minced
- Salt and black pepper ground, to taste
- 2 lbs. chicken wings
- Lime wedges, to serve
- Mayonnaise, to serve

DIRECTION

- 1. Start by throwing all the Ingredients into the large bowl and mix well.
- 2. Cover the wings and marinate them in the refrigerator for 2 hours.
- 3. Now add the wings along with their marinade into the Crockpot.
- 4. Cover it and cook for 3 hours on Low Settings.
- 5. Garnish as desired.
- 6. Serve warm.

PREPARATION	COOKING TIME	SERVINGS
10	3 *hours*	4

Barbeque Chicken Wings

NUTRITION Calories 457 , Total Fat 19.1 g , Saturated Fat 11 g , Cholesterol 262 mg , Total Carbs 8.9 g , Sugar 1.2 g , Fiber 1.7 g , Sodium 557 mg , Potassium 748 mg , Protein 32.5 g

INGREDIENTS

- 2 lbs. chicken wings
- 1/2 cup of water
- 1/2 teaspoon of basil, dried
- 3/4 cup of BBQ sauce
- 1/2 cup of lime juice
- 1 teaspoon of red pepper, crushed
- 2 teaspoons of paprika
- 1/2 cup of swerve
- Salt and black pepper- to taste
- A pinch cayenne peppers

DIRECTION

- Start by throwing all the Ingredients into the Crockpot and mix them well.
- Cover it and cook for 3 hours on Low Settings.
- Garnish as desired.
- Serve warm.

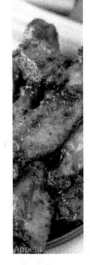

PREPARATION	COOKING TIME	SERVINGS
10	3 *hours*	4

Saucy Duck

NUTRITION Calories 338 , Total Fat 3.8 g , Saturated Fat 0.7 g , Cholesterol 22 mg , Total Carbs 8.3 g , Fiber 2.4 g , Sugar 1.2 g , Sodium 620 mg , Potassium 271 mg , Protein 15.4g

INGREDIENTS

- 1 duck, cut into small chunks
- 4 garlic cloves, minced
- 4 tablespoons of swerves
- 2 green onions, roughly diced
- 4 tablespoon of soy sauce
- 4 tablespoon of sherry wine
- 1/4 cup of water
- 1-inch ginger root, sliced
- A pinch salt
- black pepper to taste

DIRECTION

- Start by throwing all the Ingredients into the Crockpot and mix them well.
- Cover it and cook for 6 hours on Low Settings.
- Garnish as desired.
- Serve warm.

PREPARATION	COOKING TIME	SERVINGS
10	6 hours	4

Chicken Roux Gumbo

NUTRITION Calories 604 , Total Fat 30.6 g , Saturated Fat 13.1 g , Cholesterol 131 mg , Total Carbs 1.4g , Fiber 0.2 g , Sugar 20.3 g , Sodium 834 mg , Potassium 512 mg , Protein 54.6 g

INGREDIENTS

- 1 lb. chicken thighs, cut into halves
- 1 tablespoon of vegetable oil
- 1 lb. smoky sausage, sliced, crispy, and crumbled.
- Salt and black pepper- to taste
- Aromatics:
- 1 bell pepper, diced
- 2 quarts' chicken stock
- 15 oz. canned tomatoes, diced
- 1 celery stalk, diced
- salt to taste
- 4 garlic cloves, minced
- 1/2 lbs. okra, sliced
- 1 yellow onion, diced
- a dash tabasco sauce
- For the roux:
- 1/2 cup of almond flour
- 1/4 cup of vegetable oil
- 1 teaspoon of Cajun spice

DIRECTION

- 1. Start by throwing all the Ingredients except okra and roux Ingredients into the Crockpot.
- 2. Cover it and cook for 5 hours on Low Settings.
- 3. Stir in okra and cook for another 1 hour on low heat.
- 4. Mix all the roux Ingredients and add them to the Crockpot.
- 5. Stir cook on high heat until the sauce thickens.
- 6. Garnish as desired.
- 7. Serve warm.

PREPARATION	COOKING TIME	SERVINGS
10	6 hours	24

Cider-Braised Chicken

NUTRITION Calories 311, Total Fat 25.5 g , Saturated Fat 12.4 g , Cholesterol 69 mg , Total Carbs 1.4 g , Fiber 0.7 g , Sugar 0.3 g , Sodium 58 mg , Potassium 362 mg , Protein 18.4 g

INGREDIENTS

- 4 chicken drumsticks
- 2 tablespoon of olive oil
- ½ cup of apple cider vinegar
- 1 tablespoon of balsamic vinegar
- 1 chili pepper, diced
- 1 yellow onion, minced
- Salt and black pepper- to taste

DIRECTION

- Start by throwing all the Ingredients into a bowl and mix them well.
- Marinate this chicken for 2 hours in the refrigerator.
- Spread the chicken along with its marinade in the Crockpot.
- Cover it and cook for 5 hours on Low Settings.
- Garnish as desired.
- Serve warm.

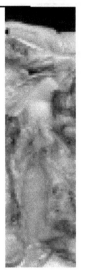

PREPARATION	COOKING TIME	SERVINGS
10	5 hours	2

Chunky Chicken Salsa

NUTRITION Calories 541 , Total Fat 34 g , Saturated Fat 8.5 g , Cholesterol 69 mg , Total Carbs 3.4 g , Fiber 1.2 g , Sugar 1 g , Sodium 547 mg , Potassium 467 mg , Protein 20.3 g

INGREDIENTS

- 1 lb. chicken breast, skinless and boneless
- 1 cup of chunky salsa
- 3/4 teaspoon of cumin
- A pinch oregano
- Salt and black pepper- to taste

DIRECTION

- Start by throwing all the Ingredients into the Crockpot and mix them well.
- Cover it and cook for 6 hours on Low Settings.
- Garnish as desired.
- Serve warm.

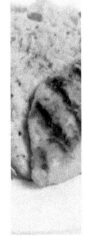

PREPARATION	COOKING TIME	SERVINGS
10	6 hours	2

Dijon Chicken

NUTRITION Calories 398 , Total Fat 13.8 g , Saturated Fat 5.1 g , Cholesterol 200 mg , Total Carbs 3.6 g , Fiber 1 g , Sugar 1.3 g , Sodium 272 mg , Potassium 531 mg , Protein 51.8 g

INGREDIENTS

- 2 lbs. chicken thighs, skinless and boneless
- 3/4 cup of chicken stock
- 1/4 cup of lemon juice
- 2 tablespoon of extra virgin olive oil
- 3 tablespoon of Dijon mustard
- 2 tablespoons of Italian seasoning
- Salt and black pepper- to taste

DIRECTION

- Start by throwing all the Ingredients into the Crockpot and mix them well.
- Cover it and cook for 6 hours on Low Settings.
- Garnish as desired.
- Serve warm.

PREPARATION	COOKING TIME	SERVINGS
10	6 hours	4

Chicken Thighs with Vegetables

NUTRITION Calories 372, Total Fat 11.8 g, Saturated Fat 4.4 g , Cholesterol 62 mg , Total Carbs 1.8 g , Fiber 0.6 g, Sugar 27.3 g , Sodium 871 mg , Potassium 288 mg , Protein 34 g

INGREDIENTS

- 6 chicken thighs
- 1 teaspoon of vegetable oil
- 15 oz. canned tomatoes, diced
- 1 yellow onion, diced
- 2 tablespoon of tomato paste
- 1/2 cup of white wine
- 2 cups of chicken stock
- 1 celery stalk, diced
- 1/4 lb. baby carrots, cut into halves
- 1/2 teaspoon of thyme, dried
- Salt and black pepper- to taste

DIRECTION

- Start by throwing all the Ingredients into the Crockpot and mix them well.
- Cover it and cook for 6 hours on Low Settings.
- Shred the slow-cooked chicken using a fork and return to the pot.
- Mix well and garnish as desired.
- Serve warm.

PREPARATION	COOKING TIME	SERVINGS
10	6 hours	6

Chicken dipped in Tomatillo Sauce

NUTRITION Calories 427 , Total Fat 31.1 g, Saturated Fat 4.2 g , Cholesterol 0 mg , Total Carbs 9 g , Sugar 12.4 g , Fiber 19.8 g , Sodium 86 mg, Potassium 100 mg, Protein 23.5 g

INGREDIENTS

- 1 lb. chicken thighs, skinless and boneless
- 2 tablespoon of extra virgin olive oil
- 1 yellow onion, sliced
- 1 garlic clove, crushed
- 4 oz. canned green chilies, diced
- 1 handful cilantro, diced
- 15 oz. cauliflower rice, already cooked
- 5 oz. tomatoes, diced
- 15 oz. cheddar cheese, grated
- 4 oz. black olives, pitted and diced
- Salt and black pepper- to taste
- 15 oz. canned tomatillos, diced

DIRECTION

- Start by throwing all the Ingredients into the Crockpot and mix them well.
- Cover it and cook for 5 6 hours on Low Settings.
- Shred the slow-cooked chicken and return to the pot.
- Mix well and garnish as desired.
- Serve warm.

PREPARATION	COOKING TIME	SERVINGS
10	6 *hours*	4

Chicken with Lemon Parsley Butter

NUTRITION Calories 379, Total Fat 29.7 g, Saturated Fat 18.6 g , Cholesterol 141 mg , Total Carbs 9.7g , Fiber 0.9 g , Sugar 1.3 g , Sodium 193 mg , Potassium 131 mg , Protein 25.2 g

INGREDIENTS

- 1 (5 – 6lbs) whole roasting chicken, rinsed
- 1 cup of water
- 1/2 teaspoon of kosher salt
- 1/4 teaspoon of black pepper
- 1 whole lemon, sliced
- 4 tablespoons of butter
- 2 tablespoons of fresh parsley, chopped

DIRECTION

- Start by seasoning the chicken with all the herbs and spices.
- Place this chicken in the Crockpot.
- Cover it and cook for 3 hours on High Settings.
- Meanwhile, melt butter with lemon slices and parsley in a saucepan.
- Drizzle the butter over the Crockpot chicken.
- Serve warm.

PREPARATION	COOKING TIME	SERVINGS
10	3 *hours*	10

Paprika Chicken

NUTRITION Calories 313 , Total Fat 134g , Saturated Fat 78 g , Cholesterol 861 mg , Total Carbs 6.3 g , Fiber 0.7 g , Sugar 19 g , Sodium 62 mg , Potassium 211 mg , Protein 24.6 g

INGREDIENTS

- 1 free-range whole chicken
- 1 tablespoon of olive oil
- 1 tablespoon of dried paprika
- 1 tablespoon of curry powder
- 1 teaspoon of dried turmeric
- 1 teaspoon of salt

DIRECTION

- Start by mixing all the spices and oil in a bowl except chicken.
- Now season the chicken with these spices liberally.
- Add the chicken and spices to your Crockpot.
- Cover the lid of the crockpot and cook for 8 hours on Low.
- Serve warm.

PREPARATION	COOKING TIME	SERVINGS
10	8 hours	8

Rotisserie Chicken

NUTRITION Calories 301, Total Fat 12.2 g, Saturated Fat 2.4 g , Cholesterol 110 mg , Total Carbs 2.5 g , Fiber 0.9 g , Sugar 1.4 g, Sodium 276 mg, Potassium 231 mg, Protein 28.8 g

INGREDIENTS

- 1 organic whole chicken
- 1 tablespoon of olive oil
- 1 teaspoon of thyme
- 1 teaspoon of rosemary
- 1 teaspoon of garlic, granulated
- salt and pepper

DIRECTION

- Start by seasoning the chicken with all the herbs and spices.
- Broil this seasoned chicken for 5 minutes in the oven until golden brown.
- Place this chicken in the Crockpot.
- Cover it and cook for 8 hours on Low Settings.
- Serve warm.

PREPARATION	COOKING TIME	SERVINGS
10	8 hours	10

Crockpot Chicken Adobo

NUTRITION Calories 249, Total Fat 11.9 g , Saturated Fat 1.7 g, Cholesterol 78 mg , Total Carbs 1.8 g , Fiber 1.1 g, Sugar 0.3 g, Sodium 79 mg, Potassium 131 mg, Protein 25 g

INGREDIENTS

- 1/4 cup of apple cider vinegar
- 12 chicken drumsticks
- 1 onion, diced into slices
- 2 tablespoons of olive oil
- 10 cloves garlic, smashed
- 1 cup of gluten-free tamari
- 1/4 cup of diced green onion

DIRECTION

- Place the drumsticks in the Crockpot and then add the remaining Ingredients on top.
- Cover it and cook for 8 hours on Low Settings.
- Mix gently, then serve warm.

PREPARATION	COOKING TIME	SERVINGS
10	8 hours	6

Chicken Ginger Curry

NUTRITION Calories 248, Total Fat 15.7 g , Saturated Fat 2.7 g , Cholesterol 75 mg, Total Carbs 8.4 g, Fiber 0g Sugar 1.1 g, Sodium 94 mg, Potassium 331 mg, Protein 14.1 g

INGREDIENTS

- 1 ½ lbs. chicken drumsticks (approx. 5 drumsticks), skin removed
- 1 (13.5 oz.) can coconut milk
- 1 onion, diced
- 4 cloves garlic, minced
- 1-inch knob fresh ginger, minced
- 1 Serrano pepper, minced
- 1 tablespoon of Garam Masala
- ½ teaspoon of cayenne
- ½ teaspoon of paprika
- ½ teaspoon of turmeric
- salt and pepper, adjust to taste

DIRECTION

- Start by throwing all the Ingredients into the Crockpot.
- Cover it and cook for 6 hours on Low Settings.
- Garnish as desired.
- Serve warm

PREPARATION	COOKING TIME	SERVINGS
10	6 hours	4

Thai Chicken Curry

NUTRITION Calories 327, Total Fat 3.5 g, Saturated Fat 0.5 g , Cholesterol 162 mg, Total Carbs 56g, Fiber 0.4 g, Sugar 0.5 g, Sodium 142 mg, Potassium 558 mg, Protein 21.5 g

INGREDIENTS

- 1 can coconut milk
- 1/2 cup of chicken stock
- 1 lb. boneless, skinless chicken thighs, diced
- 1 2 tablespoons of red curry paste
- 1 tablespoon of coconut aminos
- 1 tablespoon of fish sauce
- 2 3 garlic cloves, minced
- Salt and black pepper-to taste
- red pepper flakes as desired
- 1 bag frozen mixed veggies

DIRECTION

- Start by throwing all the Ingredient except vegetables into the Crockpot.
- Cover it and cook for 2 hours on Low Settings.
- Remove its lid and thawed veggies.
- Cover the crockpot again then continue cooking for another 30 minutes on Low settings.
- Garnish as desired.
- Serve warm.

PREPARATION	COOKING TIME	SERVINGS
10	2.5 _hours_	6

Lemongrass and Coconut Chicken Drumsticks

NUTRITION Calories 372, Total Fat 11.1 g, Saturated Fat 5.8 g, Cholesterol 610 mg, Total Carbs 0.9 g , Fiber 0.2 g , Sugar 0.2 g, Sodium 749 mg, Potassium 488 mg , Protein 63.5 g

INGREDIENTS

- 10 drumsticks, skin removed
- 1 thick stalk fresh lemongrass
- 4 cloves garlic, minced
- 1 thumb-size piece of ginger
- 1 cup of coconut milk
- 2 tablespoons of Red Boat fish sauce
- 3 tablespoons of coconut aminos
- 1 teaspoon of five-spice powder
- 1 large onion, sliced
- ¼ cup of fresh scallions, diced
- Kosher salt
- Black pepper

DIRECTION

- Start by throwing all the Ingredient into the Crockpot.
- Cover it and cook for 5 hours on Low Settings.
- Garnish as desired.
- Serve warm.

PREPARATION	COOKING TIME	SERVINGS
10	5 _hours_	5

Green Chile Chicken

NUTRITION Calories 248, Total Fat 2.4 g, Saturated Fat 0.1 g , Cholesterol 320 mg, Total Carbs 2.9 g, Fiber 0.7 g , Sugar 0.7 g, Sodium 350 mg, Potassium 255 mg, Protein 44.3 g

INGREDIENTS

- *8 chicken thighs, thawed, boneless and skinless*
- *1 (4 oz.) can green chilis*
- *2 teaspoons of garlic salt*
- *optional: add in ½ cup of diced onions*

DIRECTION

- Start by throwing all the Ingredients into the Crockpot.
- Cover it and cook for 6 hours on Low Settings.
- Garnish as desired.
- Serve warm.

PREPARATION	COOKING TIME	SERVINGS
10	6 *hours*	6

Garlic Butter Chicken with Cream Cheese Sauce

NUTRITION Calories 301, Total Fat 12.2 g, Saturated Fat 2.4 g, Cholesterol 110 mg, Total Carbs 1.5 g Fiber 0.9 g, Sugar 1.4 g, Sodium 276 mg, Potassium 375mg, Protein 28.8 g

INGREDIENTS

For the garlic chicken:
- *8 garlic cloves, sliced*
- *1.5 teaspoons of salt*
- *1 stick of butter*
- *2 2.5 lbs. of chicken breasts*
- *Optional 1 onion, sliced*

For the cream cheese sauce:
- *8 oz. of cream cheese*
- *1 cup of chicken stock*
- *salt to taste*

DIRECTION

- Start by throwing all the Ingredients for garlic chicken into the Crockpot.
- Cover it and cook for 6 hours on Low Settings.
- Now stir cook all the Ingredients for cream cheese sauce in a saucepan.
- Once heated, pour this sauce over the cooked chicken.
- Garnish as desired.
- Serve warm

PREPARATION	COOKING TIME	SERVINGS
10	6 *hours*	4

Jerk chicken

NUTRITION Calories 249, Total Fat 11.9 g , Saturated Fat 1.7 g , Cholesterol 78 mg, Total Carbs 1.8 g , Fiber 1.1g , Sugar 0.3 g, Sodium 79 mg, Potassium 264 mg, Protein 35

INGREDIENTS

- 5 drumsticks and 5 wings
- 4 teaspoons of salt
- 4 teaspoons of paprika
- 1 teaspoon of cayenne pepper
- 2 teaspoons of onion powder
- 2 teaspoons of thyme
- 2 teaspoons of white pepper
- 2 teaspoons of garlic powder
- 1 teaspoon of black pepper

DIRECTION

- Start by throwing all the Ingredients into the Crockpot.
- Cover it and cook for 6 hours on Low Settings.
- Garnish as desired.
- Serve warm.

PREPARATION	COOKING TIME	SERVINGS
10	6 *hours*	5

Spicy Wings with Mint Sauce

NUTRITION Calories 248, Total Fat 15.7 g, Saturated Fat 2.7 g , Cholesterol 75 mg, Total Carbs 0.4 g, Fiber 0g Sugar 0 g, Sodium 94 mg, Potassium 158 mg, Protein 24.9 g

INGREDIENTS

- 1 tablespoon of cumin
- 18 chicken wings, cut in half
- 1 tablespoon of turmeric
- 1 tablespoon of coriander
- 1 tablespoon of fresh ginger, finely grated
- 2 tablespoon of olive oil
- 1 tablespoon of paprika
- A pinch of cayenne pepper
- ¼ cup of chicken stock
- Salt and black pepper ground, to taste

Chutney/ Sauce:
- 1 cup of fresh mint leaves
- Juice of ½ lime
- ¾ cup of cilantro
- 1 Serrano pepper
- 1 tablespoon of water
- 1 small ginger piece, peeled and diced
- 1 tablespoon of olive oil
- Salt and black pepper ground, to taste

DIRECTION

- Start by throwing all the Ingredients for wings into the Crockpot.
- Cover it and cook for 6 hours on Low Settings.
- Meanwhile, blend all the mint sauce Ingredients in a blender jug.
- Serve the cooked wings with mint sauce.
- Garnish as desired.
- Serve warm.

PREPARATION	COOKING TIME	SERVINGS
10	6 *hours*	6

Cacciatore Olive Chicken

NUTRITION Calories 297, Total Fat 16.2 g, Saturated Fat 6.5 g , Cholesterol 35 mg, Total Carbs 5.9 g, Sugar 3.3 g Fiber 1.9 g, Sodium 575 mg, Potassium 155 mg, Protein 8.9 g

INGREDIENTS

- 28 oz. canned tomatoes and juice, crushed
- 8 chicken drumsticks, bone-in
- 1 cup of chicken stock
- 1 bay leaf
- 1 teaspoon of garlic powder
- 1 yellow onion, diced
- 1 teaspoon of oregano, dried
- salt to taste

DIRECTION

- Start by throwing all the Ingredients into the Crockpot and mix them well.
- Cover it and cook for 6 hours on Low Settings.
- Garnish as desired.
- Serve warm.

PREPARATION	COOKING TIME	SERVINGS
10	6 *hours*	4

Duck and Vegetable Stew

NUTRITION Calories 449, Total Fat 23.4 g, Saturated Fat 1.5 g, Cholesterol 210 mg, Total Carbs 0.4 g, Fiber 1.3 g Sugar 22g, Sodium 838 mg, Potassium 331 mg, Protein 28.5g

INGREDIENTS

- 1 duck, diced into medium pieces
- 1 tablespoon of wine
- 2 carrots, diced
- 2 cups of water
- 1 cucumber, diced
- 1-inch ginger pieces, diced
- Salt and black pepper- to taste

DIRECTION

- Start by throwing all the Ingredients except into the Crockpot and mix them well.
- Cover it and cook for 5 hours on Low Settings.
- Garnish with cucumber.
- Serve warm.

PREPARATION	COOKING TIME	SERVINGS
10	5 *hours*	4

Mushroom Cream Goose Curry

NUTRITION Calories 288, Total Fat 5.7g, Saturated Fat 1.8 g , Cholesterol 60 mg , Total Carbs 2.9 g , Fiber 0.2 g Sugar 0.1 g , Sodium 554 mg, Potassium 431 mg, Protein 25.6g

INGREDIENTS

- 12 oz. canned mushroom cream
- 1 goose breast, fat: trimmed off and cut into pieces
- 1 goose leg, skinless
- 1 yellow onion, diced
- 3 ½ cups of water
- 2 teaspoons of garlic, minced
- 1 goose thigh, skinless
- Salt and black pepper- to taste

DIRECTION

- Start by throwing all the Ingredients into the Crockpot except cream and mix them well.
- Cover it and cook for 6 hours on Low Settings.
- Stir in mushroom cream and cook for another 30 minutes on low heat.
- Give it a stir and garnish as desired.
- Serve warm.

PREPARATION	COOKING TIME	SERVINGS
10	6.5 *hours*	6

Colombian Chicken

NUTRITION Calories 481, Total Fat 11.1 g, Saturated Fat 0.1 g , Cholesterol 320 mg , Total Carbs 9.1 g Fiber 1.7 g , Sugar 3 g, Sodium 203 mg, Potassium 331 mg, Protein 7 g

INGREDIENTS

- 1 chicken, cut into 8 pieces
- 2 bay leaves
- 4 big tomatoes, cut into medium chunks
- 1 yellow onion, sliced
- Salt and black pepper- to taste

DIRECTION

- Start by throwing all the Ingredients into the Crockpot and mix them well.
- Cover it and cook for 6 hours on Low Settings.
- Garnish as desired.
- Serve warm.

PREPARATION	COOKING TIME	SERVINGS
10	6 *hours*	4

Chicken Curry

NUTRITION Calories 537, Total Fat 19.8 g, Saturated Fat 1.4 g, Cholesterol 10 mg, Total Carbs 5.1 g, Fiber 0.9 g Sugar 1.4 g, Sodium 719 mg, Potassium 374 mg, Protein 37.6.8 g

INGREDIENTS

- 3 lb. chicken drumsticks and thighs
- 1 yellow onion, diced
- 2 tablespoons of butter, melted
- 1/2 cup of chicken stock
- 15 oz. canned tomatoes, crushed
- 1/4 cup of lemon juice
- 4 garlic cloves, minced
- 1 lb. spinach, chopped
- 1/2 cup of heavy cream
- 1 tablespoon of ginger, grated
- 1/2 cup of cilantro, diced
- 1 ½ teaspoon of paprika
- 1 tablespoon of cumin, ground
- 1 ½ teaspoon of coriander, ground
- 1 teaspoon of turmeric, ground
- Salt and black pepper- to taste
- A pinch cayenne peppers

DIRECTION

- Start by throwing all the Ingredients into the Crockpot except lemon juice, cream, and cilantro, then mixes them well.
- Cover it and cook for 6 hours on Low Settings.
- Stir in remaining Ingredients and cook again for 1 hour on low heat.
- Garnish as desired.
- Serve warm.

PREPARATION	COOKING TIME	SERVINGS
10	6 *hours*	6

Saucy Teriyaki Chicken

NUTRITION Calories 609, Total Fat 50.5 g, Saturated Fat 11.7 g , Cholesterol 58 mg , Total Carbs 9.9 g, Fiber 1.5 g, Sugar 0.3 g, Sodium 463 mg, Potassium 531 mg, Protein 29.3 g

INGREDIENTS

- 2 lbs. chicken breasts, skinless and boneless
- 2/3 cup of teriyaki sauce
- 1 tablespoon of honey
- 1/2 cup of chicken stock
- a handful green onions, diced
- salt and black pepper - to taste

DIRECTION

- Start by throwing all the Ingredients into the Crockpot and mix them well.
- Cover it and cook for 6 hours on Low Settings.
- Garnish as desired.
- Serve warm.

PREPARATION	COOKING TIME	SERVINGS
10	6 *hours*	6

Chicken Shrimp Curry

NUTRITION Calories 240, Total Fat 22.5 g, Saturated Fat 2.7 g , Cholesterol 15 mg, Total Carbs 7.1 g, Fiber 0g Sugar 0 g, Sodium 474 mg, Potassium 244 mg, Protein 14.9 g

INGREDIENTS

- 8 oz. shrimp, peeled and deveined
- 8 oz. sausages, sliced
- 8 oz. chicken breasts, skinless, boneless and diced
- 2 tablespoon of extra virgin olive oil
- 1 teaspoon of creole seasoning
- 3 garlic cloves, minced
- 1 yellow onion, diced
- 1 green bell pepper, diced
- 3 celery stalks, diced
- 1 cup of cauliflower rice
- 1 cup of chicken stock
- 2 cups of canned tomatoes, diced
- 3 tablespoons of parsley, chopped
- 2 teaspoons of thyme, dried
- A pinch cayenne peppers
- 2 teaspoon of Worcestershire sauce
- 1 dash tabasco sauce

DIRECTION

- Start by throwing all the Ingredients into the Crockpot except shrimp and mix them well.
- Cover it and cook for 5 hours on Low Settings.
- Stir in shrimp and cook for another 1 hour on low heat.
- Garnish as desired.
- Serve warm.

PREPARATION	COOKING TIME	SERVINGS
10	6 *hours*	6

Ground Duck Chili

NUTRITION Calories 548, Total Fat 22.9 g, Saturated Fat 9 g , Cholesterol 105 mg , Total Carbs 7.5 g , Sugar 10.9 g , Fiber 6.3 g, Sodium 350 mg, Potassium 433 mg, Protein 40.1 g

INGREDIENTS

- 1 yellow onion, cut into half
- 1 garlic heat, top trimmed off
- 2 cloves
- 1 bay leaf
- 6 cups of water
- Salt- to taste

For the duck:
- 1 lb. Duck, ground
- 15 oz. Canned tomatoes and their juices, diced
- 4 oz. Canned green chilies and their juice
- 1 teaspoon of Swerve
- 1 tablespoon of Vegetable oil
- 1 yellow onion, minced
- 2 carrots, diced
- Salt and black pepper- to taste
- Handful cilantro, diced

DIRECTION

- Start by throwing all other Ingredients into the Crockpot and mix them well.
- Cover it and cook for 6 hours on Low Settings.
- Garnish as desired.
- Serve warm.

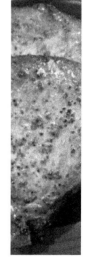

PREPARATION	COOKING TIME	SERVINGS
10	6 *hours*	8

Butter Green Peas

NUTRITION *Calories 121, fat 6.5, fiber 3, carbs 3.4, protein 0.6*

INGREDIENTS

- 1 cup green peas
- 1 teaspoon minced garlic
- 1 tablespoon butter, softened
- ½ teaspoon cayenne pepper
- 1 tablespoon olive oil
- ¾ teaspoon salt
- 1 teaspoon paprika
- 1 teaspoon garam masala
- ½ cup chicken stock

DIRECTION

- In the slow cooker, mix the peas with butter, garlic and the other Ingredients:,
- Close the lid and cook for 3 hours on High.

PREPARATION	COOKING TIME	SERVINGS
10	3 *hours*	4

Lemon Asparagus

NUTRITION Calories 139, fat 4.6., fiber 2.5, carbs 3.3, protein 3.5

INGREDIENTS

- 8 oz. asparagus
- ½ cup butter
- juice of 1 lemon
- Zest of 1 lemon, grated
- ½ teaspoon turmeric
- 1 teaspoon rosemary, dried

DIRECTION

- In your slow cooker, mix the asparagus with butter, lemon juice and the other Ingredients: and close the lid.
- Cook the vegetables on Low for 5 hours. Divide between plates and serve.

PREPARATION	COOKING TIME	SERVINGS
8	5 *hours*	2

Lime Green Beans

NUTRITION calories 67, fat 5.6, fiber 2, carbs 4, protein 2.1

INGREDIENTS

- 1-pound green beans, trimmed and halved
- 2 spring onions, chopped
- 2 tablespoons lime juice
- ½ teaspoon lime zest, grated
- 2 tablespoons olive oil
- ¼ teaspoon ground black pepper
- ¾ teaspoon salt
- ¾ cup of water

DIRECTION

- In the slow cooker, mix the green beans with the spring onions and the other Ingredients: and close the lid.
- Cook for 2.5 hours on High.

PREPARATION	COOKING TIME	SERVINGS
10	2.5 *hours*	5

Cheese Asparagus

NUTRITION calories 214, fat 6.2, fiber 1.7, carbs 3.6, protein 4.2

INGREDIENTS

- 10 oz. asparagus, trimmed
- 4 oz. Cheddar cheese, sliced
- 1/3 cup butter, soft
- 1 teaspoon turmeric powder
- ½ teaspoon salt
- ¼ teaspoon white pepper

DIRECTION

- In the slow cooker, mix the asparagus with butter and the other Ingredients, put the lid on and cook for 3 hours on High.

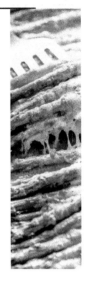

PREPARATION	COOKING TIME	SERVINGS
10	3 *hours*	4

Creamy Broccoli

NUTRITION calories 102, fat 9, fiber 1.9, carbs 4.3, protein 2.5

INGREDIENTS

- ½ cup coconut cream
- 2 cups broccoli florets
- 1 teaspoon mint, dried
- 1 teaspoon garam masala
- 1 teaspoon salt
- 1 tablespoon almonds flakes
- ½ teaspoon turmeric

DIRECTION

- In the slow cooker, mix the broccoli with the mint and the other Ingredients.
- Close the lid and cook vegetables for 1 hour on High.
- Divide between plates and serve.

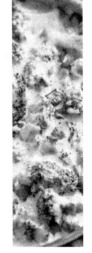

PREPARATION	COOKING TIME	SERVINGS
15	1 *hours*	4

Curry Cauliflower

NUTRITION calories 146, fat 4.3, fiber 1.9, carbs 5.7, protein 5.3

INGREDIENTS

- 1 ½ cup cauliflower, trimmed and florets separated
- 1 tablespoon curry paste
- ½ cup coconut cream
- 1 teaspoon butter
- ½ teaspoon garam masala
- ¾ cup chives, chopped
- 1 tablespoon rosemary, chopped
- 2 tablespoons Parmesan, grated

DIRECTION

- In the slow cooker, mix the cauliflower with the curry paste and the other Ingredients.
- Cook the cauliflower for 2.5 hours on High.

PREPARATION	COOKING TIME	SERVINGS
15	5.5 hours	4

Garlic Eggplant

NUTRITION calories 132, fat 2.8, fiber 4.7, carbs 8.5, protein 1.6

INGREDIENTS

- 1-pound eggplant, trimmed and roughly cubed
- 1 tablespoon balsamic vinegar
- 1 garlic clove, diced
- 1 teaspoon tarragon
- 1 teaspoon salt
- 1 tablespoon olive oil
- ½ teaspoon ground paprika
- ¼ cup of water

DIRECTION

- In the slow cooker, mix the eggplant with the vinegar, garlic and the other Ingredients, close the lid and cook on High for 2 hours.
- Divide into bowls and serve.

PREPARATION	COOKING TIME	SERVINGS
15	2 hours	4

Coconut Brussels Sprouts

NUTRITION calories 128, fat 5.6, fiber 1.7, carbs 4.4, protein 3.6

INGREDIENTS

- 2 cups Brussels sprouts, halved
- ½ cup of coconut milk
- 1 teaspoon garlic powder
- 1 teaspoon salt
- ½ teaspoon coriander, ground
- 1 teaspoon dried oregano
- 1 tablespoon balsamic vinegar
- 1 teaspoon butter

DIRECTION

- Place Brussels sprouts in the slow cooker.
- Add the rest of the Ingredients, toss, close the lid and cook the Brussels sprouts for 4 hours on Low.
- Divide between plates and serve.

PREPARATION	COOKING TIME	SERVINGS
10	4 *hours*	6

Cauliflower Pilaf with Hazelnuts

NUTRITION calories 48, fat 3.1, fiber 1.9, carbs 4.8, protein 1.6

INGREDIENTS

- 3 cups cauliflower, chopped
- 1 cup chicken stock
- 1 teaspoon ground black pepper
- ½ teaspoon turmeric
- ½ teaspoon ground paprika
- 1 teaspoon salt
- 1 tablespoon dried dill
- 1 tablespoon butter
- 2 tablespoons hazelnuts, chopped

DIRECTION

- Put cauliflower in the blender and blend until you get cauliflower rice.
- Then transfer the cauliflower rice in the slow cooker.
- Add ground black pepper, turmeric, ground paprika, salt, dried dill, and butter.
- Mix up the cauliflower rice. Add chicken stock and close the lid.
- Cook the pilaf for 2 hours on High.
- Then add chopped hazelnuts and mix the pilaf well.

PREPARATION	COOKING TIME	SERVINGS
15	2 *hours*	6

Cauliflower and Turmeric Mash

NUTRITION calories 58, fat 5.2, fiber 1.2, carbs 2.7, protein 1.1

INGREDIENTS

- 1 cup cauliflower florets
- 1 teaspoon turmeric powder
- 1 cup of water
- 1 teaspoon salt
- 1 tablespoon butter
- 1 tablespoon coconut cream
- 1 teaspoon coriander, ground

DIRECTION

- In the slow cooker, mix the cauliflower with water and salt.
- Close the lid and cook for 3 hours on High.
- Then drain water and transfer the cauliflower to a blender.
- Add the rest of the Ingredients, blend and serve.

PREPARATION	COOKING TIME	SERVINGS
10	3 *hours*	5

Spinach and Olives Mix

NUTRITION calories 189, fat 6.2, fiber 0.6, carbs 3, protein 3.4

INGREDIENTS

- 2 cups spinach
- 2 tablespoons chives, chopped
- 5 oz. Cheddar cheese, shredded
- ½ cup heavy cream
- 1 teaspoon ground black pepper
- ½ teaspoon salt
- 1 cup black olives, pitted and halved
- 1 teaspoon sage
- 1 teaspoon sweet paprika

DIRECTION

- In the slow cooker, mix the spinach with the chives and the other Ingredients, toss and close the lid.
- Cook for 3.5 hours on Low and serve.

PREPARATION	COOKING TIME	SERVINGS
15	3.5 *hours*	6

Red Cabbage and Walnuts

NUTRITION calories 112, fat 5.1, fiber 2, carbs 5.8, protein 3.5

INGREDIENTS

- 2 cups red cabbage, shredded
- 3 spring onions, chopped
- ½ cup chicken stock
- 1 tablespoon olive oil
- 1 teaspoon salt
- 1 teaspoon cumin, ground
- 1 teaspoon hot paprika
- 1 tablespoon Keto tomato sauce
- 1 oz. walnuts
- 1/3 cup fresh parsley, chopped

DIRECTION

- In the slow cooker, mix the cabbage with the spring onions and the other Ingredients.
- Close the lid and cook cabbage for 6 hours on Low.
- Divide into bowls and serve.

PREPARATION	COOKING TIME	SERVINGS
15	6 _hours_	4

Paprika Bok Choy

NUTRITION calories 128, fat 3.2, fiber 3.9, carbs 4.9, protein 4.1

INGREDIENTS

- 1-pound bok choy, torn
- ½ cup of coconut milk
- 1 tablespoon almond butter, softened
- 1 teaspoon ground paprika
- 1 teaspoon turmeric
- ½ teaspoon cayenne pepper

DIRECTION

- In the slow cooker, mix the bok choy with the coconut milk and the other Ingredients, toss and close the lid.
- Cook the meal for 2.5 hours on High.

PREPARATION	COOKING TIME	SERVINGS
15	2.5 _hours_	6

Zucchini Mix

NUTRITION calories 34, fat 1.3, fiber 3.6, carbs 4.7, protein 3.6

INGREDIENTS

- 1-pound zucchinis, roughly cubed
- 2 spring onions, chopped
- 1 teaspoon curry paste
- 1 teaspoon basil, dried
- 1 teaspoon salt
- 1 teaspoon ground black pepper
- 1 bay leaf
- ½ cup beef stock

DIRECTION

- In the slow cooker, mix the zucchinis with the onion and the other Ingredients.
- Close the lid and cook on Low for 3 hours.

PREPARATION	COOKING TIME	SERVINGS
10	3 *hours*	6

Zucchini and Spring Onions

NUTRITION calories 82, fat 5.6, fiber 2.8, carbs 5.6, protein 3.2

INGREDIENTS

- 1-pound zucchinis, sliced
- 1 teaspoon avocado oil
- 1 teaspoon salt
- 1 teaspoon white pepper
- 2 spring onions, chopped
- 1/3 cup organic almond milk
- 2 tablespoons butter
- ½ teaspoon turmeric powder

DIRECTION

- In the slow cooker, mix the zucchinis with the spring onions, oil and the other Ingredients.
- Close the lid and cook for 2 hours on High.

PREPARATION	COOKING TIME	SERVINGS
20	2 *hours*	8

Creamy Portobello Mix

NUTRITION *calories 126, fat 5.1, fiber 1.6, carbs 5.9, protein 4.4*

PREPARATION	COOKING TIME	SERVINGS
15	7 *hours*	4

INGREDIENTS

- 4 Portobello mushrooms
- ½ cup Monterey Jack cheese, grated
- ½ cup heavy cream
- 1 teaspoon curry powder
- 1 teaspoon basil, dried
- ½ teaspoon salt
- 1 teaspoon olive oil

DIRECTION

- In the slow cooker, mix the mushrooms with the cheese and the other Ingredients.
- Close the lid and cook the meal for 7 hours on Low.

Eggplant Mash

NUTRITION *calories 206, fat 6.2, fiber 3.6, carbs 7.9, protein 8.6*

PREPARATION	COOKING TIME	SERVINGS
10	2.5 *hours*	2

INGREDIENTS

- 7 oz. eggplant, trimmed
- 1 tablespoon butter
- 1 teaspoon basil, dried
- 1 teaspoon chili powder
- ½ teaspoon garlic powder
- 1/3 cup water
- ½ teaspoon salt

DIRECTION

- Peel the eggplant and rub with salt.
- Then put it in the slow cooker and water.
- Close the lid and cook the eggplant for 2.5 hours on High.
- Then drain water and mash the eggplant.
- Add the rest of the Ingredients, whisk and serve.

Cheddar Artichoke

NUTRITION *calories 135, fat 3.9, fiber 4.3, carbs 4.9, protein 4.3*

PREPARATION	COOKING TIME	SERVINGS
15	3 *hours*	6

INGREDIENTS

- 1 teaspoon garlic, diced
- 1 tablespoon olive oil
- 1-pound artichoke hearts, chopped
- 3 oz. Cheddar cheese, shredded
- 1 teaspoon curry powder
- 1 cup chicken stock
- 1 teaspoon butter
- 1 teaspoon garam masala

DIRECTION

- In the slow cooker, mix the artichokes with garlic, oil and the other Ingredients.
- Cook the artichoke hearts for 3 hours on High.
- Divide between plates and serve.

Squash and Zucchinis

NUTRITION *calories 40, fat 2.2, fiber 1.8, carbs 4.3, protein 1.1*

PREPARATION	COOKING TIME	SERVINGS
10	4 *hours*	6

DIRECTION

- In the slow cooker, mix the squash with the zucchinis, milk and the other Ingredients.
- Close the lid and cook the vegetables on Low for 4 hours.

INGREDIENTS

- 4 cups spaghetti squash, cubed
- 2 zucchinis, cubed
- ½ cup coconut milk
- ½ teaspoon ground cinnamon
- ¾ teaspoon ground ginger
- 3 tablespoons oregano
- 1 teaspoon butter

Dill Leeks

NUTRITION calories 123, fat 2.9, fiber 2.2, carbs 7.5, protein 4.3.

PREPARATION	COOKING TIME	SERVINGS
10	3 hours	3

INGREDIENTS

- 2 cups leeks, sliced
- 1 cup chicken stock
- 2 tablespoons fresh dill, chopped
- ½ teaspoon turmeric powder
- 1 teaspoon sweet paprika
- 1 tablespoon coconut cream
- 1 teaspoon butter

DIRECTION

- In the slow cooker, mix the beets with the stock, dill and the other Ingredients.
- Cook on Low for 3 hours and serve.

Vegetable Lasagna

NUTRITION calories 257, fat 15.9, fiber 4.5, carbs 10.5, protein 21.5

PREPARATION	COOKING TIME	SERVINGS
25	5 hours	4

DIRECTION

- Place coconut oil in the skillet and melt it.
- Then add sliced eggplants and roast them for 1 minute from each side.
- After this, transfer them in the bowl.
- Toss butter in the skillet.
- Place 1 beaten egg in the skillet and stir it to get the shape of a pancake.
- Roast the egg pancake for 1 minute from each side.
- Repeat the steps with remaining eggs.
- Separate the eggplants into 2 parts.
- Place 1 part of eggplants in the slow cooker. You should make the eggplant layer.
- Then add ½ cup chopped parsley and 1 egg pancake.
- Sprinkle the egg pancakes with 1/3 cup of Parmesan.
- Then add remaining eggplants and second egg pancake.
- Sprinkle it with ½ part of remaining Parmesan and top with the last egg pancake.
- Then spread it with tomato sauce, kale and sprinkle with chili flakes and ground black pepper.
- Add tomato sauce and top lasagna with remaining cheese.
- Close the lid and cook lasagna for 6 hours on Low.

INGREDIENTS

- 1 eggplant, sliced
- 1 cup kale, chopped
- 3 eggs, beaten
- 2 tablespoons Keto tomato sauce
- ½ teaspoon ground black pepper
- 1 cup Cheddar, grated
- ½ teaspoon chili flakes
- 1 tablespoon tomato sauce
- 1 teaspoon coconut oil
- ½ teaspoon butter

Cauliflower Rice Mix

NUTRITION calories 131, fat 4.5, fiber 2.1, carbs 6.2, protein 4.5

PREPARATION	COOKING TIME	SERVINGS
15	2 *hours*	6

DIRECTION

- In the slow cooker, mix the cauliflower with the butter and the other Ingredients: except the cheese, close the lid and cook on High for 1 hour.
- Add the cheese, cook on High for 1 more hour, divide between plates and serve.

INGREDIENTS

- 1 cup cauliflower rice
- 1 tablespoon coconut butter
- ¼ teaspoon salt
- ¾ teaspoon turmeric
- 1 teaspoon cayenne pepper
- 1 teaspoon curry powder
- 2 oz. Provolone cheese
- 1 ½ cups chicken stock

Vegetable Cream

NUTRITION calories 218, fat 5.6, fiber 1.9, carbs 5.6, protein 4.4

PREPARATION	COOKING TIME	SERVINGS
15	3 *hours*	4

DIRECTION

- In the slow cooker, mix the broccoli with the onion and the other Ingredients, close the lid and cook on High for 3 hours.
- Blend using an immersion blender and serve.

INGREDIENTS

- 1 cup heavy cream
- 2 cups broccoli, chopped
- 2 spring onions, chopped
- 1 teaspoon olive oil
- 1 teaspoon salt
- 1 teaspoon ground paprika
- 1 oz. celery stalk, chopped
- 1 cup chicken stock
- 1 tablespoon fresh chives, chopped
- ½ cup mushrooms

Coconut Okra

NUTRITION *calories 203, fat 6.7, fiber 2.5, carbs 6.2, protein 3.3*

PREPARATION	COOKING TIME	SERVINGS
15	3 *hours*	6

DIRECTION

- In the slow cooker, mix the okra with cream, butter and the other Ingredients.
- Cook okra for 3 hours on High.

INGREDIENTS

- 1-pound okra, trimmed
- 1/3 cup coconut cream
- 1/3 cup butter
- ½ teaspoon salt
- ½ teaspoon turmeric powder
- ¾ teaspoon ground nutmeg

Pecan Kale Mix

NUTRITION *calories 126, fat 4.8, fiber 4.6, carbs 6, protein 1.1*

PREPARATION	COOKING TIME	SERVINGS
15	4 *hours*	6

DIRECTION

- In the slow cooker, mix the kale with cilantro, pecans and the other Ingredients: and close the lid.
- Cook the mix on Low for 4 hours and serve.

INGREDIENTS

- 1 cup pecans, chopped
- 2 tablespoons butter, softened
- 1-pound kale, torn
- ¼ teaspoon salt
- 2 tablespoons cilantro, chopped
- 1 teaspoon turmeric
- ½ teaspoon onion powder
- 1/2 cup chicken stock

Mushroom Soup

NUTRITION *calories 214, fat 12...5, fiber 2.2, carbs 6.7, protein 2.3*

PREPARATION	COOKING TIME	SERVINGS
6	7 *hours*	4

DIRECTION

- In your slow cooker, mix the mushrooms with spring onions and the other Ingredients: and close the lid.
- Cook the soup for 7 hours on Low.
- When the soup is cooked, blend with an immersion blender and serve.

INGREDIENTS

- 1 cup cremini mushrooms, chopped
- 2 spring onions, chopped
- 1 garlic clove, diced
- 1 tablespoon oregano, chopped
- 1 teaspoon olive oil
- ¾ teaspoon ground black pepper
- 2 cups of water
- 1 cup of coconut milk

Artichoke and Asparagus Mix

NUTRITION *calories 122, fat 5.9, fiber 4.5, carbs 5.2, protein 8.4*

PREPARATION	COOKING TIME	SERVINGS
15	2 *hours*	4

DIRECTION

- In the slow cooker, mix the artichokes with the asparagus, onion and the other Ingredients, close the lid and cook on Low for 2 hours.

INGREDIENTS

- 2 artichokes, trimmed and halved
- 1-pound asparagus, trimmed and roughly chopped
- 2 spring onions, chopped
- 1 tablespoon almond butter
- ½ cup coconut cream
- ½ teaspoon salt
- 1 teaspoon chili pepper
- ¼ jalapeno pepper, minced
- ½ cup chicken stock

Butter Green Beans

NUTRITION calories 175, fat 15.5, fiber 2.5, carbs 7, protein 2.8

PREPARATION	COOKING TIME	SERVINGS
5	4.5 *hours*	6

INGREDIENTS

- 2 cups green beans, trimmed and halved
- ½ cup butter
- 1 teaspoon salt

DIRECTION

- Mix up together snap peas with salt and transfer them in the slow cooker.
- Add butter and close the lid.
- Cook the vegetables on Low for 4.5 hours.

Hot Eggplant Mix

NUTRITION calories 202, fat 5.2, fiber 6.5, carbs 4.5, protein 5.1

PREPARATION	COOKING TIME	SERVINGS
15	2 *hours*	4

DIRECTION

- In the slow cooker, mix the eggplants with the coconut oil and the other Ingredients: and close the lid.
- Cook the eggplant mix for 2 hours on Low.

INGREDIENTS

- 1 teaspoon coconut oil, melted
- 3 eggplants, sliced
- 1 teaspoon minced garlic
- 1 red chili pepper, minced
- 1 teaspoon Keto tomato sauce
- 1 tablespoon butter
- 1 teaspoon hot paprika
- 1 teaspoon chives, chopped

Zucchini Balls

NUTRITION calories 207, fat 5.5, fibre 1.8, carbs 4.5, protein 3.6

PREPARATION	COOKING TIME	SERVINGS
20	30 *mins*	4

INGREDIENTS

- 1 cup zucchini, grated
- ½ cup almond flour
- ¼ cup Parmesan, grated
- 1 egg, whisked
- 1 tablespoon avocado oil
- ¾ cup of coconut milk
- ½ teaspoon salt

DIRECTION

- In the mixing bowl zucchinis with flour and the other Ingredients: except the coconut milk and the oil and shape medium balls.
- Preheat avocado oil in the skillet and add zucchini balls.
- Roast them for 2 minutes from each side.
- After this, transfer the zucchini balls in the slow cooker. Add coconut milk and close the lid.
- Cook the meal for 30 minutes on High.

Homemade Vegetable Stock

NUTRITION Calories: 11, Protein: 0g, Carbs: 3g, Fat: 0g, Fiber: 0g

PREPARATION	COOKING TIME	SERVINGS
15	12 *hours* 30 *mins*	4

DIRECTION

- Put everything in your slow cooker and cover. Do not turn on; let it sit for 30 minutes.
- Cook on low for 12 hours. Strain the broth and discard the solids.
- Before using, keep the stock in a container in the fridge for 2-3 hours.

INGREDIENTS

- 4 quarts cold filtered water
- 12 whole peppercorns
- 3 peeled and chopped carrots
- 3 chopped celery stalks
- 2 bay leaves
- 4 smashed garlic cloves
- 1 large quartered onion
- 2 tablespoons apple cider vinegar
- Any other vegetable scraps

Cream of Zucchini Soup

NUTRITION Calories: 96, Protein: 7g, Carbs: 11g, Fat: 5g, Fiber: 2.3g

PREPARATION	COOKING TIME	SERVINGS
15	2 hours 10 mins	4

INGREDIENTS

- 3 cups vegetable stock
- 2 pounds chopped zucchini
- 2 minced garlic cloves
- ¾ cup chopped onion
- ¼ cup basil leaves
- 1 tablespoon extra-virgin olive oil
- Salt and pepper to taste

DIRECTION

- Heat-up olive oil in a skillet. When hot, cook garlic and onion for about 5 minutes.
- Pour into your slow cooker with the rest of the fixings. Close the lid.
- Cook on low for 2 hours. Puree the soup with an immersion blender. Serve.

Tomato Soup

NUTRITION Calories: 165, Protein: 3g, Carbs: 15g, Fat: 13g, Fiber: 3.7g

PREPARATION	COOKING TIME	SERVINGS
15	4 hours	4

DIRECTION

- Put all the fixings except heavy cream in the slow cooker, then cook on low for 4 hours.
- Blend then stir in the cream using an immersion blender. Taste and season with more salt and pepper if necessary.

INGREDIENTS

- 1 can crushed tomatoes
- 1 cup vegetable broth
- ½ cup heavy cream
- 2 tablespoons chopped parsley
- ½ teaspoon onion powder
- ½ teaspoon garlic powder
- Salt and pepper to taste

Vegetable Korma

PREPARATION	COOKING TIME	SERVINGS
15	8 *hours*	4

DIRECTION

- Add vegetables into your slow cooker. Mix coconut milk with seasonings.
- Pour into the slow cooker. Sprinkle over coconut flour and mix until blended.
- Close and cook on low for 8 hours. Taste and season more if necessary. Serve!

INGREDIENTS

- 1 head's worth of cauliflower florets
- ¾ can of full-fat coconut milk
- 2 cups chopped green beans
- ½ chopped onion
- 2 minced garlic cloves
- 2 tablespoons curry powder
- 2 tablespoons coconut flour
- 1 teaspoon garam masala
- Salt and pepper to taste

Zoodles with Cauliflower-Tomato Sauce

PREPARATION	COOKING TIME	SERVINGS
15	3 *hours* 31 *mins*	4

DIRECTION

- Put everything but the zoodles into your slow cooker. Cook on high for 3 ½ hours.
- Smash into a chunky sauce with a potato masher or another utensil.
- To cook the zoodles, boil a large pot of water. When boiling, cook zoodles for just 1 minute, then drain—Season with salt and pepper. Serve sauce over zoodles!

INGREDIENTS

- 5 large spiralized zucchinis
- Two 24-ounce cans of diced tomatoes
- 2 small heads' worth of cauliflower florets
- 1 cup chopped sweet onion
- 4 minced garlic cloves
- ½ cup veggie broth
- 5 teaspoons Italian seasoning
- Salt and pepper to taste
- Enough water to cover zoodles

Spaghetti Squash Carbonara

NUTRITION *Calories: 211, Protein: 5g, Carbs: 26g, Fat: 11g, Fiber: 5.1g*

PREPARATION	COOKING TIME	SERVINGS
15	8 10	4
	hours *mins*	

DIRECTION

- Put squash in your cooker and pour in 2 cups of water. Close the lid.
- Cook on low for 8-9 hours. When the spaghetti squash cools, mix egg, cream, milk, and cheese in a bowl.
- When the squash is cool enough for you to handle with oven mitts, cut it open lengthwise and scrape out noodles. Mix in the egg mixture right away.
- Add spinach and seasonings. Top with coconut bacon and enjoy!

INGREDIENTS

- 2 cups of water
- One 3-pound spaghetti squash
- ½ cup coconut bacon
- ½ cup fresh spinach leaves
- 1 egg
- 3 tablespoons heavy cream
- 3 tablespoons unsweetened almond milk
- ½ cup grated Parmesan cheese
- 1 teaspoon garlic powder
- Salt and pepper to taste

Summery Bell Pepper + Eggplant Salad

NUTRITION *Calories: 128, Protein: 5g, Carbs: 27g, Fat: 1g, Fiber: 9.7g*

PREPARATION	COOKING TIME	SERVINGS
15	7	4
	hours	

DIRECTION

- Mix all the fixings in your slow cooker. Close the lid. Cook on low for 7-8 hours.
- When time is up, serve warm, or chill in the fridge for a few hours before eating.

INGREDIENTS

- One 24-ounce can of whole tomatoes
- 2 sliced yellow bell peppers
- 2 small eggplants (smaller ones tend to be less bitter)
- 1 sliced red onion
- 1 tablespoon paprika
- 2 teaspoons cumin
- Salt and pepper to taste
- A squeeze of lime juice

Stuffed Eggplant

NUTRITION Calories 241, Fat 13.1, Fiber 0.1, Carbs 0.6, Protein 30.5

PREPARATION
15

COOKING TIME
1   30
hours   mins

SERVINGS
6

INGREDIENTS

- 1 seeded and chopped green bell pepper
- 1 tbsp. tomato paste
- 1 tsp. cumin
- 1 tsp. raw coconut sugar
- 2 chopped red onions
- 3 tbsp. chopped parsley
- 4 chopped tomatoes
- 4 minced garlic cloves
- 4 tbsp. olive oil
- 6 eggplants

DIRECTION

- Remove eggplant skins with a vegetable peeler. Slice eggplants lengthwise and sprinkle with salt. Set aside for half an hour to sweat.
- Place eggplants into your slow cooker. Cook on high 20 minutes.
- Sauté onions in a heated pan with olive oil. Stir bell pepper and garlic with onions and sauté for an additional 1 to 2 minutes.
- Pour mixture into eggplants into the slow cooker—Cook 20 minutes on high.
- Put pepper plus salt and add parsley, tomato paste, cumin, sugar, and tomato. Cook another 10 minutes, stir well and serve!

Bacon Cheddar Broccoli Salad

NUTRITION Calories: 189, Carbs: 8g, Fat: 21g, Protein: 8g

PREPARATION	COOKING TIME	SERVINGS
15	2 *hours*	15

DIRECTION

- For the dressing, whisk all dressing components together, adjusting taste pepper and salt, and add to your slow cooker.
- Set to a low setting to cook for 2 hours until everything is combined.
- Serve warm!

INGREDIENTS

- Dressing:
- ¼ C. sweetener of choice
- 1 C. keto mayo
- 2 tbsp. organic vinegar
- Broccoli Salad:
- ½ diced red onion
- 4 ounces cheddar cheese
- ½ pound bacon, cooked and chopped
- 1 large head broccoli
- 1/8 C. sunflower seeds
- 1/8 C. pumpkin seeds

Cracked-Out Keto Slaw

NUTRITION Calories: 360, Carbs: 5g, Fat: 33g, Protein: 7g

PREPARATION	COOKING TIME	SERVINGS
15	1 *hours* 35 *mins*	2

DIRECTION

- Toss cabbage with chili paste, sesame oil, vinegar, and tamari. Add to slow cooker.
- Add minced garlic and mix well. Set to cook on high 1 ½ hours.
- Stir in macadamia nuts. Cook 5 minutes more. Garnish with sesame seeds before serving.

INGREDIENTS

- ½ C. chopped macadamia nuts
- 1 tbsp. sesame oil
- 1 tsp. chili paste
- 1 tsp. vinegar
- 2 garlic cloves
- 2 tbsp. tamari
- 4 C. shredded cabbage

Zucchini Pasta

NUTRITION Calories: 181, Carbs: 6g, Fat: 13g, Protein: 5g

PREPARATION	COOKING TIME	SERVINGS
15	2 *hours*	4

DIRECTION

- Sauté onion and garlic 3 minutes till fragrant in olive oil.
- Add zucchini noodles to your slow cooker and season with pepper and salt—Cook 60 minutes on high heat.
- Mix in tomatoes, basil, onion, garlic, and red pepper. Cook another 20 minutes.
- Add parmesan cheese to slow cooker. Mix thoroughly and cook 10 minutes to melt the cheese. Devour!

INGREDIENTS

- ¼ C. olive oil
- ½ C. basil
- ½ tsp. red pepper flakes
- 1-pint halved cherry tomatoes
- 1 sliced red onion
- 2 pounds spiralized zucchini
- 4 minced garlic cloves

Twice Baked Spaghetti Squash

NUTRITION Calories: 230, Carbs: 4g, Fat: 17g, Protein: 12g

PREPARATION	COOKING TIME	SERVINGS
15	6 *hours*	4

DIRECTION

- Cut spaghetti squash in half lengthwise, discarding innards. Set gently into your pot.
- Cook on high heat for 4 hours.
- Take squash innards and mix with parmesan cheese and butter. Then mix in pepper, salt, garlic, and oregano.
- Add squash innards mixture to the middle of cooked squash halves.
- Cook on high for another 1-2 hours till middles are deliciously bubbly.

INGREDIENTS

- ¼ tsp. Pepper
- ¼ tsp. salt
- ½ C. grated parmesan cheese
- 1 tsp. oregano
- 2 minced garlic cloves
- 2 small spaghetti squashes
- 2 tbsp. butter
- 4 slices Provolone cheese

Mushroom Risotto

NUTRITION *Calories: 438, Carbs: 5g, Fat: 17g, Protein: 12g*

PREPARATION	COOKING TIME	SERVINGS
15	4 *hours*	4

INGREDIENTS

- ¼ C. vegetable broth
- 1-pound sliced Portobello mushrooms
- 1-pound sliced white mushrooms
- 1/3 C. grated parmesan cheese
- 2 diced shallots
- 3 tbsp. chopped chives
- 3 tbsp. coconut oil
- 4 ½ C. riced cauliflower
- 4 tbsp. butter

DIRECTION

- Heat-up oil and sauté mushrooms 3 minutes till soft. Discard liquid and set it to the side.
- Add oil to skillet and sauté shallots 60 seconds.
- Pour all recipe components into your pot and mix well to combine.
- Cook 3 hours on high heat. Serve topped with parmesan cheese.

Vegan Bibimbap

NUTRITION *Calories: 119, Carbs: 0g, Fat: 18g, Protein: 8g*

PREPARATION	COOKING TIME	SERVINGS
15	45 *mins*	4

DIRECTION

- In a bowl, combine tempeh squares with 1 tbsp. soy sauce and 2 tbsp. vinegar. Set aside to soak. Slice veggies.
- Add carrot, broccoli, and peppers to slow cooker. Cook on high 30 minutes.
- Add cauliflower rice to the slow cooker; cook 5 minutes.
- Add sweetener, oil, soy sauce, vinegar, and sriracha to slow cooker. Don't hesitate to add a bit of water if you find the mixture to be too thick.

INGREDIENTS

- ½ cucumber, sliced into strips
- 1 grated carrot
- 1 sliced red bell pepper
- 1 tbsp. soy sauce
- 1 tsp. sesame oil
- 10-ounces riced cauliflower
- 2 tbsp. rice vinegar
- 2 tbsp. sesame seeds
- 2 tbsp. sriracha sauce
- 4-5 broccoli florets
- 7-ounces tempeh, sliced into squares
- Liquid sweetener

Avocado Pesto Kelp Noodles

NUTRITION Calories: 321, Carbs: 1g, Fat: 32g , Protein: 2g

PREPARATION	COOKING TIME	SERVINGS
15	1 30 hours mins	2

INGREDIENTS

- Pesto:
- ¼ C. basil
- ½ C. extra-virgin olive oil
- 1 avocado
- 1 C. baby spinach leaves
- 1 tsp. salt
- 1-2 garlic cloves
- 1 package of kelp noodles

DIRECTION

- Add kelp noodles to slow cooker with just enough water to cover them. Cook on high 45-60 minutes.
- In the meantime, combine pesto Ingredients: in a blender, blending till smooth and incorporated.
- Stir in pesto and heat noodle mixture 10 minutes.

Vegan Cream of Mushroom Soup

NUTRITION Calories: 281, Carbs: 3g, Fat: 16g, Protein: 11g

PREPARATION	COOKING TIME	SERVINGS
15	1 40 hours mins	2

INGREDIENTS

- ¼ tsp sea salt
- ½ diced yellow onion
- ½ tsp. extra-virgin olive oil
- 1 ½ C. chopped white mushrooms
- 1 2/3 C. unsweetened almond milk
- 1 tsp. onion powder
- 2 C. cauliflower florets

DIRECTION

- Add cauliflower, pepper, salt, onion powder, and milk to slow cooker. Stir and set to cook on high 1 hour.
- With olive oil, sauté onions and mushrooms together 8 to 10 minutes till softened.
- Allow cauliflower mixture to cool off a bit and add to blender. Blend until smooth. Then blend in mushroom mixture.
- Pour back into the slow cooker and heat 30 minutes.

Creamy Curry Sauce Noodle Bowl

NUTRITION Calories: 110 , Carbs: 1g , Fat: 9g , Protein: 7g

PREPARATION	COOKING TIME	SERVINGS
15	2 hours	4

DIRECTION

- Add all Ingredients, minus curry sauce components, to your slow cooker. Set to cook on high 1-2 hours.
- In the meantime, add all of the curry sauce Ingredients to a blender. Puree until smooth.
- Pour over veggie and noodle mixture. Stir well to coat.

INGREDIENTS

- ½ head chopped cauliflower
- 1 diced red bell pepper
- 1 pack of Kanten Noodles
- 2 chopped carrots
- 2 handfuls of mixed greens
- Chopped cilantro
- Curry Sauce:
- ¼ C. avocado oil mayo
- ¼ C. water
- ¼ tsp./ ginger
- ½ tsp. pepper
- 1 ½ tsp. coriander
- 1 tsp. cumin
- 1 tsp turmeric
- 2 tbsp. apple cider vinegar
- 2 tbsp. avocado oil
- 2 tsp. curry powder

Spinach Artichoke Casserole

NUTRITION Calories: 141, Carbs: 7g, Fat: 9g, Protein: 10g

PREPARATION	COOKING TIME	SERVINGS
15	4 hours	10

DIRECTION

- Grease the inside of your slow cooker.
- Whisk ½ of parmesan cheese, pepper, salt, garlic, artichoke hearts, spinach, eggs, and almond milk.
- Add baking powder and coconut flour, combining well.
- Spread into the slow cooker. Sprinkle with remaining parmesan cheese.
- Cook within 2 to 3 hours on high, or you can cook 4 to 6 hours on a lower heat setting.

INGREDIENTS

- ½ tsp. pepper
- ¾ C. coconut flour
- ¾ C. unsweetened almond milk
- 1 C. grated parmesan cheese
- 1 tbsp. baking powder
- 1 tsp. salt
- 3 minced garlic cloves
- 5-ounces chopped spinach
- 6-ounces chopped artichoke hearts
- 8 eggs

Asparagus with Lemon

NUTRITION Calories: 78, Fat: 2 g, Carbs: 3.7 g, Protein: 9 g

PREPARATION	COOKING TIME	SERVINGS
15	2 *hours*	2

INGREDIENTS

- 1 lb. asparagus spears
- 1 tbsp. lemon juice

DIRECTION

- Prepare the seasonings: 2 crushed cloves of garlic and salt and pepper to taste.
- Put the asparagus spears on the bottom of the crockpot. Add the lemon juice and the seasonings.
- Cook on low for 2 hours.

Veggie-Noodle Soup

NUTRITION Calories: 56, Fat: 0.5 g, Carbs: 0.5 g, Protein: 3 g

PREPARATION	COOKING TIME	SERVINGS
15	8 *hours*	2

DIRECTION

- Except for the zucchini and spinach, add all the Ingredients: to the crockpot.
- Add 3 cups of water.
- Cover and cook within 8 hours on low. Add the zucchini and spinach at the last 10 minutes of cooking.

INGREDIENTS

- 1/2 cup chopped carrots, chopped
- 1/2 cup chopped celery, chopped
- 1 tsp Italian seasoning
- 7 oz. zucchini, cut spiral
- 2 cups spinach leaves, chopped

Zucchini and Yellow Squash

NUTRITION Calories: 122, Fat: 9.9 g, Carbs: 3.7 g, Protein: 4.2 g

PREPARATION   COOKING TIME   SERVINGS

15   6   2

hours

INGREDIENTS

- 2/3 cup zucchini, sliced
- 2/3 cups yellow squash, sliced
- 1/3 tsp Italian seasoning
- 1/8 cup butter

DIRECTION

- Place zucchini and squash on the bottom of the slow cooker.
- Sprinkle with the Italian seasoning with salt, pepper, and garlic powder to taste. Top with butter.
- Cover and cook within 6 hours on low.

Gluten-Free Zucchini Bread

NUTRITION Calories: 174, Fat: 13 g, Carbs: 2.9 g, Protein: 4 g

PREPARATION   COOKING TIME   SERVINGS

DIRECTION   15   3   2

hours

INGREDIENTS

- Combine all dry Ingredients: and add a pinch of salt and sweetener of choice. Combine the dry Ingredients: with the eggs and mix thoroughly.
- Fold in zucchini and spread inside the slow cooker. Cover and cook within 3 hours on high.

- 1/2 cup coconut flour
- 1/2 tsp baking powder and baking soda
- 1 egg, whisked
- 1/4 cup butter
- 1 cup zucchini, shredded

Eggplant Parmesan

NUTRITION
Calories: 159, Fat: 12 g, Carbs: 8 g, Protein: 14 g

PREPARATION	COOKING TIME	SERVINGS
40	4 hours	2

DIRECTION

- Put salt on each side of the eggplant, then let stand for 30 minutes.
- Spread some of the marinara on the bottom of the slow cooker and season with salt and pepper, garlic powder, and Italian seasoning.
- Spread the eggplants on a single the slow cooker and pour over some of the marinara sauce. Repeat up to 3 layers. Top with Parmesan. Cover and cook for 4 hours.

INGREDIENTS

- 1 large eggplant, 1/2-inch slices
- 1 egg, whisked
- 1 tsp Italian seasoning
- 1 cup marinara
- 1/4 cup Parmesan cheese, grated

Zucchini Lasagna

NUTRITION
Calories: 251, Fat: 13.9 g, Carbs: 4.8 g, Protein: 20.8 g

PREPARATION	COOKING TIME	SERVINGS
15	4 hours	2

DIRECTION

- Mix egg with spinach and parmesan. Spread some of the tomato sauce inside the slow cooker and season with salt and pepper.
- Spread the zucchini on a single the slow cooker and pour over some of the tomato sauce. Repeat until 3 layers.
- Top with Parmesan.
- Cover and cook for 4 hours.

INGREDIENTS

- 1 large egg, whisked
- 1/8 cup Parmesan cheese, grated
- 1 cup spinach, chopped
- 2 cups tomato sauce
- 2 zucchinis, 1/8-inch thick, pre-grilled

Cauliflower Bolognese on Zucchini Noodles

NUTRITION *Calories: 164, Fat: 5 g, Carbs: 6 g, Protein: 12 g*

PREPARATION	COOKING TIME	SERVINGS
15	4 *hours*	2

INGREDIENTS

- 1 cauliflower head, floret cuts
- 1 tsp dried basil flakes
- 28 oz. diced tomatoes
- 1/2 cup vegetable broth
- 5 zucchinis, spiral cut

DIRECTION

- Place Ingredients: in the slow cooker except for the zucchini. Season with 2 garlic cloves, 3.4 diced onions, salt, pepper to taste, and desired spices. Cover and cook for 4 hours.
- Smash florets of the cauliflower with a fork to form "Bolognese."
- Transfer the dish on top of the zucchini noodles.

Garlic Ranch Mushrooms

NUTRITION *Calories: 97, Fat: 20 g, Carbs: 3 g, Protein: 10 g*

PREPARATION	COOKING TIME	SERVINGS
15	2 *hours*	2

DIRECTION

- Place 5 cloves of garlic at the bottom of the slow cooker and pour in the melted butter.
- Add in the mushrooms and pour the dressing—season with salt and pepper to taste.
- Cover and cook on high within 2 hours.

INGREDIENTS

- 1 package of Ranch Dressing
- 4 packages of whole mushrooms
- 1 cube butter, melted

Easy Creamed Spinach

NUTRITION *Calories: 165, Fat: 13.22 g, Carbs: 3.63 g, Protein: 7.33 g*

PREPARATION
15

COOKING TIME
3
hours

SERVINGS
2

INGREDIENTS

- 10 oz. spinach, defrosted
- 3 tbsp. Parmesan cheese
- 3 oz. cream cheese
- 2 tbsp. sour cream

DIRECTION

- Combine all the fixings in the slow cooker.
- Add some seasonings: salt and pepper to taste and half a teaspoon of onion and garlic powder. Mix thoroughly—cover and cook within 3 hours on low.

Low Carb Greek Spinach and Eggs

NUTRITION *Calories: 481, Fat: 43g, m, Protein: 6g, Carbs: 1g*

PREPARATION
30

COOKING TIME
1.5
hours

SERVINGS
2

DIRECTION

- Grease the inside of the slow cooker with the oil and butter.
- Add the spinach and lightly season with salt and pepper. Set to cook on high heat for 1 hour.
- Add the eggs and feta cheese along with the rest of the herbs. Give everything a whisk and cook for another 20 minutes in high heat.
- Serve as it is on the plate and garnish optionally with some cherry tomatoes.

INGREDIENTS

- 4 large eggs, lightly beaten
- 3 cups fresh spinach, washed and drained
- 2 tbsp. of butter
- 1 tbsp. of olive oil
- 1 cup of crumbled feta cheese
- 1 tsp of oregano
- 1 minced garlic
- Salt/Pepper

Cauliflower Hash Browns

NUTRITION Calories: 165, Fat: 12g, Carbs: 6g, Protein: 7g.

PREPARATION   COOKING TIME   SERVINGS

30   1.5   4
                    hours

INGREDIENTS

- 3 cups of shredded cauliflower
- 1 cup of cheddar cheese
- 2 large eggs, beaten
- 1 tsp of mustard powder
- Salt/Pepper

DIRECTION

- Combine the eggs with the cauliflower in the slow cooker along with the mustard powder and salt and pepper to taste.
- Set to cook for 50 minutes on high heat.
- Add the cheddar cheese on top.
- Whisk lightly and cook for another 20-25 minutes in high heat.
- Scoop out the hash brown mixture and form as you wish e.g. squares or balls

Veggies and "Cheese" Filling

NUTRITION Calories: 189, Fat: 8g, Carbs: 10g, Protein: 9, 8 g.

PREPARATION COOKING TIME   SERVINGS

DIRECTION   30   1.5   4
                                 hours

- Combine in a bowl the nutritional yeast with coconut milk and the seasonings. Whisk and set aside.
- Lightly saute the chopped veggies in a pan (no more than 2 minutes) till they change a bit of color but they are still crunchy enough.
- Add to the slow cooker and cook on high heat for 40 minutes. Add the nutritional yeast mixture and cook on high heat for another 20 minutes
- Remove and add a filling to coconut flour tortillas.

INGREDIENTS

- 1 large green pepper, thickly chopped
- 1 large red onion, thinly chopped
- 1 large red pepper, thickly chopped
- 2 tbsp. of nutritional yeast
- 1 cup of coconut cream
- 1 tbsp. of sugar-free fajita seasoning
- 1 tbsp. of butter
- Salt
- Pepper
- 2 coconut flour tortillas

CoconutFlour"Porridge" With Blueberries and Cinnamon

NUTRITION *Calories: 453, Fat: 39g, Carbs: 12g, Protein: 14g.*

PREPARATION	COOKING TIME	SERVINGS
40	2.5 *hours*	4

INGREDIENTS

- ⅔ cups of coconut flour
- ⅓ cup flaxseed flour
- ⅔ cup unsweetened, coconut cream
- 1 tbsp. of ghee
- 1 tsp of agave syrup
- 1 tbsp. of blueberries
- 1 tsp of cinnamon

DIRECTION

- Place all the first four Ingredients together in the slow cooker to make a thick paste.
- Set to cook on low heat for 2 ½ hours to make a thick, creamy porridge.
- Transfer onto a big bowl (or two smaller bowls) and drizzle with a bit of agave syrup. Add the cinnamon and blueberries on top.

Chapter 10.Beef

Kalua Pork with Cabbage

NUTRITION Calories 264 , Fat 18.4 g , Carbohydrates 4.4 g , Sugar 2.4 g , Protein 20.5 g , Cholesterol 71 mg

INGREDIENTS

- 1 medium cabbage head, chopped
- 1 lbs. pork shoulder butt roast, trimmed
- bacon slices
- 1 tbsp. sea salt

DIRECTION

- Place 4 bacon slices into the bottom of the slow cooker.
- Spread pork roast on top of bacon slices and season with salt.
- Arrange remaining bacon slices on top of the pork roast layer.
- Cover slow cooker with lid and cook on low for 8 hours or until meat is tender.
- Add chopped cabbage. Cover again and cook on low for 1 hour.
- Remove pork from the slow cooker and shred using a fork.
- Return shredded pork to the slow cooker and stir well.
- Serve warm and enjoy.

PREPARATION	COOKING TIME	SERVINGS
10	9 *hours*	12

Creamy Pork Chops

NUTRITION Calories 280, Fat 15.1 g, Carbohydrates 7.4 g , Sugar 1 g , Protein 29.1 g , Cholesterol 64 mg

INGREDIENTS

- boneless pork chops
- ½ cup chicken stock
- 1 oz. dry ranch dressing
- oz. chicken soup
- garlic cloves, minced
- Pepper

DIRECTION

- Season pork chops with pepper and place in a slow cooker.
- In a bowl, mix together chicken soup, ranch dressing, stock, and garlic.
- Pour chicken soup mixture over top of pork chops.
- Cover slow cooker with lid and cook on low for 6 hours.
- Serve hot and enjoy.

PREPARATION	COOKING TIME	SERVINGS
10	6 *hours*	4

Beef Taco Filling

NUTRITION Calories 75 , Fat 2.4 g , Carbohydrates 0.9 g , Sugar 0.6 g , Protein 11.7 g , Cholesterol 34 mg

INGREDIENTS

- 1 lb. ground beef
- oz. can tomato with green chilies
- 1 envelope taco seasoning

DIRECTION

- Add all Ingredients: to the slow cooker and stir well.
- Cover slow cooker with lid and cook on low for 6 hours.
- Serve and enjoy.

PREPARATION	COOKING TIME	SERVINGS
10	6 *hours*	12

Flavorful Steak Fajitas

NUTRITION Calories 333 , Fat 9.7 g , Carbohydrates 11.9 g , Sugar 5 g , Protein 47.8 g , Cholesterol 135 mg

INGREDIENTS

- 2 lbs. beef, sliced
- 2 tbsp. fajita seasoning
- 20 oz. salsa
- 1 large onion, sliced
- 1 bell pepper, sliced

DIRECTION

- Add salsa into the slow cooker.
- Add remaining Ingredients: on top of the salsa and stir to mix.
- Cover slow cooker with lid and cook on low for 6 hours.
- Stir well and serve.

PREPARATION	COOKING TIME	SERVINGS
10	6 *hours*	6

Garlic Herb Pork

NUTRITION Calories 359, Fat 27.8 g , Carbohydrates 2.1 g , Sugar 1.1 g , Protein 23.2 g

INGREDIENTS

- lbs. pork shoulder roast, boneless and cut into 4 pieces
- ½ tbsp. cumin
- ½ tbsp. fresh oregano
- 2/3 cup grapefruit juice
- garlic cloves
- Pepper and salt

DIRECTION

- Add pork roast into the slow cooker. Season with pepper and salt.
- Add garlic, cumin, oregano, and grapefruit juice into the blender and blend until smooth.
- Pour blended mixture over pork and stir well.
- Cover slow cooker with lid and cook on low for 8 hours.
- Remove pork from the slow cooker and shred using a fork.
- Return shredded pork into the slow cooker and stir well.
- Serve warm and enjoy.

PREPARATION	COOKING TIME	SERVINGS
10	8 *hours*	10

Garlic Thyme Lamb Chops

NUTRITION Calories 40 , Fat 1.9 g , Carbohydrates 2.3 g , Sugar 0.6 g , Protein 3.4 g , Cholesterol 0 mg

INGREDIENTS

- lamb chops
- 1 tsp dried oregano
- 2 garlic cloves, minced
- ½ tsp dried thyme
- 1 medium onion, sliced
- Pepper and salt

DIRECTION

- Add sliced onion into the slow cooker.
- Combine together thyme, oregano, pepper, and salt. Rub over lamb chops.
- Place lamb chops in the slow cooker and top with garlic.
- Pour ¼ cup water around the lamb chops.
- Cover slow cooker with lid and cook on low for 6 hours.
- Serve and enjoy.

PREPARATION	COOKING TIME	SERVINGS
10	6 *hours*	8

Pork Tenderloin

NUTRITION Calories 196 , Fat 4 g , Carbohydrates 3.1 g , Sugar 0.9 g , Protein 29.9 g ,
Cholesterol 83 mg

INGREDIENTS

- 1 ½ lbs. pork tenderloin, trimmed and cut in half lengthwise
- garlic cloves, chopped
- 1 oz enveloppe dry onionsoup mix
- ¾ cup red wine
- 1 cup water
- Pepper and salt

DIRECTION

- Place pork tenderloin into the slow cooker.
- Pour red wine and water over pork.
- Sprinkle dry onion soup mix on top of pork tenderloin.
- Top with chopped garlic and season with pepper and salt.
- Cover slow cooker with lid and cook on low for 4 hours.
- Stir well and serve.

PREPARATION	COOKING TIME	SERVINGS
10	4 *hours*	6

Smoky Pork with Cabbage

NUTRITION Calories 484 , Fat 21.5 g , Carbohydrates 3.5 g , Sugar 1.9 g , Protein 65.4 g ,
Cholesterol 195 mg

INGREDIENTS

- lbs. pastured pork roast
- 1/3 cup liquid smoke
- 1/2 cabbage head, chopped
- 1 cup water
- 1 tbsp. kosher salt

DIRECTION

- Rub pork with kosher salt and place into the slow cooker.
- Pour liquid smoke over the pork. Add water.
- Cover slow cooker with lid and cook on low for 7 hours.
- Remove pork from the slow cooker and add cabbage to the bottom of the slow cooker.
- Now place pork on top of the cabbage.
- Cover again and cook for 1 hour more.
- Shred pork with a fork and serves.

PREPARATION	COOKING TIME	SERVINGS
10	8 *hours*	6

Simple Roasted Pork Shoulder

NUTRITION Calories 664 , Fat 48.5 g , Carbohydrates 0.3 g , Sugar 0.1 g , Protein 52.9 g , Cholesterol 204 mg

INGREDIENTS

- lbs. pork shoulder
- 1 tsp garlic powder
- 1/2 cup water
- 1/2 tsp black pepper
- 1/2 tsp sea salt

DIRECTION

- Season pork with garlic powder, pepper, and salt and place in a slow cooker. Add water.
- Cover slow cooker with lid and cook on high for 1 hour, then turn heat to low and cook for 8 hours.
- Remove meat from the slow cooker and shred using a fork.
- Serve and enjoy.

PREPARATION	COOKING TIME	SERVINGS
10	9 *hours*	8

Flavors Pork Chops

NUTRITION Calories 386 , Fat 32.9 g , Carbohydrates 2.9 g , Sugar 0.7 g , Protein 19.7 g

INGREDIENTS

- pork chops
- 2 garlic cloves, minced
- 1 cup chicken broth
- 1 tbsp. poultry seasoning
- 1/4 cup olive oil
- Pepper and salt

DIRECTION

- In a bowl, whisk together olive oil, poultry seasoning, garlic, broth, pepper, and salt.
- Pour olive oil mixture into the slow cooker, then place pork chops into the slow cooker.
- Cover slow cooker with lid and cook on high for 4 hours.
- Serve and enjoy.

PREPARATION	COOKING TIME	SERVINGS
10	4 *hours*	4

Beef Stroganoff

NUTRITION Calories 471, Fat 25.3 g , Carbohydrates 8.6 g , Sugar 3.1 g , Protein 48.9 g , Cholesterol 109 mg

INGREDIENTS

- 1/2 lb. beef stew meat
- 1/2 cup sour cream
- 2.5 oz. mushrooms, sliced
- oz. mushroom soup
- 1 medium onion, chopped
- Pepper and salt

DIRECTION

- Add all Ingredients: except sour cream into the slow cooker and mix well.
- Cover slow cooker with lid and cook on low for 8 hours.
- Add sour cream and stir well.
- Serve and enjoy.

PREPARATION	COOKING TIME	SERVINGS
10	8 *hours*	2

Chili Lime Beef

NUTRITION Calories 355 , Fat 16.8 g , Carbohydrates 14 g , Sugar 11.3 g , Protein 35.5 g , Cholesterol 120 mg

INGREDIENTS

- 1 lb. beef chuck roast
- 1 tsp chili powder
- 2 cups lemon-lime soda
- 1 fresh lime juice
- 1 garlic clove, crushed
- 1/2 tsp salt

DIRECTION

- Place beef chuck roast into the slow cooker.
- Season roast with garlic, chili powder, and salt.
- Pour lemon-lime soda over the roast.
- Cover slow cooker with lid and cook on low for 6 hours. Shred the meat using a fork.
- Add lime juice over shredded roast and serve.

PREPARATION	COOKING TIME	SERVINGS
10	6 *hours*	4

Beef in Sauce

NUTRITION 231 calories, 35g protein, 4.6g carbohydrates, 7.1g fat, 0.7g fiber, 101mg cholesterol, 79mg sodium, 507mg potassium

INGREDIENTS

- 1-pound beef stew meat, chopped
- 1 teaspoon gram masala
- 1 cup of water
- 1 tablespoon flour
- 1 teaspoon garlic powder
- 1 onion, diced

DIRECTION

- Whisk flour with water until smooth and pour the liquid into the slow cooker.
- Add gram masala and beef stew meat.
- After this, add onion and garlic powder.
- Close the lid and cook the meat on low for 9 hours.
- Serve the cooked beef with thick gravy from the slow cooker.

PREPARATION	COOKING TIME	SERVINGS
10	9 *hours*	4

Beef with Greens

NUTRITION 177 calories, 26.3g protein, 1.1g carbohydrates, 7g fat, 0.6g fiber, 76mg cholesterol, 95mg sodium, 449mg potassium.

INGREDIENTS

- 1 cup fresh spinach, chopped
- oz. beef stew meat, cubed
- 1 cup Swiss chard, chopped
- 2 cups of water
- 1 teaspoon olive oil
- 1 teaspoon dried rosemary

DIRECTION

- Heat olive oil in the skillet.
- Add beef and roast it for 1 minute per side.
- Then transfer the meat to the slow cooker.
- Add Swiss chard, spinach, water, and rosemary.
- Close the lid and cook the meal on Low for 8 hours.

PREPARATION	COOKING TIME	SERVINGS
15	8 *hours*	3

Beef and Scallions Bowl

NUTRITION 258 calories, 36.4g protein, 0.4g carbohydrates, 7.7g fat, 2g fiber, 101mg cholesterol, 99mg sodium, 697mg potassium.

INGREDIENTS

- 1 teaspoon chili powder
- 2 oz. scallions, chopped
- 1-pound beef stew meat, cubed
- 1 cup corn kernels, frozen
- 1 cup of water
- 2 tablespoons tomato paste
- 1 teaspoon minced garlic

DIRECTION

- Mix water with tomato paste and pour the liquid into the slow cooker.
- Add chili powder, beef, corn kernels, and minced garlic.
- Close the lid and cook the meal on high for 5 hours.
- When the meal is cooked, transfer the mixture to the bowls and top with scallions.

PREPARATION	COOKING TIME	SERVINGS
10	5 hours	4

Beef and Artichokes Bowls

NUTRITION 313 calories, 36.5g protein, 4.6g carbohydrates, 5.9g fat, 17.8g fiber, 76mg cholesterol, 1527mg sodium, 1559mg potassium.

INGREDIENTS

- 2 lbs. beef, sliced
- 2 tbsp. fajita seasoning
- 20 oz. salsa
- 1 large onion, sliced
- 1 bell pepper, sliced

DIRECTION

- Mix meat with white pepper and cayenne pepper. Transfer it to the slow cooker bowl.
- Add salt, artichoke hearts, and water.
- Close the lid and cook the meal on Low for 7 hours.

PREPARATION	COOKING TIME	SERVINGS
10	7 hours	2

Mustard Beef

NUTRITION 267 calories, 35.9g protein, 2.1g carbohydrates, 12.1g fat, 0.9g fiber, 101mg cholesterol, 140mg sodium, 496mg potassium.

INGREDIENTS

- 1-pound beef sirloin, chopped
- 1 tablespoon capers, drained
- 1 cup of water
- 2 tablespoons mustard
- 1 tablespoon coconut oil

DIRECTION

- Mix meat with mustard and leave for 10 minutes to marinate.
- Then melt the coconut oil in the skillet.
- Add meat and roast it for 1 minute per side on high heat.
- After this, transfer the meat to the slow cooker.
- Add water and capers.
- Cook the meal on Low for 8 hours.

PREPARATION	COOKING TIME	SERVINGS
10	8 hours	4

Beef Masala

NUTRITION 283 calories, 35.3g protein, 2.2g carbohydrates, 14.4g fat, 0.9g fiber, 101mg cholesterol, 82mg sodium, 560mg potassium.

INGREDIENTS

- 1-pound beef sirloin, sliced
- 1 teaspoon gram masala
- 2 tablespoons lemon juice
- 1 teaspoon ground paprika
- ½ cup of coconut milk
- 1 teaspoon dried mint

DIRECTION

- In the bowl, mix coconut milk with dried mint, ground paprika, lemon juice, and gram masala.
- Then add beef sirloin and mix the mixture. Leave it for at least 10 minutes to marinate.
- Then transfer the mixture to the slow cooker.
- Cook it on Low for 9 hours.

PREPARATION	COOKING TIME	SERVINGS
15	9 hours	6

Beef Sauté with Endives

NUTRITION 238 calories, 35.4g protein, 6.4g carbohydrates, 7.2g fat, 1.9g fiber, 101mg cholesterol, 175mg sodium, 689mg potassium.

INGREDIENTS

- 1-pound beef sirloin, chopped
- oz. endives, roughly chopped
- 1 teaspoon peppercorns
- 1 carrot, diced
- 1 onion, sliced
- 1 cup of water
- ½ cup tomato juice

DIRECTION

- Mix beef with onion, carrot, and peppercorns.
- Place the mixture in the slow cooker.
- Add water and tomato juice.
- Then close the lid and cook it on High for 5 hours.
- After this, add endives and cook the meal for 3 hours on Low.

PREPARATION	COOKING TIME	SERVINGS
10	8 _hours_	4

Sweet Beef

NUTRITION 227 calories, 34.5g protein, 3.8g carbohydrates, 7.2g fat, 0.2g fiber, 101mg cholesterol, 78mg sodium, 483mg potassium.

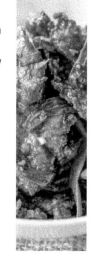

INGREDIENTS

- 1-pound beef roast, sliced
- 1 tablespoon maple syrup
- 2 tablespoons lemon juice
- 1 teaspoon dried oregano
- 1 cup of water

DIRECTION

- Mix water with maple syrup, lemon juice, and dried oregano.
- Then pour the liquid into the slow cooker.
- Add beef roast and close the lid.
- Cook the meal on High for 5 hours.

PREPARATION	COOKING TIME	SERVINGS
10	5 _hours_	4

Thyme Beef

NUTRITION 274 calories, 34.5g protein0.9g carbohydrates, 14.2g fat, 0.5g fiber 101mg cholesterol, 1240mg sodium, 469mg potassium

INGREDIENTS

- oz. beef sirloin, chopped
- 1 tablespoon dried thyme
- 1 tablespoon olive oil
- ½ cup of water
- 1 teaspoon salt

DIRECTION

- Preheat the skillet well.
- Then mix beef with dried thyme and olive oil.
- Put the meat in the hot skillet and roast for 2 minutes per side on high heat.
- Then transfer the meat to the slow cooker.
- Add salt and water.
- Cook the meal on High for 5 hours.

PREPARATION	COOKING TIME	SERVINGS
15	5 hours	2

Hot Beef

NUTRITION 241 calories, 34.4g protein, 0.1g carbohydrates, 10.6g fat, 0g fiber, 101mg cholesterol, 266mg sodium, 467mg potassium.

INGREDIENTS

- 1-pound beef sirloin, chopped
- 2 tablespoons hot sauce
- 1 tablespoon olive oil
- ½ cup of water

DIRECTION

- In the shallow bowl, mix hot sauce with olive oil.
- Then mix beef sirloin with hot sauce mixture and leave for 10 minutes to marinate.
- Put the marinated beef in the slow cooker.
- Add water and close the lid.
- Cook the meal on Low for 8 hours.

PREPARATION	COOKING TIME	SERVINGS
15	8 hours	4

Beef Chops with Sprouts

NUTRITION 175 calories, 25.2g protein, 1.6g carbohydrates, 7.8g fat, 0.3g fiber, 64mg cholesterol, 526mg sodium, 386mg potassium.

INGREDIENTS

- 1-pound beef loin
- ½ cup bean sprouts
- 1 cup of water
- 1 tablespoon tomato paste
- 1 teaspoon chili powder
- 1 teaspoon salt

DIRECTION

- Cut the beef loin into 5 beef chops and sprinkle the beef chops with chili powder and salt.
- Then place them in the slow cooker.
- Add water and tomato paste. Cook the meat on low for 7 hours.
- Then transfer the cooked beef chops onto the plates, sprinkle with tomato gravy from the slow cooker, and top with bean sprouts.

PREPARATION	COOKING TIME	SERVINGS
10	7 *hours*	5

Beef Ragout with Beans

NUTRITION 321 calories, 37.7g protein, 28g carbohydrates, 6.2g fat, 7.3g fiber, 81mg cholesterol, 81mg sodium, 959mg potassium.

INGREDIENTS

- 1 tablespoon tomato paste
- 1 cup mug beans, canned
- 1 carrot, grated
- 1-pound beef stew meat, chopped
- 1 teaspoon ground black pepper
- 2 cups of water

DIRECTION

- Pour water into the slow cooker.
- Add meat, ground black pepper, and carrot.
- Cook the mixture on High for 4 hours.
- Then add tomato paste and mug beans. Stir the meal and cook it on high for 1 hour more.

PREPARATION	COOKING TIME	SERVINGS
10	5 *hours*	5

Braised Beef

239 calories, 33.1g protein, 1.2g carbohydrates, 10.4g fat, 0.3g fiber, 104mg cholesterol, 1238mg sodium, 431mg potassium.

INGREDIENTS

- oz. beef tenderloin, chopped
- 1 garlic clove, peeled
- 1 teaspoon peppercorn
- 1 teaspoon salt
- 1 tablespoon dried basil
- 2 cups of water

DIRECTION

- Put all Ingredients: from the list above in the slow cooker.
- Gently stir the mixture and close the lid.
- Cook the beef on low for 9 hours.

PREPARATION	COOKING TIME	SERVINGS
8	9 hours	2

Coconut Beef

NUTRITION 303 calories, 27.6g protein, 3.5g carbohydrates, 19.9g fat, 1.4g fiber, 83mg cholesterol, 66mg sodium, 495mg potassium.

INGREDIENTS

- 1 cup baby spinach, chopped
- 1 cup of coconut milk
- 1-pound beef tenderloin, chopped
- 1 teaspoon avocado oil
- 1 teaspoon dried rosemary
- 1 teaspoon garlic powder

DIRECTION

- Roast meat in the avocado oil for 1 minute per side on high heat.
- Then transfer the meat in the slow cooker.
- Add garlic powder, dried rosemary, coconut milk, and baby spinach.
- Close the lid and cook the meal on Low for 8 hours.

PREPARATION	COOKING TIME	SERVINGS
10	8 hours	5

Beef Roast

NUTRITION 354 calories, 23.9g protein, 1.8g carbohydrates, 27.3g fat, 0.2g fiber, 94mg cholesterol, 119mg sodium, 230mg potassium.

INGREDIENTS

- 1-pound beef chuck roast
- 1 tablespoon ketchup
- 1 tablespoon mayonnaise
- 1 teaspoon chili powder
- 1 teaspoon olive oil
- 1 teaspoon lemon juice
- ½ cup of water

DIRECTION

- 1-pound beef chuck roast
- 1 tablespoon ketchup
- 1 tablespoon mayonnaise
- 1 teaspoon chili powder
- 1 teaspoon olive oil
- 1 teaspoon lemon juice
- ½ cup of water

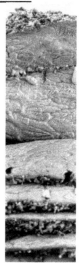

PREPARATION	COOKING TIME	SERVINGS
10	6 *hours*	5

Lunch Beef

NUTRITION 179 calories, 19.3g protein, 7.8g carbohydrates, 7.4g fat, 1.8g fiber, 53mg cholesterol, 520mg sodium, 146mg potassium.

INGREDIENTS

- ½ white onion, sliced
- 1 teaspoon brown sugar
- 1 teaspoon chili powder
- 1 teaspoon hot sauce
- ½ cup okra, chopped
- 1 cup of water
- oz. beef loin, chopped

DIRECTION

- Mix the beef loin with hot sauce, chili powder, and brown sugar.
- Transfer the meat to the slow cooker.
- Add water, okra, and onion.
- Cook the meal on Low for 8 hours.

PREPARATION	COOKING TIME	SERVINGS
10	8 *hours*	2

Braised Beef Strips

NUTRITION 173 calories, 19.6g protein, 3.2g carbohydrates, 9.4g fat, 0.8g fiber, 50mg cholesterol, 624mg sodium, 316mg potassium.

INGREDIENTS

- ½ cup mushroom, sliced
- 1 onion, sliced
- 1 cup of water
- 1 tablespoon coconut oil
- 1 teaspoon salt
- 1 teaspoon white pepper
- oz. beef loin, cut into strips

DIRECTION

- Melt the coconut oil in the skillet.
- Add mushrooms and roast them for 5 minutes on medium heat.
- Then transfer the mushrooms to the slow cooker.
- Add all remaining Ingredients: and close the lid.
- Cook the meal on High for 5 hours

PREPARATION	COOKING TIME	SERVINGS
10	5 *hours*	4

Beef Dip

NUTRITION 118 calories, 8.6g protein, 2.5g carbohydrates, 8.2g fat, 0.4g fiber, 41mg cholesterol, 78mg sodium, 126mg potassium.

INGREDIENTS

- ½ cup heavy cream
- 1 onion, diced
- 1 teaspoon cream cheese
- ½ cup Cheddar cheese, shredded
- 1 teaspoon garlic powder
- oz. dried beef, chopped
- ½ cup of water

DIRECTION

- Put all Ingredients: in the slow cooker.
- Gently stir the Ingredients: and close the lid.
- Cook the dip on Low for 10 hours.

PREPARATION	COOKING TIME	SERVINGS
10	10 *hours*	6

Beef and Sauerkraut Bowl

NUTRITION 202 calories, 15.5g protein, 1.7g carbohydrates, 14.2g fat, 1g fiber, 71mg cholesterol, 1240mg sodium, 236mg potassium

INGREDIENTS

- *1 cup sauerkraut*
- *1-pound corned beef, chopped*
- *¼ cup apple cider vinegar*
- *1 cup of water*

DIRECTION

- Pour water and apple cider vinegar into the slow cooker.
- Add corned beef and cook it on High for 5 hours.
- Then chop the meat roughly and put in the serving bowls.
- Top the meat with sauerkraut.

PREPARATION	COOKING TIME	SERVINGS
10	5 *hours*	4

Sweet Passata Dipped Steaks

NUTRITION Calories 371, Total Fat 17.2 g, Saturated Fat 9.4 g, Cholesterol 141 mg, Sodium 153 mg, Total Carbs 6 g, Fiber 0.9 g, Sugar 1.4 g, Protein 32 g

INGREDIENTS

- *¼ cup of Tomato passata*
- *1 teaspoon of Ginger, grated*
- *1 tablespoon of Mustard*
- *1 Garlic clove, minced*
- *1 teaspoon of Garlic, minced*
- *1 tablespoon of Stevia*
- *1 tablespoon of Olive oil*
- *1 and ½ lbs. Beef steaks*

DIRECTION

- Start by putting all the Ingredients: into your Crockpot.
- Cover it and cook for 2 hours on High settings.
- Once done, uncover the pot and mix well.
- Garnish as desired.
- Serve warm.

PREPARATION	COOKING TIME	SERVINGS
10	2 *hours*	4

Mushroom Beef Goulash

NUTRITION Calories 291 , Total Fat 14.2 g , Saturated Fat 4.4 g , Cholesterol 180 mg , Sodium 154 mg , Total Carbs 5.3 g , Fiber 3.1 g , Sugar 3.6 g , Protein 20.8 g

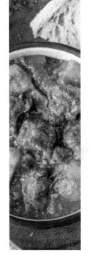

INGREDIENTS

- 1 and ½ lbs. beef, cubed
- 1 red bell pepper, diced
- 1 yellow onion, diced
- 2 garlic cloves, minced
- 2 teaspoons of sweet paprika
- 3 oz. mushrooms halved
- 2 bay leaves
- a drizzle of olive oil
- ½ cup of beef stock
- ½ cup of coconut cream

DIRECTION

- Start by putting all the Ingredients: into your Crockpot.
- Cover it and cook for 8 hours on Low settings.
- Once done, uncover the pot and mix well.
- Remove and discard the bay leaves.
- Garnish as desired.
- Serve warm.

PREPARATION	COOKING TIME	SERVINGS
10	8 hours	3

Beef Onion Stew

NUTRITION Calories 41 , Total Fat 13.2 g, Saturated Fat 21.4 g , Cholesterol 140 mg , Sodium 161 mg , Total Carbs 3.5 g , Fiber 2.9 g, Sugar 3.4 g , Protein 36.2 g

INGREDIENTS

- 1 tablespoon of olive oil
- 1 yellow onion, diced
- 1 lb. beefsteak, cut into strips
- 2 springs onions, diced
- 1 cup of tomato passata
- Salt and black pepper- to taste

DIRECTION

- Start by putting all the Ingredients: into your Crockpot except the spring onions.
- Cover it and cook for 4 hours on medium settings.
- Once done, uncover the pot and mix well.
- Garnish with spring onions.
- Serve warm.

PREPARATION	COOKING TIME	SERVINGS
10	4 hours	2

Beef Steaks with Peppercorn Sauce

NUTRITION Calories 351, Total Fat 12.2 g, Saturated Fat 2.4 g , Cholesterol 110 mg , Sodium 276 mg , Total Carbs 5.4 g , Fiber 0.9 g, Sugar 1.4 g , Protein 15.8 g

INGREDIENTS

- 2 medium sirloin beef steaks
- 1 teaspoon of black peppercorns
- ¼ cup of sugar-free tomato sauce
- Salt and black pepper- to taste
- 1 tablespoon of olive oil

DIRECTION

- Start by putting all the Ingredients: into your Crockpot.
- Cover it and cook for 8 hours on Low settings.
- Once done, uncover the pot and mix well.
- Garnish as desired.
- Serve warm.

PREPARATION	COOKING TIME	SERVINGS
10	8 hours	2

Pumpkin Beef Chili

NUTRITION Calories 238, Total Fat 13.8 g, Saturated Fat 1.7 g , Cholesterol 221 mg, Sodium 120 mg, Total Carbs 4.3 g, Fiber 2.4 g, Sugar 11.2 g, Protein 34.4g

INGREDIENTS

- 1 tablespoon of Olive oil
- 1 green bell pepper, diced
- 1 ½ lb. Beef, ground
- 6 garlic cloves, minced
- 28 oz. canned tomatoes, diced
- 14 oz. pumpkin puree
- 1 cup of chicken stock
- 2 tablespoon of Chili powder
- 1 ½ teaspoon of Cumin, ground
- 1 teaspoon of Cinnamon powder
- Salt and black pepper- to taste

DIRECTION

- Start by putting all the Ingredients: into your Crockpot.
- Cover it and cook for 4 hours on Low settings.
- Once done, uncover the pot and mix well.
- Garnish as desired.
- Serve warm.

PREPARATION	COOKING TIME	SERVINGS
10	3 hours	6

Olives Beef Stew

NUTRITION Calories 359, Total Fat 34 g, Saturated Fat 10.3 g , Cholesterol 112 mg , Total Carbs 8.5 g, Sugar 2 g Fiber 1.3 g, Sodium 92 mg, Protein 27.5 g

INGREDIENTS

- 28 oz. beefsteak, cubed
- 1 tablespoon of olive oil
- 1 tablespoon of parsley, chopped
- Salt and black pepper- to taste
- 8 oz. tomato passata
- 1 yellow onion, diced
- 1 cup of green olives pitted and sliced

DIRECTION

- Start by putting all the Ingredients: into your Crockpot.
- Cover it and cook for 10 hours on Low settings.
- Once done, uncover the pot and mix well.
- Garnish as desired.
- Serve warm.

PREPARATION	COOKING TIME	SERVINGS
10	10 hours	4

Beef Cabbage Casserole

NUTRITION Calories 204, Total Fat 10.6 g, Saturated Fat 13.1 g , Cholesterol 131 m, Sodium 141 mg, Total Carbs 2.4 g, Fiber 0.2 g, Sugar 14.3 g, Protein 12.6 g

INGREDIENTS

- ½ cabbage head, shredded
- 1 yellow onion, diced
- 3 garlic cloves, minced
- 1 ½ lb. beef, ground
- 1 ½ cups of tomatoes, crushed
- 2 cups of cauliflower rice
- A drizzle of olive oil
- Salt and black pepper- to taste
- ½ teaspoon of Red pepper, crushed
- ½ cup of parsley, chopped

DIRECTION

- Start by putting all the Ingredients: into your Crockpot.
- Cover it and cook for 8 hours on Low settings.
- Once done, uncover the pot and mix well.
- Garnish as desired.
- Serve warm.

PREPARATION	COOKING TIME	SERVINGS
10	8 hours	6

Vegetable Beef Stew

NUTRITION Calories 31, Total Fat 25.5 g, Saturated Fat 12.4 g, Cholesterol 69 mg, Sodium 58 mg, Total Carbs 1.4 g, Fiber 0.7 g, Sugar 7.3 g, Protein 3.4 g, Protein 17.5 g

INGREDIENTS

- ½ lb. beef meat, cubed
- ½ yellow onion, diced
- 3 oz. tomato paste
- 1 garlic clove, minced
- ½ tablespoon of thyme, diced
- 1 carrot, diced
- 1.5 celery stalks, diced
- 1 tablespoon of parsley, chopped
- 1 tablespoon of white vinegar
- salt and black pepper to taste

DIRECTION

- Start by putting all the Ingredients: into your Crockpot.
- Cover it and cook for 8 hours on Low settings.
- Once done, uncover the pot and mix well.
- Garnish as desired.
- Serve warm.

PREPARATION	COOKING TIME	SERVINGS
10	8 hours	2

Spicy Mexican Luncheon

NUTRITION Calories 338, Total Fat 34 g, Saturated Fat 8.5 g , Cholesterol 69 mg, Sodium 217 mg, Total Carbs 5.1 g , Fiber 1.2 g, Sugar 12 g, Protein 30.3 g

INGREDIENTS

- 2 lbs. beef stew meat, cubed
- 6 tomatoes, diced
- 2 red onion, diced
- 10 oz. canned green chilies, diced
- 4 teaspoon of chili powder
- 2 teaspoon of cumin powder
- 2 teaspoons of oregano, dried
- 4 cups of vegetable broth
- salt and black pepper to taste

DIRECTION

- Start by putting all the Ingredients: into your Crockpot.
- Cover it and cook for 8 hours on Low settings.
- Once done, uncover the pot and mix well.
- Garnish as desired.
- Serve warm.

PREPARATION	COOKING TIME	SERVINGS
10	8 hours	4

Beef & Broccoli

NUTRITION Calories 527, Total Fat 49 g, Saturated Fat 14 g , Cholesterol 83 mg , Sodium 92 mg, Total Carbs 3 g Sugar 1 g, Fiber 1 g, Protein 19 g

INGREDIENTS

- 2 lbs. flank steak, slice into 2" chunks
- 2/3 cup of liquid aminos
- 1 cup of beef broth
- 3 tablespoons of swerve
- 1 teaspoon of freshly grated ginger
- 3 garlic cloves, minced
- 1/4   1/2 teaspoons of red pepper flakes
- 1/2 teaspoons of salt
- 1 head broccoli, diced
- 1 red bell pepper, diced
- 1 teaspoon of sesame seeds

DIRECTION

- Start by putting all the Ingredients: into your Crockpot except the broccoli and bell pepper.
- Cover it and cook for 10 hours on Low settings.
- Once done, uncover the pot and mix well.
- Stir in broccoli and bell pepper then continue cooking for 1 hour on low heat.
- Serve warm.

PREPARATION	COOKING TIME	SERVINGS
10	10 *hours*	4

Beef Mushroom Stroganoff

NUTRITION Calories 416, Total Fat 19.2 g, Saturated Fat 2.4 g , Cholesterol 14 mg , Sodium 261 mg, Total Carbs 3 g, Fiber 2.3 g, Sugar 5.4 g, Protein 41.1 g

INGREDIENTS

- 1 brown onion sliced and quartered
- 2 cloves garlic, smashed
- 2 slices streaky bacon diced
- 1 lb. beef, stewing steak cubed
- 1 teaspoon of smoked paprika
- 3 tablespoons of tomato paste
- 1 cup of beef stock
- ½ cup of mushrooms quartered

DIRECTION

- Start by putting all the Ingredients into your Crockpot.
- Cover it and cook for 8 hours on Low settings.
- Once done, uncover the pot and mix well.
- Serve warm.

PREPARATION	COOKING TIME	SERVINGS
10	8 *hours*	2

Garlic Beef Stewwith Olives, Capers, and Tomatoes

NUTRITION Calories 378, Total Fat 18.2 g, Saturated Fat 3.1 g, Cholesterol 320 mg, Sodium 130 mg , Total Carbs 2.2 g, Fiber 0.7 g, Sugar 2.7 g, Protein 34.3 g

INGREDIENTS

- 2 3 lb. beef chuck roast, cut into pieces
- 1 2 tablespoons of olive oil
- 1 can beef broth
- 1 cup of garlic cloves, peeled and cut into lengthwise slivers
- 1 cup of Kalamata Olives, cut in half lengthwise
- 2 tablespoons of capers, rinsed
- 3 bay leaves
- 1 teaspoon of dried Greek oregano
- 1 can (14.5 oz.) tomatoes with juice
- 1 small can (8 oz.) sugar-free tomato sauce
- 2 tablespoons of tomato paste

DIRECTION

- Start by putting all the Ingredients: into your Crockpot.
- Cover it and cook for 4 hours on High settings.
- Once done, uncover the pot and mix well.
- Serve warm.

PREPARATION	COOKING TIME	SERVINGS
10	4 *hours*	6

Mexican Chili

NUTRITION Calories 429, Total Fat 15.1 g, Saturated Fat 9.4 g , Cholesterol 130 mg, Sodium 132 mg, Total Carbs 7 g, Fiber 2.9 g, Sugar 2.4 g, Protein 33.1 g

INGREDIENTS

- 2 1/2 lbs. ground beef
- 1 medium red onion, diced and divided
- 4 tablespoons of minced garlic
- 3 large ribs of celery, diced
- ¼ cup of pickled jalapeno slices
- 6 oz. can tomato paste
- 14.5 oz. can tomato and green chilies
- 14.5 oz. can stew tomatoes with Mexican seasoning
- 2 tablespoons of Worcestershire sauce or Coconut Aminos
- 4 tablespoons of chili powder
- 2 tablespoons of cumin, mounded
- 2 teaspoons of salt
- 1/2 teaspoons of cayenne
- 1 teaspoon of garlic powder
- 1 teaspoon of onion powder1 teaspoon of oregano
- 1 teaspoon of black pepper
- 1 bay leaf

DIRECTION

- Start by putting all the Ingredients: into your Crockpot.
- Cover it and cook for 8 hours on Low settings.
- Once done, uncover the pot and mix well.
- Serve warm.

PREPARATION	COOKING TIME	SERVINGS
10	8 *hours*	6

Green Chile Shredded Beef Cabbage Bowl

NUTRITION Calories 429, Total Fat 11.9 g, Saturated Fat 1.7 g, Cholesterol 78 mg, Sodium 79 mg, Total Carbs 1.8 g, Fiber 1.1 g, Sugar 0.3 g, Protein 35 g

INGREDIENTS

For Crockpot Beef:
- *2 lb. beef chuck roast, well-trimmed and cut into thick strips*
- *1 tablespoon of Kalyn's taco seasoning 2 3 teaspoons of olive oil*
- *2 cans (4 oz. can) diced chilis with juice*

For Cabbage Slaw and Dressing:
- *1 small head green cabbage*
- *1/2 small head red cabbage*
- *1/2 cup of sliced green onion*
- *6 tablespoons of mayo or light mayo*
- *4 teaspoons of fresh-squeezed lime juice*
- *2 teaspoons of green Tabasco sauce*

DIRECTION

- Start by putting all the Ingredients: for beef into your Crockpot.
- Cover it and cook for 4 hours on High settings.
- Once done, uncover the pot and mix well.
- Now toss all the coleslaw Ingredients: in a salad bowl.
- Serve the beef with coleslaw.

PREPARATION	COOKING TIME	SERVINGS
10	4 *hours*	4

Chipotle Barbacoa Recipe

NUTRITION Calories 248, Total Fat 15.7 g, Saturated Fat 2.7 g, Cholesterol 75 mg, Sodium 94 mg, Total Carbs 4.4 g, Fiber 0.2 g, Sugar 0.1 g, Protein 43.2 g

INGREDIENTS

- *3 lb. beef brisket or chuck roast*
- *1/2 cup of beef broth*
- *2 medium chipotle chilis in adobo*
- *5 cloves garlic*
- *2 tablespoons of apple cider vinegar*
- *2 tablespoons of lime juice*
- *1 tablespoon of oregano, dried*
- *2 teaspoons of cumin*
- *2 teaspoons of salt*
- *1 teaspoon of black pepper*
- *1/2 teaspoons of cloves, ground*
- *2 whole bay leaf*

DIRECTION

- Start by putting all the Ingredients: into your Crockpot.
- Cover it and cook for 10 hours on Low settings.
- Once done, uncover the pot and mix well.
- Shred the slow-cooked beef and return it to the pot.
- Serve warm.

PREPARATION	COOKING TIME	SERVINGS
10	10 *hours*	6

Chapter 11. Pork Recipes

Pulled Pork

NUTRITION Net Carbs: 2g; Calories: 233; Total Fat: 12g; Saturated Fat: 3g; Protein: 20g; Carbs: 2g; Fiber: 0g; Sugar: 0g

INGREDIENTS

- 3 pounds pasture-raised pork shoulder, boneless and fat trimmed
- 2 teaspoons onion powder
- 2 teaspoons garlic powder
- 2 teaspoons salt
- 2 teaspoons paprika
- 1 tablespoon parsley
- 2 teaspoons cumin
- ½ cup beer

DIRECTION

- Place pork in a 6-quart slow cooker and switch it on.
- Stir together remaining Ingredients: except for beer and then rub this mixture all over the pork until evenly coated on all sides.
- Pour in beer, then shut with lid and cook for 8 hours at low heating setting or 4 hours at high heat setting.
- When done, shred pork with two forks; stir well until coated with sauce and serve.

PREPARATION	COOKING TIME	SERVINGS
5	8 *hours*	8

Pork Roast

NUTRITION Net Carbs: 3g; Calories: 579; Total Fat: 51g; Saturated Fat: 12g; Protein: 28g; Carbs: 4g; Fiber: 1g; Sugar: 0.1g

INGREDIENTS

- 30-ounce pasture-raised pork shoulder, fat trimmed
- 1 teaspoon minced garlic
- ½ teaspoon grated ginger
- ½ tablespoon salt
- ½ teaspoon ground black pepper
- 2 teaspoons dried thyme
- 1 tablespoon paprika powder
- 5 black peppercorns
- 1 bay leaf
- 1 tablespoon avocado oil
- 1 cup water

DIRECTION

- Place pork in a 6-quart slow cooker, season with salt and thyme, add peppercorns and bay leaf and then pour in water.
- Plug in the slow cooker, then shut with its lid and cook for 8 hours at low heat setting or 4 hours at high heat setting.
- When done, transfer pork to a baking dish and reserve cooking sauce in a saucepan.
- Set oven to 450 degrees F and let preheat.
- In the meantime, stir together remaining Ingredients: in a small bowl until combined and then brush mixture all over pork.
- Place the baking sheet into the oven to bake pork for 10 to 15 minutes or until roasted.
- Cut roasted pork into thin slices and serve with reserved cooking sauce.

PREPARATION	COOKING TIME	SERVINGS
5	8 hours 15 mins	6

Chinese Pulled Pork

NUTRITION Net Carbs: 2g; Calories: 447; Total Fat: 35g; Saturated Fat: 13g; Protein: 30g; Carbs: 3g; Fiber: 1g; Sugar: 2g

INGREDIENTS

- 2.2-pound pasture-raised pork shoulder, fat trimmed
- 2 tablespoons garlic paste
- 2 teaspoons ginger paste
- 1 teaspoon smoked paprika
- 5 drops Erythritol sweetener
- 4 tablespoons soy sauce
- 1 tablespoon tomato paste
- 4 tablespoons tomato sauce, sugar-free
- 1 cup chicken broth

DIRECTION

- Place pork in a 6-quart slow cooker.
- Whisk together remaining Ingredients: until smooth and then pour over the pork.
- Plug in the slow cooker, then shut with lid and cook for 7 hours at low heat setting or until pork is tender.
- Then shred pork with two forks and stir well until evenly coated with sauce.
- Continue cooking pork for 30 minutes or more at low heating setting until sauce is thicken to desired consistency.
- Serve straightaway.

PREPARATION	COOKING TIME	SERVINGS
5	7.5 hours	6

Bacon Wrapped Pork Loin

NUTRITION Net Carbs: 0g; Calories: 639; Total Fat: 41g; Saturated Fat: 19g; Protein: 69g; Carbs: 0g; Fiber: 0g; Sugar: 0g

INGREDIENTS

- 2-pound pasture-raised pork loin roast, fat-trimmed
- 4 strips of bacon, uncooked
- 3 tablespoon dried onion soup mix, organic
- 1/4 cup water

DIRECTION

- Pour water into a 6-quart slow cooker.
- Rub seasoning mix on all sides of pork, then wrap with bacon and place into the slow cooker.
- Plug in the slow cooker, then shut with lid and cook for seven hours at low heat setting or 5 hours at high heat setting.
- Serve straightaway.

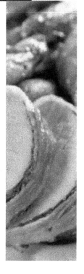

PREPARATION	COOKING TIME	SERVINGS
5	7 hours	4

Lasagna

NUTRITION Net Carbs: 6g; Calories: 720; Total Fat: 53g; Saturated Fat: 17g; Protein: 50g; Carbs: 11g; Fiber: 5g; Sugar: 5g

INGREDIENTS

- 2 pounds minced pasture-raised pork, browned and fat drained
- 16 slices of chicken thin deli slices
- 24-ounce marinara sauce, organic and sugar-free
- 15-ounce ricotta cheese
- 12 slices of mozzarella cheese
- 1 ½ cups shredded mozzarella cheese

DIRECTION

- Stir together pork and marinara sauce in a bowl and spread 1/3 of this mixture into the bottom of a 6-quarts slow cooker.
- Top with 8 slices of chicken and then top with 6 slices of mozzarella cheese.
- Spread half of the remaining meat mixture over mozzarella cheese layer and then evenly top with dollops of half of the ricotta cheese.
- Add more layers by starting with chicken slices, slices of mozzarella, remaining meat sauce and ricotta cheese in the end.
- Top with shredded mozzarella cheese, then plug in the slow cooker, shut with lid and cook for 2 to 3 hours at low heat setting or until cheeses melt completely.
- When done, let the slow cooker cool for 1 hour and then slice lasagna and serve immediately.

PREPARATION	COOKING TIME	SERVINGS
10	3 hours	8

Meatballs Stuffed With Cheese

NUTRITION Net Carbs: 6.5g; Calories: 548; Total Fat: 34g; Saturated Fat: 10g; Protein: 49g; Carbs: 9.5g; Fiber: 3g; Sugar: 4g

INGREDIENTS

- 2 1/2 pounds ground pork, pasture-raised
- 1/2 cup pork rinds, crushed
- 1/2 teaspoon garlic powder
- 1/2 teaspoon salt
- 1/2 teaspoon ground black pepper
- 2 tablespoons Italian seasonings
- 2 cup marinara sauce, sugar-free and organic
- 2 eggs
- 1/2 cup grated Parmesan cheese
- 8 ounces block of mozzarella cheese, cut into 24 pieces

DIRECTION

- Crack eggs in a large bowl, add pork rind, garlic powder, salt, black pepper, and Italian seasoning and whisk until combined.
- Add ground meat, then mix until combined and shape the mixture into 24 meatballs.
- Place a piece of cheese into the center of each meatball and then wrap meat around it.
- Pour half of the marinara sauce into the bottom of a 6-quart slow cooker, then arrange meatballs and cover with remaining sauce.
- Plug in the slow cooker, shut with lid and cook meatballs for 6 hours at low heat setting or 3 hours at high heat setting.
- Serve straightaway.

PREPARATION	COOKING TIME	SERVINGS
5	6 *hours*	4

Kalua Pig

NUTRITION Net Carbs: 0g; Calories: 349; Total Fat: 27g; Saturated Fat: 10g; Protein: 26.6g; Carbs: 0g; Fiber: 0g; Sugar: 0g

INGREDIENTS

- 5 pounds pasture-raised pork shoulder, bone-in, and fat-trimmed
- 3 slices of bacon
- 5 cloves of garlic, peeled
- 2 tablespoons sea salt

DIRECTION

- Make some cuts into the pork, then tuck garlic in them and season with salt.
- Line a 6-quarts slow cooker with bacon slices, then top with seasoned pork and shut with lid.
- Plug in the slow cooker and cook for 16 hours at low heat setting until very tender.
- When done, transfer pork to a cutting board and shred pork with two forks.
- Then taste pork to adjust seasoning and add cooking liquid to adjust seasoning.
- Serve straightaway.

PREPARATION	COOKING TIME	SERVINGS
5	16 *hours*	8

Balsamic Pork Tenderloin

NUTRITION Net Carbs: 0.6g; Calories: 224; Total Fat: 10g; Saturated Fat: 1.6g; Protein: 33g; Carbs: 0.6g; Fiber: 0g; Sugar: 0.3g

INGREDIENTS

- 2 pounds pasture-raised pork tenderloin
- 2 teaspoons minced garlic
- 1/2 teaspoon sea salt
- 1/2 teaspoon red pepper flakes
- 1 tablespoon Worcestershire sauce
- 2 tablespoons avocado oil
- 1/2 cup balsamic vinegar
- 2 tablespoons coconut aminos

DIRECTION

- Grease a 6-quart slow cooker with oil and set aside.
- Sprinkle garlic all over the pork and then place it into the slow cooker.
- Whisk together remaining Ingredients, then pour over pork and shut with lid.
- Plug in the slow cooker and cook pork for 6 hours at low heat setting or 4 hours at high setting until tender.
- When done, transfer pork to serving plate, pour ½ cup of cooking liquid over pork and serve.

PREPARATION	COOKING TIME	SERVINGS
5	6 *hours*	8

Spicy Pork

NUTRITION Net Carbs: 1.2g; Calories: 344.5; Total Fat: 25g; Saturated Fat: 10.7g; Protein: 28.4g; Carbs: 1.7g; Fiber: 0.5g; Sugar: 1.1g

INGREDIENTS

- 2 pasture-raised pork shoulder, boneless and fat trimmed
- ½ of jalapeno, deseeded and cored, chopped
- 6 ounce crushed tomatoes
- ¼ cup chopped green onion
- 3 clove of garlic, peeled and sliced in half
- 1 tablespoon sea salt
- ½ teaspoon ground black pepper
- 1 ½ tablespoon paprika, divided
- ½ tablespoon dried oregano
- ½ tablespoon ground cumin
- 2 limes, juiced
- 2 tablespoons avocado oil

DIRECTION

- Place pork in a 6-quart slow cooker, season with salt, black pepper, paprika, oregano, and cumin until seasoned well.
- Then add remaining Ingredients and stir until combined.
- Plug in the slow cooker, shut it with the lid and cook for 8 to 10 hours at low heat setting or 4 to 5 hours at high heat setting until very tender.
- Serve straightaway.

PREPARATION	COOKING TIME	SERVINGS
5	10 *hours*	6

Zesty Garlic Pulled Pork

NUTRITION Net Carbs: 1.2g; Calories: 616; Total Fat: 43g; Saturated Fat: 11.5g; Protein: 55.4g; Carbs: 1.5g; Fiber: 0.3g; Sugar: 0g

INGREDIENTS

- 3-pound pasture-raised pork shoulder
- 5 cloves of garlic, peeled and sliced
- 1 tablespoon of salt
- 1/2 teaspoon ground black pepper
- 1 teaspoon oregano
- 1/2 teaspoon cumin
- 1 lime, zested and juiced

DIRECTION

- Make cut into the meat of pork and stuff with garlic slices.
- Stir together garlic, salt, black pepper, oregano, cumin, lime zest, and juice until smooth paste comes together and then brush this paste all over the pork.
- Place pork into a large resealable bag, seal it and let marinate in the refrigerator for overnight.
- When ready to cook, transfer pork to a 6-quart slow cooker and shut with lid.
- Plug in the slow cooker and cook for 8 hours at low heat setting or until pork is very tender.
- When done, shred pork with two forks and serve as a lettuce wrap.

PREPARATION	COOKING TIME	SERVINGS
5	8 hours	6

Ranch Pork Chops

NUTRITION Net Carbs: 4g; Calories: 479; Total Fat: 27g; Saturated Fat: 12g; Protein: 54g; Carbs: 5g; Fiber: 1g; Sugar: 1.5g

INGREDIENTS

- 8-ounce sliced mushrooms
- 2 pounds pasture-raised pork loin
- 2 tablespoons ranch dressing mix
- 2 tablespoons avocado oil
- 21 ounce cream of chicken soup
- 2 cups water

DIRECTION

- Add ranch dressing, oil chicken soup, and water into the bowl, whisk until smooth, then add mushrooms and stir until combined.
- Cut pork into 6 slices and layer into the bottom of a slow cooker.
- Evenly pour in prepared chicken soup mixture and shut with lid.
- Plug in the slow cooker and cook for eight hours at low heat setting or until pork is cooked through.
- Serve straightaway.

PREPARATION	COOKING TIME	SERVINGS
5	8 hours	6

Chapter 12. Lamb

Smoked Lamb Chili

NUTRITION Calories 511, Total Fat 18.5 g, Saturated Fat 11.5 g, Cholesterol 51 mg , Sodium 346 mg, Total Carbs 22 g , Sugar 0.5 g, Fiber 0.4 g, Potassium 123 mg, Protein 11.5 g

INGREDIENTS

- 2 lbs. grass-fed ground lamb
- 8 bacon strips, diced
- 1 small onion, diced
- 3 tablespoons of chili powder
- 2 tablespoons of smoked pa-prika
- 4 teaspoons of cumin, ground
- 2 red bell pepper, seeded and diced
- Black pepper, to taste
- 4 garlic cloves, minced

DIRECTION

- Start by putting all the Ingredients into your Crockpot.
- Cover its lid and cook for 8 hours on Medium settings.
- Once done, remove its lid and mix well.
- Garnish as desired.
- Serve warm.

PREPARATION	COOKING TIME	SERVINGS
10	8 hours	4

Lamb Chops Curry

NUTRITION Calories 184, Total Fat 12.7 g, Saturated Fat 7.3 g, Cholesterol 35 mg, Sodium 222 mg Total Carbs 6.3 g, Sugar 2.7 g, Fiber 1.6 g, Potassium 342mg, Protein 12.2 g

PREPARATION	COOKING TIME	SERVINGS
10	6 hours	2

DIRECTION

- Start by putting all the Ingredients into your Crockpot.
- Cover its lid and cook for 6 hours on Low settings.
- Once done, remove its lid and mix well.
- Garnish as desired.
- Serve warm.

INGREDIENTS

- 1 lb. lamb loin chops
- 1 garlic clove, crushed
- ½ cup of bone broth
- 3/4 teaspoon of rosemary, dried, crushed
- 1 tablespoon of xanthan gum
- 1 ½ tablespoons of butter
- ½ small onion, sliced
- 3/4 cup of Sugar-free diced tomatoes
- 1 cup of carrots, peeled and sliced
- Salt and black pepper
- ½ tablespoon of cold water

Dinner Lamb Shanks

NUTRITION Calories 188, Total Fat 12.5 g, Saturated Fat 4.4 g, Cholesterol 53 mg, Sodium 1098 mg, Total Carbs 4.9 g , Sugar 0.3 g, Fiber 2 g, Potassium 332mg, Protein 14.6 g

PREPARATION	COOKING TIME	SERVINGS
15	2 hours	2

DIRECTION

- Start by putting all the Ingredients into your Crockpot.
- Cover its lid and cook for 8 hours on Low settings.
- Once done, remove its lid and mix well.
- Garnish as desired.
- Serve warm.

INGREDIENTS

- 1 ½ lb. grass-fed lamb shanks, trimmed
- 1 tablespoon of olive oil
- 3/4 cup of bone broth
- ½ teaspoon of rosemary, dried, crushed
- 1 tablespoon of melted butter
- 3 whole garlic cloves, peeled
- Salt and black pepper, to taste
- 3/4 tablespoon of Sugar-free tomato paste
- 1 ¼ tablespoon of fresh lemon juice

Coconut Lamb Stew

NUTRITION Calories 141, Total Fat 11.3 g, Saturated Fat 3.8 g, Cholesterol 181 mg , Sodium 334 mg, Total Carbs 0.6 g , Sugar 0.5 g, Fiber 0 g, Potassium 332 mg, Protein 8.9 g

PREPARATION	COOKING TIME	SERVINGS
10	10 *hours*	2

DIRECTION

- Start by putting all the Ingredients into your Crockpot except basil.
- Cover its lid and cook for 10 hours on Low settings.
- Once done, remove its lid and mix well.
- Garnish with basil
- Serve warm.

INGREDIENTS

- 1 lb. grass-fed lamb shoulder, cut into bite-sized pieces
- 1 tablespoon of curry powder, divided
- ¼ cup of unsweetened coconut milk
- 2 tablespoons of coconut cream
- 1 tablespoon of coconut oil
- 1 medium yellow onion, diced
- ½ cup of chicken broth
- 1 tablespoon of fresh lemon juice
- Salt and black pepper, to taste
- 2 tablespoons of fresh basil, diced

Herbed Lamb Stew

NUTRITION Calories 260, Total Fat 22.9 g, Saturated Fat 7.3 g , Cholesterol 0 mg , Sodium 9 mg, Total Carbs 47 g , Sugar 1.8 g , Fiber 1.4 g , Protein 5.6 g

PREPARATION	COOKING TIME	SERVINGS
10	9 *hours*	2

DIRECTION

- Start by putting all the Ingredients into your Crockpot.
- Cover its lid and cook for 9 hours on Low settings.
- Once done, remove its lid and mix well.
- Garnish as desired.
- Serve warm.

INGREDIENTS

- 1 lb. grass-fed lamb shoulder, trimmed and cubed into 2-inch size
- 3/4 tablespoon of olive oil
- 1 celery stalk, diced
- 1 cup of tomatoes, diced
- 1 ½ tablespoon of fresh lemon juice
- ½ teaspoon of salt
- ½ teaspoon of black pepper
- ½ large green bell pepper, cut into 8 slices
- ½ large red bell pepper, cut into 8 slices
- ½ cup of bone broth
- ½ small onion, diced
- ½ tablespoon of garlic, minced
- ½ teaspoon of oregano, dried, crushed
- ½ teaspoon of dried basil, crushed

Vegetable Lamb Stew

NUTRITION Calories 108 , Total Fat 9 g , Saturated Fat 4.3 g , Cholesterol 180 mg , Sodium 146 mg, Total Carbs 1.1 g , Sugar 0.5 g , Fiber 0.1 g, Protein 6 g

PREPARATION	COOKING TIME	SERVINGS
10	10.5 *hours*	2

DIRECTION

- Start by putting all the Ingredients into your Crockpot except zucchini.
- Cover its lid and cook for 10 hours on Low settings.
- Once done, remove its lid and mix well.
- Stir in zucchini and continue cooking for 30 minutes on high heat.
- Garnish as desired.
- Serve warm.

INGREDIENTS

- 1 lb. cubed lamb stew meat
- 1 tablespoon of fresh ginger, grated
- ½ teaspoon of lime juice
- ¼ teaspoon of black pepper
- 3/4 cup of diced tomatoes
- ½ teaspoon of turmeric powder
- 1 ½ medium carrots, sliced
- 2 garlic cloves, minced
- ½ cup of coconut milk
- ¼ teaspoon of salt
- 1 tablespoon of olive oil
- ½ medium onion, diced
- ½ medium zucchini, diced

Lamb Leg with Thyme

NUTRITION Calories 112, Total Fat 4.9 g, Saturated Fat 1.9 g , Cholesterol 10 mg , Sodium 355 mg, Total Carbs 1.9 g , Sugar 0.8 g , Fiber 0.4 g, Protein 3 g

PREPARATION	COOKING TIME	SERVINGS
15	2 *hours*	2

DIRECTION

- Start by putting all the Ingredients into your Crockpot.
- Cover its lid and cook for 10 hours on Low settings.
- Once done, remove its lid and mix well.
- Garnish as desired.
- Serve warm.

INGREDIENTS

- 2 lbs. leg of lamb
- 1 teaspoon of fine salt
- 2 ½ tablespoons of olive oil
- 6 sprigs thyme
- 1 ½ cup of bone broth
- 6 garlic cloves, minced
- 1 ½ teaspoon of black pepper
- 1 ½ small onion
- 3/4 cup of vegetable stock

Full Meal Turmeric Lamb

NUTRITION Calories 132, Total Fat 10.9 g, Saturated Fat 2.7 g , Cholesterol 164 mg , Sodium 65 mg , Total Carbs 3.3 g , Sugar 0.5 g , Fiber 2.3 g, Protein 6.3 g

PREPARATION
10

COOKING TIME
6
hours

SERVINGS
2

INGREDIENTS

- ½ lb. ground lamb meat
- ½ cup of onion diced
- ½ tablespoon of garlic
- ½ tablespoon of minced ginger
- ¼ teaspoon of turmeric
- ¼ teaspoon of ground coriander
- ½ teaspoon of salt
- ¼ teaspoon of cumin
- ¼ teaspoon of cayenne pepper

DIRECTION

- Start by putting all the Ingredients into your Crockpot.
- Cover its lid and cook for 6 hours on Low settings.
- Once done, remove its lid and mix well.
- Garnish as desired.
- Serve warm.

Lamb Cauliflower Curry

NUTRITION Calories 118, Total Fat 9.7 g, Saturated Fat 4.3 g , Cholesterol 228 mg , Sodium 160 mg , Total Carbs 0.5 g , Fiber 0 g, Sugar 0.5 g , Protein 7.4 g

PREPARATION
10

COOKING TIME
10
hours

SERVINGS
4

DIRECTION

- Start by putting all the Ingredients into your Crockpot.
- Cover its lid and cook for 10 hours on Low settings.
- Once done, remove its lid and mix well.
- Garnish as desired.
- Serve warm.

INGREDIENTS

- 2 lbs. lamb roasted Wegmans
- 1 cup of onion soup
- ¼ cup of carrots
- 1 cup of cauliflower
- 1 cup of beef broth

Irish Chop Stew

NUTRITION Calories 280 , Total Fat 23 g, Saturated Fat 13.8 g , Cholesterol 82 mg , Sodium 28 mg, Total Carbs 3.1 g , Fiber 2.5 g , Sugar 0.5 g , Protein 3.9 g

PREPARATION	COOKING TIME	SERVINGS
15	4 hours	2

INGREDIENTS

- 8 lamb shoulder chops, cubed
- 8 large onions, sliced into thin rounds
- 4 cups of water
- 4 tablespoons of olive oil
- 9 large carrots, chunked
- 4 sprigs thyme
- 2 teaspoons of salt
- 2 teaspoons of black pepper

DIRECTION

- Start by putting all the Ingredients into your Crockpot.
- Cover its lid and cook for 10 hours on Low settings.
- Once done, remove its lid and mix well.
- Garnish as desired.
- Serve warm.

Picante Glazed Chops

NUTRITION Calories 206, Total Fat 20.8 g, Saturated Fat 14.2 g , Cholesterol 315 mg , Sodium 35 mg Total Carbs 2.6 g , Fiber 0.1 g, Sugar 1.5 g , Protein 4.2 g

PREPARATION	COOKING TIME	SERVINGS
10	6 hours	6

DIRECTION

- Start by putting all the Ingredients into your Crockpot.
- Cover its lid and cook for 6 hours on Low settings.
- Once done, remove its lid and mix well.
- Garnish as desired.
- Serve warm.

INGREDIENTS

- 6 lamb chops, bone-in
- 1 ¼ cup of Picante sauce
- 1 cup of cherry tomatoes
- 3 tablespoons of olive oil
- 3 tablespoons of almond flour
- 3 tablespoons of brown swerve, packed

Pomegranate Lamb

NUTRITION Calories 225, Total Fat 20.4 g, Saturated Fat 8.7 g , Cholesterol 30 mg , Sodium 135 mg, Total Carbs 7.7 g , Fiber 4.3 g, Sugar 2.2 g , Protein 5.2 g

PREPARATION	COOKING TIME		SERVINGS
10	10 *hours*	15 *mins*	4

DIRECTION

- Start by throwing all the Ingredients except the pomegranate seeds, butter, and flour into your Crockpot.
- Cover its lid and cook for 10 hours on Low settings.
- Once done, remove its lid and mix well.
- Slice the slow-cooked lamb then transfer to a plate
- Mix flour with butter in a small bowl then pour into the crockpot.
- Continue cooking the remaining sauce for 15 minutes on high heat.
- Pour this sauce around the slices lamb.
- Garnish with pomegranate seeds.
- Serve warm.

INGREDIENTS

- 1 leg of lamb, boneless (tied)
- 1 cup of pomegranate juice
- 1 cup of white wine
- 1 cup of chicken stock
- ½ cup of pomegranate seeds
- 4 mint leaves
- 4 cloves garlic, peeled and minced
- 1 teaspoon of black pepper, ground
- 1 teaspoon of salt
- 3 tablespoons of olive oil

Persian Lamb Curry

NUTRITION Calories 376, Total Fat 12.1 g, Saturated Fat 14.2 g , Cholesterol 195 mg , Sodium 73 mg, Total Carbs 4.6 g , Fiber 3.1 g, Sugar 2.1 g , Protein 25.7 g

PREPARATION	COOKING TIME	SERVINGS
10	10 *hours*	6

DIRECTION

- Start by putting all the Ingredients into your Crockpot except cilantro.
- Cover its lid and cook for 10 hours on Low settings.
- Once done, remove its lid and mix well.
- Garnish with cilantro.
- Serve warm.

INGREDIENTS

- 1 tablespoon of turmeric
- 2 teaspoons of black pepper
- 1 teaspoon of salt
- 1 teaspoon of crushed red pepper flakes
- 3 tablespoons of extra virgin olive oil
- 2 medium onions, minced
- 3 lbs. lamb meat, cut into chunks
- 3 tablespoons of tomato paste
- ¼ cup of cilantro, diced

Indian Lamb Stew

NUTRITION Calories 265, Total Fat 26.1 g, Saturated Fat 7.8 g , Cholesterol 143 mg , Sodium 65 mg Total Carbs 5.9 g , Fiber 3.2 g, Sugar 1.3 g , Protein 6.1 g

PREPARATION	COOKING TIME	SERVINGS
10	10 *hours* 15 *mins*	8

DIRECTION

- Start by throwing all the Ingredients except the butter and flour into your Crockpot.
- Cover its lid and cook for 10 hours on Low settings.
- Once done, remove its lid and mix well.
- Mix corn starch and water in a small bowl then pour into the crockpot.
- Continue cooking the remaining sauce for 15 minutes on high heat until it thickens.
- Garnish as desired.
- Serve warm.

INGREDIENTS

- 2 tablespoons of sweet paprika
- 1 ½ teaspoons of cayenne pepper
- 1 cup of Greek yogurt
- ¼ cup of vegetable oil
- 4 lbs. boneless lamb shoulder
- 1 ½ teaspoons of ground ginger
- 1 ½ teaspoon of ground coriander
- ½ teaspoon of ground turmeric
- ¼ teaspoon of cloves, ground
- 2 small cinnamon sticks
- 8 cardamom pods
- 1 medium tomato, diced
- Black pepper
- 1 tablespoon of xanthan gum
- 2 tablespoons of water

Chapter 13. Seafood & Fish Recipes

Clam Chowder

NUTRITION *Calories: 427, Fat: 33g, Carbs: 5g, Protein: 27g*

PREPARATION	COOKING TIME	SERVINGS
10	2 *hours*	4

DIRECTION

- Except for the cream, add everything in the Crock-Pot.
- Cover and cook on high for 1 hour and 45 minutes.
- Then add the cream and cook on high for 15 minutes more.
- Serve.

INGREDIENTS

- Chopped celery – ½ cup
- Chopped onion – ½ cup
- Chicken broth – 1 cup
- Whole baby clams with juice – 2 cans
- Heavy whipping cream – 1 cup
- Salt – ½ tsp.
- Ground thyme – ½ tsp.
- Pepper – ½ tsp.

Creamy Seafood Chowder

NUTRITION *Calories: 225, Fat: 9.6g, Carbs: 5.6g, Protein: 21.4g*

PREPARATION	COOKING TIME	SERVINGS
10	5 *hours*	6

DIRECTION

- Drizzle oil into the Crock-Pot.
- Add the white fish, shrimp, prawns, onion, garlic, cream, wine, salt, and pepper into the pot. Stir to mix.
- Cover with the lid and cook on low for 5 hours.
- Sprinkle with fresh parsley and serve.

INGREDIENTS

- Garlic – 5 cloves, crushed
- Small onion – 1, finely chopped
- Prawns – 1 cup
- Shrimp – 1 cup
- Whitefish – 1 cup
- Full-fat cream – 2 cups
- Dry white wine – 1 cup
- A handful of fresh parsley, finely chopped
- Olive oil – 2 tbsp.

Salmon Cake

NUTRITION Calories: 277, Fat: 20.8g , Carbs: 1.1g, Protein: 22.5g

PREPARATION	*COOKING TIME*	*SERVINGS*
10	4 hours	4

INGREDIENTS
- 1. Salmon Cake

DIRECTION

- Drizzle oil into the Crock-Pot.
- Place the spinach, cream, beaten egg, salmon, salt, and pepper into the pot and mix to combine.
- Cover with the lid and cook on low for 4 hours.

Lemon-Butter Fish

NUTRITION Calories: 202, Fat: 13.4g, Carbs: 1.3g, Protein: 20.3g

PREPARATION	*COOKING TIME*	*SERVINGS*
10	5 hours	4

DIRECTION

- Combine the butter, garlic, zest of one lemon, and chopped parsley to a bowl.
- Drizzle oil into the Crock-Pot.
- Season the fish with salt and pepper and place into the pot.
- Place a dollop of lemon butter onto each fish fillet and gently spread it out.
- Cover with the lid and cook on low for 5 hours.
- Serve each fish fillet with a generous spoonful of melted lemon butter from the bottom of the pot. Drizzle with lemon juice and serve.

INGREDIENTS
- Fresh white fish – 4 fillets
- Butter - 1 ½ ounce, soft but not melted
- Garlic cloves – 2, crushed
- Lemon – 1 (juice and zest)
- A handful of fresh parsley, finely chopped
- Salt and pepper to taste
- Olive oil – 2 tbsp.

Salmon with Green Beans

NUTRITION Calories: 278, Fat: 17.8g, Carbs: 8.1g, Protein: 24.5g

PREPARATION	COOKING TIME	SERVINGS
10	3 *hours*	4

INGREDIENTS

- Salmon fillets – 4, skin on
- Garlic – 4 cloves, crushed
- Broccoli – ½ head, cut into florets
- Frozen green beans – 2 cups
- Olive oil – 3 tbsp., divided
- Salt and pepper to taste
- Water – ¼ cup

DIRECTION

- Add the olive oil into the Crock-Pot.
- Season the salmon with salt and pepper and place into the pot (skin-side down). Add the water.
- Place garlic, beans, and broccoli on top of the salmon. Season with salt and pepper.
- Drizzle some more oil over the veggies and fish.
- Cover with the lid and cook on high for 3 hours.
- Serve.

Coconut Fish Curry

NUTRITION Calories: 562, Fat: 49.9g, Carbs: 13g, Protein: 20.6g

PREPARATION	COOKING TIME	SERVINGS
10	4 *hours*	4

DIRECTION

- Add olive oil into the Crock-Pot.
- Add the coconut milk, stock, fish, curry paste, turmeric, onion, garlic, salt, and pepper to the pot. Stir to combine.
- Cover with the lid and cook on high for 4 hours.
- Drizzle with lime juice and fresh coriander and serve.

INGREDIENTS

- Large white fish fillets – 4, cut into chunks
- Garlic cloves – 4, crushed
- Small onion – 1, finely chopped
- Ground turmeric – 1 tsp.
- Yellow curry paste – 2 tbsp.
- Fish stock – 2 cups
- Full-fat coconut milk – 2 cans
- Lime – 1
- Fresh coriander as needed, roughly chopped
- Olive oil – 2 tbsp.
- Salt and pepper to taste

Coconut Lime Mussels

NUTRITION Calories: 342, Fat: 30.2g, Carbs: 11.3g, Protein: 10.9g

PREPARATION	COOKING TIME	SERVINGS
10	2.5 *hours*	4

INGREDIENTS

- Fresh mussels – 16
- Garlic – 4 cloves
- Full-fat coconut milk – 1 ½ cups
- Red chili – ½, finely chopped
- Lime – 1, juiced
- Fish stock – ½ cup
- A handful of fresh coriander
- Olive oil – 2 tbsp.
- Salt and pepper to taste

DIRECTION

- Add olive oil into the Crock-Pot.
- Add the coconut milk, garlic, chili, fish stock, salt, pepper, and juice of one lime to the pot. Stir to mix.
- Cover with the lid and cook on high for 2 hours.
- Remove the lid, place mussels into the liquid, and cover with the lid.
- Cook until mussels open, about 20 minutes.
- Serve the mussels with pot sauce. Garnish with fresh coriander.

Calamari, Prawn, and Shrimp Pasta Sauce

NUTRITION Calories: 372, Fat: 14.6g , Carbs: 8.5g , Protein: 55.1g

PREPARATION	COOKING TIME	SERVINGS
10	3 *hours*	4

DIRECTION

- Add oil into the Crock-Pot.
- Add the tomatoes, garlic, shrimp, prawns, calamari, mixed herbs, balsamic vinegar, water, salt, and pepper. Stir to mix.
- Cover with the lid and cook on high for 3 hours.
- Serve with zucchini noodles or veggies.

INGREDIENTS

- Calamari – 1 cup
- Prawns – 1 cup
- Shrimp – 1 cup
- Garlic – 6 cloves, crushed
- Tomatoes – 4, chopped
- Dried mixed herbs – 1 tsp.
- Balsamic vinegar – 1 tbsp.
- Olive oil – 2 tbsp.
- Salt and pepper to taste
- Water – ½ cup

Sesame Prawns

NUTRITION Calories: 236 , Fat: 7.7g , Carbs: 4.3g , Protein: 37.4g

PREPARATION	COOKING TIME	SERVINGS
10	2 *hours*	4

INGREDIENTS

- Large prawns – 3 cups
- Garlic – 4 cloves, crushed
- Sesame oil – 1 tbsp.
- Toasted sesame seeds – 2 tbsp.
- Red chili – ½, finely chopped
- Fish stock – ½ cup
- Salt and pepper to taste
- Chopped herbs for serving

DIRECTION

- Drizzle the sesame oil into the Crock-Pot.
- Add the garlic, prawns, sesame seeds, chili, and fish stock to the pot. Mix to coat.
- Cover with the lid and cook on high for 2 hours.
- Serve hot with fresh herbs and cauliflower rice.

Tuna Steaks

NUTRITION Calories: 269, Fat: 8.6g, Carbs: 2.9g, Protein: 40.4g

PREPARATION	COOKING TIME	SERVINGS
10	3 *hours*	4

DIRECTION

- Reduce the white wine in a pan by simmering until the strong alcohol smell is cooked off.
- Rub the tuna steaks with olive oil, and season with salt and pepper.
- Place the tuna steaks into the Crock-Pot.
- Sprinkle the crushed garlic on top of the tuna steaks.
- Place 2 lemon slices on top of each tuna steak.
- Pour the reduced wine into the pot.
- Cover with the lid and cook on high for 3 hours.
- Transfer fish on serving plates. Drizzle with pot liquid and serve.

INGREDIENTS

- Tuna steaks – 4
- Garlic – 3 cloves, crushed
- Lemon – 1, sliced into 8 slices
- White wine – ½ cup
- Olive oil – 2 tbsp.
- Salt and pepper to taste

Creamy Smoked Salmon Soup

NUTRITION Calories: 309, Fat: 26.4g, Carbs: 7g, Protein: 12.3g

PREPARATION	COOKING TIME	SERVINGS
10	3 *hours*	4

INGREDIENTS

- Smoked salmon – ½ lb., roughly chopped
- Garlic – 3 cloves, crushed
- Small onion – 1, finely chopped
- Leek – 1, finely chopped
- Heavy cream – 1 ½ cups
- Olive oil – 2 tbsp.
- Salt and pepper to taste
- Fish stock – 1 ½ cups

DIRECTION

- Add oil into the Crock-Pot.
- Add fish stock, leek, salmon, garlic, and onion into the pot.
- Cover with the lid and cook on low for 2 hours.
- Add the cream and stir. Cook for 1 hour more.
- Adjust seasoning and serve.

Cheeseand Prawns

NUTRITION Calories: 238, Fat: 13.5g, Carbs: 9g, Protein: 20g

PREPARATION	COOKING TIME	SERVINGS
10	1 *hours* 20 *mins*	4

DIRECTION

- Melt butter in a skillet over medium heat. Then add shallots and sauté for a few minutes until translucent.
- Add prawns and sauté for 2 minutes. Set aside.
- Grease the inside of the pot with a little butter.
- Sprinkle garlic over it and add cheese.
- In a bowl, mix almond meal, apple cider, and hot sauce. Pour the mixture into the Crock-Pot. Stir.
- Cover and cook on low for 1 hour.
- Add the prawn shallot mixture and stir.
- Cover and cook on low for 10 minutes.
- Stir again and sprinkle parsley over it.
- Serve.

INGREDIENTS

- Shallots – 2, finely chopped
- Apple cider vinegar – ¼ cup
- Butter – 2 tbsp.
- Raw prawns – 4 lbs., peeled, rinsed, patted dry
- Almond meal – 2 tsp.
- Swiss cheese – 1 cup, grated
- Garlic – 2 cloves, peeled, thinly sliced
- Hot pepper sauce – ¼ tsp.
- Salt to taste
- Fresh parsley to serve

Cheesy Salmon Bites

NUTRITION Calories: 195, Fat: 17.1g, Carbs: 3.7g, Protein: 7.9g

PREPARATION	COOKING TIME	SERVINGS
10	2 hours	8

INGREDIENTS

- Smoked salmon – 4 strips, cut in half lengthways
- Firm cream cheese – ¼ lb., cut into 8 chunks
- Mozzarella cheese – ¼ lb., cut into 8 chunks
- Spring onion – 1, finely chopped
- Lemon – 1, zest
- Olive oil – 2 tbsp.

DIRECTION

- Press one piece of mozzarella and one piece of cream cheese together. Sprinkle with a small amount of spring onion.
- Wrap the cheese bundle in smoked salmon.
- Repeat the process with the remaining Ingredients.
- Drizzle oil into the Crock-Pot and place salmon bites in one layer into the pot.
- Secure the lid and cook on low for 2 hours.
- Garnish with lemon zest and serve.

Chapter 14. Appetizers & Snacks

Asparagus Bacon Bouquet

NUTRITION Calories 345, Carbs 2 g , Fat 27 g, Protein 22 g, Sodium 1311 mg, Sugar 0 g

PREPARATION	COOKING TIME	SERVINGS
15	4 hours	4

INGREDIENTS

- asparagus spears, trimmed
- slices bacon
- 1 tsp black pepper
- Extra virgin olive oil

DIRECTION

- Coat slow cooker with extra virgin olive oil.
- Slice spears in half, and sprinkle with black pepper
- Wrap three spear halves with one slice bacon, and set inside the slow cooker.
- Cook for 4 hours on medium.

Creamy Asiago Spinach Dip

NUTRITION Calories 214, Carbs 4 g, Fat 19 g, Protein 8 g, Sodium 380 mg, Sugar 1 g

PREPARATION	COOKING TIME	SERVINGS
15	4 hours	6

DIRECTION

- Coat slow cooker with olive oil.
- Place cream cheese and almond milk in a blender, and mix until smooth.
- Finely chop spinach, add to blender along with salt and black pepper, and mix.
- Place spinach mixture in a blender, add artichoke hearts and mix in with a spatula.
- Sprinkle Asiago cheese on top, and cook on medium for 4 hours.
- Serve dip with a selection of veggies like broccoli florets and carrot sticks.

INGREDIENTS

- cups spinach, wash, chopped
- ½ cup artichoke hearts
- ½ cup cream cheese
- ½ cup Asiago cheese, grated
- ½ cup almond milk
- 1 tsp black pepper
- Extra virgin olive oil

Madras Curry Chicken Bites

NUTRITION Calories 234, Carbs 3 g, Fat 8 g, Protein 38 g, Sodium 782 mg, Sugar 0 g

PREPARATION	COOKING TIME	SERVINGS
15	7 *hours*	4

DIRECTION

- Cube chicken breast into ½" pieces, and sprinkle with ½ tsp salt and ½ tsp black pepper.
- Heat 3 tbsp. extra virgin olive oil in a skillet, add chicken breasts, and brown.
- Place chicken breasts in a slow cooker.
- Add chicken stock, garlic, lemon juice, spices, and salt.
- Cook on low for 7 hours.

INGREDIENTS

- 1 lb. chicken breasts, skinless, boneless
- cloves garlic, grated
- 1 tsp ginger, grated
- 2 cups low-sodium chicken stock
- 2 lemons, juiced
- 1 tsp coriander, crushed
- 1 tsp cumin
- ½ tsp fenugreek
- 1 tbsp. curry powder
- ½ tsp cinnamon
- 1½ tsp salt
- 1 tsp black pepper
- Extra virgin olive oil

Spiced Jicama Wedges with Cilantro Chutney

NUTRITION Calories 94, Carbs 5.2 g, Fat 8 g, Protein 1 g, Sodium 879 mg, Sugar 1 g

PREPARATION	COOKING TIME	SERVINGS
15	4 *hours*	8

DIRECTION

- Slice jicama into 1" wedges, and submerge in a bowl of cold water for 20 minutes.
- Place the paprika, oregano, salt, black pepper in a bowl, and toss with jicama.
- Add 5 tbsp. extra virgin olive oil into a bowl and coat well.
- Place jicama in the slow cooker, and cook on high for 4 hours.
- Combine Ingredients for chutney in blender, mix, and refrigerate until jicama wedges are ready to serve.

INGREDIENTS

- 1 lb. jicama, peeled
- 1 tsp paprika
- ½ tsp dried parsley
- 2 tsp salt
- 2 tsp black pepper
- Extra virgin olive oil
- Cilantro Chutney
- 1 tsp dill chopped
- ¼ cup cilantro
- ½ tsp salt
- 1 tsp paprika
- 1tsp black pepper
- 2 lemons, juiced
- ¼ cup extra virgin olive oil

Teriyaki Chicken Wings

NUTRITION *Calories 354, Carbs 5.5 g, Fat 16 g, Protein 45 g, Sodium 730 mg, Sugar 0 g*

PREPARATION	COOKING TIME	SERVINGS
15	4 hours	4

INGREDIENTS

- 2 lb. chicken wings
- 2 tsp ginger, grated
- cloves garlic, grated
- ¼ cup of soy sauce
- dates, pitted
- Extra virgin olive oil

DIRECTION

- Processed the dates in a food processor along with 2 tbsp. soy sauce, and mix until pasty.
- Combine ginger, garlic, soy sauce, and dates in a bowl, add chicken wings, coat, and refrigerate overnight.
- Coat slow cooker with a little sesame oil, add chicken wings and cook on high for 4 hours.

Portabella Pizza Bites

NUTRITION *Calories 106, Carbs 5.6 g, Fat 3 g, Protein 13 g, Sodium 421 mg, Sugar 2 g*

PREPARATION	COOKING TIME	SERVINGS
15	5 hours	8

DIRECTION

- Coat 6 qt. slow cooker with extra virgin olive oil
- Heat 3 tbsp. extra virgin olive oil in a skillet, add pork, brown.
- Mix crushed tomato with salt, black pepper, oregano, parmesan, and garlic.
- Spoon a little tomato-parmesan mixture into each mushroom, add a little ground pork, and sprinkle with Mozzarella.
- Place each mushroom in a slow cooker. Cook pizza bites on medium for 5 hours.
- Sprinkle a little parsley on top before serving.

INGREDIENTS

- Portabella Mushrooms
- ½ lb. ground pork
- 1 medium onion, diced
- cloves garlic, grated
- 2 cups crushed tomato
- ½ cup Mozzarella, shredded
- ¼ cup Parmesan
- ½ tsp oregano
- 1 tsp salt
- 1 tsp black pepper
- Garnish
- ½ cup parsley, chopped

Candied Walnuts

NUTRITION Calories: 22, Carbohydrates: 10.5, Protein: 6.9, Fat: 22.5, Sugar: 7, Sodium: 42m, Fiber: 2.1g

PREPARATION	COOKING TIME	SERVINGS
15	2.5 hours	16

INGREDIENTS

- ½ cup unsalted butter
- 1-pound walnuts
- ½ cup Splenda, granular
- 1½ teaspoons ground cinnamon
- ¼ teaspoon ground allspice
- ¼ teaspoon ground ginger
- 1/8 teaspoon ground cloves

DIRECTION

- Set a slow cooker on high and preheat for about 15 minutes. Add butter and walnuts and stir to combine.
- Add the Splenda and stir to combine well. Cook, covered, for about 15 minutes.
- Uncover the slow cooker and stir the mixture. Set to cook on low, uncovered, within 2 hours, stirring occasionally.
- Transfer the walnuts to a bowl. In another small bowl, mix spices.
- Sift spice mixture over walnuts and toss to coat evenly. Set aside to cool before serving.

Flavorful Pecans

NUTRITION Calories: 225, Carbohydrates: 4.5, Protein: 3.2, Fat: 23.2, Sugar: 1.1, Sodium: 37m, Fiber: 3.3g

PREPARATION	COOKING TIME	SERVINGS
15	2.5 hours	16

DIRECTION

- Combine all fixings in a large slow cooker.
- Cook in the slow cooker on high and cook, covered, for about 15 minutes.
- Uncover the slow cooker and stir the mixture.
- Cook on low, uncovered, within 2 hours, mixing occasionally.
- Transfer the pecans into a bowl and keep aside to cool before serving.

INGREDIENTS

- 1-pound pecan halves
- ¼ cup butter, melted
- 1 teaspoon dried oregano
- 1 teaspoon dried basil
- 1 teaspoon dried thyme
- 1 tablespoon red chili powder
- ½ teaspoon onion powder
- ¼ teaspoon garlic powder
- ¼ teaspoon cayenne pepper
- Salt, to taste

Herb Flavored Almonds

NUTRITION Calories: 7, Carbohydrates: 2.8, Protein: 2.5, Fat: 6.9, Sugar: 0.5, Sodium: 12m, Fiber: 1.6g

PREPARATION | COOKING TIME | SERVINGS
15 | 2 *hours* | 16

INGREDIENTS

- 2 cups of raw almonds
- 1 tablespoon olive oil
- 1 tablespoon dried rosemary
- 1 tablespoon dried thyme
- Salt
- ground black pepper

DIRECTION

- Mix all the fixings in a large slow cooker.
- Cook in the slow cooker on high and cook, covered, for about 1½ hours, stirring after every 30 minutes. Cool before serving.

Ultra-Spicy Almonds

NUTRITION Calories: 8, Carbohydrates: 2.9, Protein: 2.6, Fat: 7.1, Sugar: 0.6, Sodium: 6m, Fiber: 1.6g

PREPARATION COOKING TIME | SERVINGS
15 | 2.5 *hours* | 32

DIRECTION

- Set a slow cooker on high and preheat for about 25 minutes.
- Add all Ingredients and stir to combine.
- Cook on low, uncovered, for about 2 hours, stirring occasionally.
- Then, in high and cook, uncovered, within 30 minutes.
- Cool before serving.

INGREDIENTS

- 2½ tablespoons coconut oil
- cups of raw almonds
- garlic cloves, minced
- 1 teaspoon smoked paprika
- 2 teaspoons red chili powder
- 1 teaspoon ground cumin
- 1 teaspoon onion powder
- Salt
- ground black pepper

214

Tastier Nuts Combo

NUTRITION Calories: 101, Carbohydrates: 3.1g, Protein: 2.1g, Fat: 0.6g, Sugar: 0.6g, Sodium: 14mg, Fiber: 1.2g

PREPARATION	COOKING TIME	SERVINGS
15	2 hours	32

INGREDIENTS

- 1 cup hazelnuts, toasted and skins removed
- 1 cup whole almonds, toasted
- 1 cup pecan halves, toasted
- 1 cup whole cashews
- ½ cup Erythritol
- 1/3 cup butter, melted
- ½ teaspoon ground cinnamon
- ½ teaspoon ground ginger
- ¼ teaspoon ground cloves
- ¼ teaspoon cayenne pepper

DIRECTION

- In a large slow cooker, add all fixings and stir to combine.
- Set on low, covered, cook for about 2 hours, stirring once after 1 hour.
- Uncover the slow cooker and stir nuts again.
- Transfer nuts onto a sheet of buttered foil to cool for at least 1 hour before serving.

Zesty Chicken Wings

NUTRITION Calories: 456, Carbohydrates: 12.6g, Protein: 66.8g, Fat: 16.9g, Sugar: 8.6g, Sodium: 1084mg, Fiber: 0.2g

PREPARATION	COOKING TIME	SERVINGS
15	7 hours 12 mins	8

DIRECTION

- For the sauce: Put all sauce fixings in a large bowl, and beat until well combined.
- Put chicken wings at the bottom of a slow cooker, and top with sauce evenly.
- Set on low setting and cook, covered, for about 6-7 hours.
- Dissolve arrowroot starch in water in a small bowl.
- Uncover the slow cooker and stir in arrowroot mixture until well combined.
- Cook on high, covered, for about 10-12 minutes.
- Serve immediately.

INGREDIENTS

For Sauce:
- ¼ cup low-sodium soy sauce
- ¼ cup fresh lime juice
- tablespoons Erythritol
- 1 teaspoon Sriracha
- 1 teaspoon ginger powder
- 2 garlic cloves, minced
- 1 teaspoon fresh lime zest, grated finely
- For Wings:
- 2 pounds grass-fed chicken wings
- teaspoons arrowroot starch
- 1 tablespoon water

Buffalo Chicken Meatballs

NUTRITION Calories: 28, Carbohydrates: 3, Protein: 36.1, Fat: 13.5, Sugar: 0.6, Sodium: 224m, Fiber: 1.2g

PREPARATION	COOKING TIME	SERVINGS
15	2 hours	4

INGREDIENTS

- 1-pound ground grass-fed chicken
- 1 organic egg
- 1/3 cup almond meal
- scallions, sliced thinly
- 2 garlic cloves, minced
- Salt
- black pepper, ground
- ¾ cup sugar-free buffalo sauce

DIRECTION

- Preheat the oven to 400 degrees F.
- In a bowl, add all Ingredients except buffalo sauce and mix until well combined.
- Make 1½-inch balls from chicken mixture.
- Arrange meatballs onto a baking sheet and bake for about 5 minutes.
- Remove from oven and transfer meatballs into a slow cooker with buffalo sauce, stir.
- Cook on low, then covered, for about 2 hours. Serve immediately.

Foolproof Beef Meatballs

NUTRITION Calories: 264, Carbohydrates: 10.8g, Protein: 36.1g, Fat: 11.7g, Sugar: 0.7g, Sodium: 508mg, Fiber: 0g

PREPARATION	COOKING TIME		SERVINGS
15	7 hours	5 mins	8

DIRECTION

- Mix all items except oil in a bowl. Make desired size balls from the mixture.
- Heat-up oil over medium-high heat in a large skillet, then cook meatballs for 4-5 minutes or until golden brown from all sides.
- Transfer the meatballs into a greased slow cooker.
- Cook in the slow cooker on low, covered, for about 7 hours. Serve hot.

INGREDIENTS

- pounds ground lean grass-fed beef
- 2 organic eggs, beaten
- 1 medium yellow onion, chopped
- 2 garlic cloves, minced
- ¼ cup fresh parsley leaves, chopped
- ½ teaspoon red pepper flakes, crushed
- ¼ teaspoon cayenne pepper
- Salt
- ground black pepper
- 2 tablespoons olive oil

Super-Tasty Pork Meatballs

NUTRITION Calories: 358, Carbohydrates: 1.9, Protein: 29.2g, Fat: 25.8g, Sugar: 0.8, Sodium: 398mg, Fiber: 0.2g

PREPARATION	COOKING TIME	SERVINGS
15	6 20 hours mins	8

INGREDIENTS

- pounds lean ground pork
- 1 cup Cheddar cheese, shredded
- 1 large organic egg
- ¼ cup yellow onion, chopped
- ¼ teaspoon ground allspice
- 1 tablespoon water
- tablespoons unsalted butter
- 1½ cups heavy whipping cream
- 1½ cups homemade chicken broth
- 1 tablespoon Worcestershire sauce
- 1 tablespoon Dijon mustard

DIRECTION

- Warm-up, the oven to 400 degrees F, then line a large baking dish with parchment paper.
- In a large bowl, add ground pork, cheddar cheese, egg, onion, allspice, and water and mix until well combined.
- Make 1½-inch balls from pork mixture.
- Arrange the meatballs onto a prepared baking dish and bake for about 20 minutes.
- Meanwhile, in a small skillet, add butter, heavy cream, and broth and bring to a gentle boil over medium heat.
- Adjust to low and simmer for about 20 minutes, stirring occasionally.
- Stir in Worcestershire sauce and mustard and remove from heat.
- In a slow cooker, add sauce and meatballs and stir.
- Cook in the slow cooker on low, covered, for about 4-6 hours. Serve immediately.

Inspiring Sausage Sliders

NUTRITION Calories: 36, Carbohydrates: 13.7, Protein: 19, Fat: 26.2, Sugar: 11.8, Sodium: 1280m, Fiber: 0.5g

PREPARATION	COOKING TIME	SERVINGS
15	5 hours	10

DIRECTION

- In a large slow cooker, add all items and stir to combine.
- Cook on low, covered, for about 4-5 hours.
- Serve immediately.

INGREDIENTS

- cups sugar-free ketchup
- ¼ cup Erythritol
- 1 tablespoon Worcestershire sauce
- 2 teaspoons mustard
- 1 teaspoon hot sauce
- 1 medium yellow onion, chopped finely
- ½ cup homemade chicken broth
- 2 pounds pork sausage, cut into ½-inch rounds

Potluck Party Peppers

NUTRITION Calories: 24, Carbohydrates: 9.6, Protein: 15.6, Fat: 16g, Sugar: 7.5g, Sodium: 824mg, Fiber: 1.8g

PREPARATION	COOKING TIME	SERVINGS
15	9 *hours*	10

INGREDIENTS

- 1½ pounds mini sweet peppers, seeded and tops removed
- 1-pound ground Italian sausage
- 1 (24-ounce) jar sugar-free spaghetti sauce
- 8-ounce mozzarella cheese, shredded

DIRECTION

- Stuff each pepper evenly with sausage.
- Lightly greased slow cooker, arrange peppers. Cook on low, covered, for about 6-8 hours.
- Uncover the crockpot and top each pepper with mozzarella cheese.
- Cook, covered for about 10 minutes. Serve hot.

Perfect Eggplant Tapenade

NUTRITION Calories: 46, Carbohydrates: 10.1g, Protein: 2g, Fat: 0.4g, Sugar: 5g, Sodium: 170mg, Fiber: 4.2g

PREPARATION	COOKING TIME	SERVINGS
15	9 *hours*	2

DIRECTION

- In a slow cooker, add eggplant, tomatoes, garlic, and capers and mix well.
- Cook on low, covered, for about 7-9 hours.
- Uncover the slow cooker and stir in the remaining Ingredients
- Serve hot.

INGREDIENTS

1. Perfect Eggplant Tapenade

Swiss Style Cheese Fondue

NUTRITION Calories: 47, Carbohydrates: 6.1g, Protein: 32.6g, Fat: 36g, Sugar: 1.8g, Sodium: 700mg, Fiber: 0.5g

PREPARATION	COOKING TIME	SERVINGS
15	3 hours 10 mins	6

INGREDIENTS

- 1 clove garlic, cut in half
- 2½ cups homemade chicken broth
- tablespoons fresh lemon juice
- 16 ounces Swiss cheese, shredded
- ounces Cheddar cheese, shredded
- tablespoons almond flour
- Pinch of ground nutmeg
- Pinch of paprika
- Pinch of ground black pepper

DIRECTION

- Rub a pan evenly with cut garlic halves. Add broth and place pan over medium heat.
- Cook until mixture is just beginning to bubble. Adjust to low, then stir in lemon juice.
- Meanwhile, in a bowl, mix cheeses and flour. Slowly, add cheese mixture to broth, stirring continuously.
- Cook until cheese mixture becomes thick, stirring continuously. Transfer the cheese mixture to a greased crockpot and sprinkle with nutmeg, paprika, and black pepper.
- Cook in the slow cooker on low, covered, for about 1-3 hours.

Tex-Mex Cheese Dip

NUTRITION Calories: 11, Carbohydrates: 5.2, Protein: 7, Fat: 8.1, Sugar: 3.4g, Sodium: 577mg, Fiber: 0.3g

PREPARATION	COOKING TIME	SERVINGS
15	1.5 hours	3

INGREDIENTS

- ounces Velveeta cheese, cubed
- ¾ cup diced tomatoes with green chili peppers
- 1 teaspoon taco seasoning

DIRECTION

- In a slow cooker, place Velveeta cheese cubes.
- Cook on low and cook, covered, for about 30-60 minutes, stirring occasionally.
- Uncover the slow cooker and stir in tomatoes and taco seasoning. Cook, covered, for about 30 minutes
- Serve hot.

2-Ingredient Cheese Dip

NUTRITION Calories: 71, Carbohydrates: 3.9g, Protein: 4.4g, Fat: 4.9g, Sugar: 2.3g, Sodium: 460mg, Fiber: 0.4g

INGREDIENTS

- 16 ounces Velveeta cheese, cubed
- 1 (16-ounce) jar salsa

DIRECTION

- In a large slow cooker, place cheese and salsa and stir gently to combine.
- Cook on high, covered, for about 2 hours, stirring occasionally. Serve hot.

PREPARATION	COOKING TIME	SERVINGS
15	2 *hours*	20

Garlic Parmesan Chicken Wings

NUTRITION Calories: 426 , Fat: 34g , Carbohydrates: 1g , Proteins: 27g

INGREDIENTS

- 1 cup Parmesan Cheese, shredded
- lb. Chicken Wings
- ¼ tsp. Black Pepper, grounded
- ½ cup Butter, preferably organic
- 1 tsp. Sea Salt
- Garlic cloves, finely minced

DIRECTION

- Begin by placing the chicken wings in the bottom portion of the slow cooker. After that, butter a large skillet over medium heat, and to this, add the garlic.
- Sauté the garlic for 30 to 50 seconds or until aromatic. Spoon in the oil over the chicken wings and coat them well.
- Now, cook them for 3 hours on low heat. Toward the end time, preheat the oven to broil.
- Line the baking sheet using a parchment paper. Once the chicken is cooked, transfer them to the baking sheet in a single layer.
- Broil it within 5 minutes or until the chicken is golden brown in color and crispy. Bring the baking sheet out after 5 minutes and top it with the cheese.
- Return the sheet to oven and bake for another 2 minutes or until melted.

PREPARATION	COOKING TIME	SERVINGS
10	3 20 *hours mins*	8

Candied Pecans

NUTRITION Calories: 257, Fat: 26g , Carbohydrates: 4g , Proteins: 4g

INGREDIENTS

- 1 cup Sukrin Gold
- 1 Egg White, medium-sized
- cups Pecan
- ¼ cup Water
- tsp. Vanilla Extract
- 1 ½ tbsp. Cinnamon

DIRECTION

- First, butter the insides of the slow cooker and transfer the pecans to it.
- After that, mix vanilla extract and egg white in a mixing bowl until just combined and foamy.
- Spoon this egg mixture over the pan. Stir them so that they coat the pecans well. Now, combine the cinnamon with the Sukrin Gold until well incorporated.
- Pour the batter over the pecans and stir them again.
- Then, close the lid and cook for 3 hours on low heat while stirring them every quarter of an hour.
- Once the time is up, transfer the pecans to a baking sheet in a single layer and allow it to cool. Serve and enjoy.

PREPARATION	COOKING TIME	SERVINGS
5	3 _hours_	12

Cocoa Nuts

NUTRITION Calories: 218, Fat: 21g , Carbohydrates: 2g , Proteins: 4g

INGREDIENTS

- ½ cup Walnuts
- tbsp. Swerve
- ½ cup Almonds, slivered
- tbsp. Butter softened
- ½ cup Pecans, halved
- 2 tbsp. Cocoa Powder, unsweetened
- 1 tsp. Vanilla Extract

DIRECTION

- First, place all the Ingredients needed to make this snack in a large mixing bowl. Mix well until well combined.
- Transfer the nut mixture to the slow cooker— Cook within 1 hour on high heat.
- Once the cooking time is up, place them on a baking sheet and cool before storing.

PREPARATION	COOKING TIME	SERVINGS
3	1 _hours_	6

Thai Curry Nuts

NUTRITION Calories: 54, Fat: 57g, Carbohydrates: 5g, Proteins: 5.41g

INGREDIENTS

- cups Nuts, raw
- ½ tsp. Salt
- ¼ cup Coconut Oil
- 1 tbsp. Curry Paste
- 1 tbsp. Swerve Sweetener

DIRECTION

- Start by heating the crockpot to high heat. Add coconut oil to crockpot and once the oil has melted, stir in curry paste, salt, and sugar. Mix well.
- Once the spice paste has dissolved, add the raw nuts. Stir them well so that the syrup coats the nuts well. Then, cover the lid and cook for 1 ½ hour on high heat.
- Finally, transfer the nuts to a baking sheet and allow them to cool completely before storing.

PREPARATION	COOKING TIME	SERVINGS
5	1 30 hours mins	8

Pumpkin Spiced Nuts

NUTRITION Calories: 38, Fat: 34.66g, Carbohydrates: 7g, Proteins: 10.92g

INGREDIENTS

- 1 cup Walnuts, raw & halved
- Egg Whites, large
- cups Almonds, raw & unsalted
- 1 ½ tbsp. Pumpkin Pie Spice
- 2 cups Cashews, raw & unsalted
- 1 cup Brazil Nuts, raw & unsalted
- 1 ½ cup Coconut Sugar

DIRECTION

- First, grease the insides of the slow cooker with oil or butter.
- After that, combine the nuts with the pumpkin pie spice and coconut sugar. Mix well.
- Then, add the egg whites into it until everything comes together. Now, transfer the nut mixture to the slow cooker.
- Cook for 2 hours on low heat. Make sure to stir them every 45 minutes or so.
- Once the nuts are done with cooking, place them on a baking sheet and allow it to cool completely.

PREPARATION	COOKING TIME	SERVINGS
15	2 hours	4

Turkey Meatballs

NUTRITION Calories: 9, Fat: 7.14g, Carbohydrates: 1.85g, Proteins: 10.18g

INGREDIENTS

- 1lb. Turkey
- Garlic cloves, crushed
- ½ tsp. Onion Powder
- 1 tbsp. Red Wine Vinegar
- ½ tsp. Rosemary
- 1 lb. Turkey sausage, grounded
- 1 Egg, large & organic
- ½ tsp. Thyme
- 1 tsp. Salt
- ½ of 1 Onion, large & diced
- ½ tsp. Garlic powder
- 1 tsp. Basil
- 1 × 28 oz. Can have crushed Tomatoes
- ½ tsp. Oregano
- ½ cup Almond Meal

DIRECTION

- First, you need to mix turkey and sausage in a large bowl until well combined.
- After that, stir together onion powder, basil, almond meal, oregano, garlic powder, and rosemary in another bowl until mixed well.
- Then, put the almond meal batter to the meat mixture and give everything a good stir.
- Mix in the egg until well incorporated. Now, form a ball out of this mixture and place them on the baking sheet.
- Place them in the oven and broil them for 2 to 3 minutes. Once broiled, add the meatballs to the crockpot.
- Top the meatballs with garlic, onion, vinegar, tomatoes, and salt.
- Close the lid and cook them for 6 hours on low heat. Finally, garnish them with basil before serving.

PREPARATION	COOKING TIME	SERVINGS
15	6 *hours*	20

Bok Choy Brownies

NUTRITION Calories: 23, Fat: 20.82g, Carbohydrates: 5.39g, Proteins: 6.68g

INGREDIENTS

- 1 packet of Bok Choy, trimmed and stems coarsely chopped
- ½ cup Swerve Sweetener
- Eggs, large & organic
- ½ tsp. Salt
- 1 tsp. Baking powder
- 1 cup Almond Flour
- 1 tsp. Vanilla Extract
- ½ cup Cocoa Powder
- 1/3 cup Coconut Oil
- ½ tsp. Espresso powder

DIRECTION

- To begin with, grease the insides of the slow cooker. Heat saltwater in a saucepan over medium heat and place the bok choy into it.
- Simmer for 5 minutes or until the stems are cooked well.
- Now, transfer the cooked bok choy to a blender and blend until it becomes a smooth puree. Mix all the dry fixing in a large mixing bowl.
- Add the wet fixing one by one until everything comes together. Put the batter inside the slow cooker and close the lid.
- Cook within 4 hours on low heat or until the center is set and a toothpick inserted comes clean.
- Allow them to cool in the slow cooker itself and then slice them into small pieces. Serve warm or cold.

PREPARATION	COOKING TIME	SERVINGS
10	4 *hours*	8

Lemon Custard

NUTRITION Calories: 31, Fat: 30g, Carbohydrates: 3g, Proteins: 7g

INGREDIENTS

- Egg yolks, large & organic
- 1 tsp. Vanilla Extract
- cups Whipping Cream
- 1 tbsp. Lemon zest
- ½ tsp. Liquid Stevia
- ¼ cup Lemon Juice, freshly squeezed

DIRECTION

- Combine egg yolks, liquid stevia, lemon juice, and zest and vanilla extract in a medium-sized mixing bowl.
- Once well combined, add whipping cream to the bowl and stir them again. Divide the mixture into 4 ramekins.
- After that, place a rack into the slow cooker and arrange the ramekins on it. Put water inside the slow cooker, so it reaches halfway up the sides of the ramekins.
- Cook within 3 hours on low heat. Finally, remove the ramekins from the slow cooker and allow them to cool at room temperature.
- Chill them in the refrigerator.

PREPARATION	COOKING TIME	SERVINGS
10	3 hours	4

Buffalo Chicken Dip

NUTRITION Calories: 34, Fat: 25.3g, Carbohydrates: 5.3g , Proteins: 22.39g

INGREDIENTS

- 1 tbsp. Ranch Seasoning
- cups cooked chicken, diced
- 1 cup Hot Sauce
- oz. Blue Cheese, crumbled
- 1 cup Sour Cream
- ½ cup Green Onion, thinly sliced
- 1 × 8 oz. Cream Cheese, chopped into cubes
- cups Mozzarella Cheese, shredded

DIRECTION

- 1 Start by greasing the insides of the slow cooker. Stir in all the remaining Ingredients: into the slow cooker and mix well.
- 2 Cook for 2 hours on high heat or until the cheese is melted. Garnish with green onions and serve it along with celery stalks.

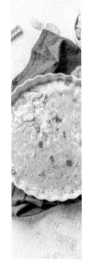

PREPARATION	COOKING TIME	SERVINGS
10	2 hours	8

Chapter 15. Soups and Stews

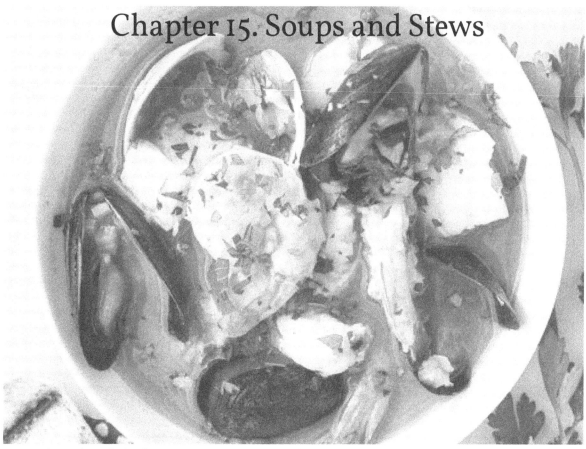

Herbed Chicken& Green Chiles Soup

NUTRITION Calories: 180.02, Total Fat: 7.04 g, Saturated Fat: 1.19 g, Cholesterol: 18.28 mg, Sodium: 831.99 mg, Potassium: 599.6 mg, Total Carbohydrates: 9.82 g, Fiber: 3.93 g, Sugar: 1.6 g, Protein: 13.02 g

INGREDIENTS

- 2 chicken breasts, boneless, skinless
- ½ teaspoon cumin, ground
- 1 teaspoon onion powder
- 1 teaspoon chili powder
- 1 teaspoon garlic powder
- ½ teaspoon white pepper, ground
- ¼ teaspoon cayenne pepper
- 4 ounces green chilies
- 1 cup beans
- 3 cups water
- ½ avocado, cubed
- 2 tablespoons extra virgin olive oil
- 1 small carrot, diced

DIRECTION

- Grease the bottom of Crock-Pot with olive oil and place chicken inside pot.
- Mix white pepper, cumin, garlic, onion, and chili powder.
- Sprinkle evenly over the chicken. Place the chilies on top of chicken.
- Pour in water and add beans and carrot and stir. Close the lid and cook on HIGH for an hour.
- Open the lid and give a good stir. Close the lid and continue to cook on HIGH for 5 hours.
- Serve hot with avocado.

PREPARATION	COOKING TIME	SERVINGS
15	6	8
	hours	

Turmeric Squash Soup

NUTRITION 194 calories, 22.6g protein, 8.4g carbohydrates, 5.8g fat, 3.2g fiber, 65mg cholesterol, 78mg sodium, 551mg potassium

INGREDIENTS

- 3 chicken thighs, skinless, boneless, chopped
- 3 cups butternut squash, chopped
- 1 teaspoon ground turmeric
- 1 onion, sliced
- 1 oz. green chilies, chopped, canned
- 6 cups of water

DIRECTION

- Put chicken thighs in the bottom of the Slow Cooker and top them with green chilies.
- Then add the ground turmeric, butternut squash, and water. Add sliced onion and close the lid.
- Cook the soup on low for 9 Hours.

PREPARATION	COOKING TIME	SERVINGS
15	9 *hours*	6

Celery Stew

NUTRITION 267 calories, 35.3g protein, 2.7g carbohydrates, 12g fat, 1.2g fiber, 104g cholesterol, 124mg sodium, 660mg potassium.

INGREDIENTS

- 3 cups of water
- 1-pound beef stew meat, cubed
- 2 cups celery, chopped
- ½ cup cremini mushrooms, sliced
- 2 tablespoons sour cream
- 1 teaspoon smoked paprika
- 1 teaspoon cayenne pepper
- 1 tablespoon sesame oil

DIRECTION

- Mix beef stew meat with cayenne pepper and put in the hot skillet.
- Add sesame oil and roast the meat for 1 minute per side on high heat.
- Transfer the meat in the Slow Cooker.
- Add celery, cremini mushrooms, sour cream, smoked paprika, and water.
- Close the lid and cook the stew on high for 6 hours.

PREPARATION	COOKING TIME	SERVINGS
15	6 *hours*	4

Barley Soup

NUTRITION 126 calories, 8.3g protein, 10.1g carbohydrates, 6g fat, 2.2g fiber, 33mg cholesterol, 797mg sodium, 249mg potassium.

INGREDIENTS

- ¼ cup barley
- 5 cups chicken stock
- 4 oz. pork tenderloin, chopped
- 1 tablespoon dried cilantro
- 1 tablespoon tomato paste
- 3 oz. carrot, grated
- ½ cup heavy cream

DIRECTION

- Put pork tenderloin in the Slow Cooker.
- Add barley, chicken stock, tomato paste, carrot, and heavy cream.
- Carefully stir the soup mixture and close the lid.
- Cook it on Low for 8 hours.

PREPARATION	COOKING TIME	SERVINGS
15	8 *hours*	5

Cabbage Stew

NUTRITION 57 calories, 2.8g protein, 13.3g carbohydrates, 0.2g fat, 3.9g fiber, 0mg cholesterol, 196mg sodium, 503mg potassium.

INGREDIENTS

- 2 cups white cabbage, shredded
- ½ cup tomato juice
- 1 teaspoon ground white pepper
- 1 cup cauliflower, chopped
- ½ cup potato, chopped
- 1 cup of water

DIRECTION

- Put cabbage, potato, and cauliflower in the Slow Cooker.
- Add tomato juice, ground white pepper, and water. Stir the stew Ingredients: and close the lid.
- Cook the stew on high for hours.

PREPARATION	COOKING TIME	SERVINGS
15	3 *hours*	2

Sweet Potato & Sausage Soup

NUTRITION Calories: 126.71, Total Fat: 2.02 g, Saturated Fat: 0.99 g, Cholesterol: 18.33 mg, Sodium: 787.22 mg, Potassium: 215.12 mg, Total Carbohydrates: 6.95 g, Fiber: 0.52 g, Sugar: 1.26 g, Protein: 15.3 g

INGREDIENTS

- 3 cups water
- Salt and pepper to taste and other seasonings
- 1 cup of bacon, cooked, cubed
- 1 cup smoked ham, cooked, cubed
- 1 red pepper, diced

DIRECTION

- Chop the onion into cubes. Grease a frying pan and sauté onion until golden in color, for about six minutes.
- Add the cubed ham and bacon. Add cubed potatoes and salt and pepper to taste.
- Pour in wine and stir. Place all Ingredients: in Slow Cooker.
- Add the water and cover and cook on LOW for 6-7 hours.
- Add the chopped pepper and tomato sauce and cook on LOW for an additional 30 minutes more.
- Serve hot.

PREPARATION	COOKING TIME	SERVINGS
15	7 35 hours mins	6

Coconut Cod Stew

NUTRITION 158 calories, 14.7g protein, 3.3g carbohydrates, 10.3g fat, 1.3g fiber, 37mg cholesterol, 55mg sodium, 138mg potassium.

INGREDIENTS

- 1-pound cod fillet, chopped
- 2 oz. scallions, roughly chopped
- 1 cup coconut cream
- 1 teaspoon curry powder
- 1 teaspoon garlic, diced

DIRECTION

- Mix curry powder with coconut cream and garlic.
- Add scallions and gently stir the liquid. After this, pour it in the Slow Cooker and add cod fillet.
- Stir the stew mixture gently and close the lid.
- Cook the stew on low for 6hours.

PREPARATION	COOKING TIME	SERVINGS
15	6.5 hours	6

German Style Soup

NUTRITION 137 calories, 16.1g protein, 4.3g carbohydrates, 5.8g fat, 1.1g fiber, 41mg cholesterol, 503mg sodium, 93mg potassium.

INGREDIENTS

- 1-pound beef loin, chopped
- 6 cups of water
- 1 cup sauerkraut
- 1 onion, diced
- 1 teaspoon cayenne pepper
- ½ cup Greek yogurt

DIRECTION

- Put beef and onion in the Slow Cooker.
- Add yogurt, water, and cayenne pepper.
- Cook the mixture on low for 8 hours.
- When the beef is cooked, add sauerkraut and stir the soup carefully.
- Cook the soup on high for 30 minutes.

PREPARATION	COOKING TIME	SERVINGS
15	8.5 *hours*	6

Shrimp Chowder

NUTRITION 277 calories, 27.4g protein, 6.1g carbohydrates, 16.3g fat, 1.8g fiber, 239mg cholesterol, 297mg sodium, 401mg potassium.

INGREDIENTS

- 1-pound shrimps
- ½ cup fennel bulb, chopped
- 1 bay leaf
- ½ teaspoon peppercorn
- 1 cup of coconut milk
- 3 cups of water
- 1 teaspoon ground coriander

DIRECTION

- Put all Ingredients: in the Slow Cooker.
- Close the lid and cook the chowder on High for 1 hour.

PREPARATION	COOKING TIME	SERVINGS
15	1 *hours*	4

Ground Pork Soup

NUTRITION 318 calories, 25.7g protein, 10.9g carbohydrates, 16.6g fat, 4.1g fiber, 74mg cholesterol, 651mg sodium, 706mg potassium.

INGREDIENTS

- 1 cup ground pork
- ½ cup red kidney beans, canned
- 1 cup tomatoes, canned
- 4 cups of water
- 1 tablespoon dried cilantro
- 1 teaspoon salt

DIRECTION

- Put ground pork in the Slow Cooker.
- Add tomatoes, water, dried cilantro, and salt. Close the lid and cook the Ingredients: on High for 5 hours.
- Then add canned red kidney beans and cook the soup on high for 30 minutes more.

PREPARATION	COOKING TIME	SERVINGS
15	5 30	4
	hours mins	

Chinese Style Cod Stew

NUTRITION 139 calories, 18.9g protein, 7.4g carbohydrates, 4.2g fat, 2.2g fiber, 42mg cholesterol, 1926mg sodium, 359mg potassium.

INGREDIENTS

- 6 oz. cod fillet
- 1 teaspoon sesame seeds
- 1 teaspoon olive oil
- 1 garlic clove, chopped
- ¼ cup of soy sauce
- ¼ cup fish stock
- 4 oz. fennel bulb, chopped

DIRECTION

- Pour fish stock in the Slow Cooker.
- Add soy sauce, olive oil, garlic, and sesame seeds.
- Then chop the fish roughly and add in the Slow Cooker.
- Cook the meal on Low for 5 hours.

PREPARATION	COOKING TIME	SERVINGS
15	5	2
	hours	

Beans Stew

NUTRITION 74 calories, 3.4g protein, 7.9g carbohydrates, 3.6g fat, 2.4g fiber, 7mg cholesterol, 109mg sodium, 218mg potassium.

INGREDIENTS

- ½ cup sweet pepper, chopped
- ¼ cup onion, chopped
- 1 cup edamame beans
- 1 cup tomatoes
- 1 teaspoon cayenne pepper
- 5 cups of water
- 2 tablespoons cream cheese

DIRECTION

- Mix water with cream cheese and pour the liquid in the Slow Cooker.
- Add cayenne pepper, edamame beans, and onion.
- Then chop the tomatoes roughly and add in the Slow Cooker.
- Close the lid and cook the stew on high for 5 hours.

PREPARATION	COOKING TIME	SERVINGS
15	5 *hours*	3

Creamy Bacon Soup

NUTRITION calories 187, fat 4, fiber 4, carbs 7, protein 8

INGREDIENTS

- 1 tablespoon olive oil
- 6 bacon slices, chopped
- 1 sweet onion, chopped
- 1 1/2 pounds potatoes, peeled and cubed
- 1 parsnip, diced
- 1/2 celery root, cubed
- 2 cups chicken stock
- 3 cups water
- Salt and pepper to taste

DIRECTION

- Heat the oil in a skillet and add the bacon. Cook until crisp then remove the bacon on a plate.
- Pour the fat of the bacon in your Slow Cooker and add the remaining Ingredients.
- Adjust the taste with salt and pepper and cook on high settings for 1 1/2 hours.
- When done, puree the soup with an immersion blender until smooth.
- Pour the soup in a bowl and top with bacon.
- Serve right away.

PREPARATION	COOKING TIME	SERVINGS
15	13/4 *hours*	6

Seafood Stew

NUTRITION calories 270, fat 4, fiber 4, carbs 12, protein 3

INGREDIENTS

- *28 ounces canned tomatoes, crushed*
- *4 cups veggie stock*
- *3 garlic cloves, minced*
- *1 pound sweet potatoes, cubed*
- *½ cup yellow onion, chopped*
- *2 pounds mixed seafood*
- *1 teaspoon thyme, dried*
- *1 teaspoon cilantro, dried*
- *1 teaspoon basil, dried*
- *Salt and black pepper to the taste*
- *A pinch of red pepper flakes, crushed*

DIRECTION

- In your Slow Cooker, mix tomatoes with stock, garlic, sweet potatoes, onion, thyme, cilantro, basil, salt, pepper and pepper flakes, stir, cover and cook on Low for 6 hours.
- Add seafood, stir, cover, and cook on High for 1 more hour, divide stew into bowls and serve for lunch.

PREPARATION	COOKING TIME	SERVINGS
15	7 *hours*	4

Chapter 16. Side Dish Recipes

Garlic Carrots Mix

NUTRITION calories 219, fat 8, fiber 4, carbs 8, protein 17

INGREDIENTS

- 1 pound carrots, sliced
- 2 garlic cloves, minced
- 1 red onion, chopped
- 1 tablespoon olive oil
- ½ cup tomato sauce
- A pinch of salt and black pepper
- ½ teaspoon oregano, dried
- 2 teaspoons lemon zest, grated
- 1 tablespoon lemon juice
- 1 tablespoon chives, chopped

DIRECTION

- In your Crock Pot, mix the carrots with the garlic, onion and then add the other Ingredients, toss, put the lid on and cook on Low for 4 hours.
- Divide the mix between plates and serve.

PREPARATION	COOKING TIME	SERVINGS
15	4 *hours*	2

Marjoram Rice Mix

NUTRITION calories 200, fat 2, fiber 3, carbs 7, protein 5

INGREDIENTS

- 1 cup wild rice
- 2 cups chicken stock
- 1 carrot, peeled and grated
- 2 tablespoons marjoram, chopped
- 1 tablespoon olive oil
- A pinch of salt and black pepper
- 1 tablespoon green onions, chopped

DIRECTION

- In your Crock Pot, mix the rice with the stock and after that add the other Ingredients, toss, put the lid on and cook on Low for 6 hours.
- Divide between plates and serve.

PREPARATION	COOKING TIME	SERVINGS
15	6 *hours*	2

Green Beans and Mushrooms

NUTRITION calories 162, fat 4, fiber 5, carbs 8, protein 4

INGREDIENTS

- 1 pound fresh green beans, trimmed
- 1 small yellow onion, chopped
- 6 ounces bacon, chopped
- 1 garlic clove, minced
- 1 cup chicken stock
- 8 ounces mushrooms, sliced
- Salt and black pepper to the taste
- A splash of balsamic vinegar

DIRECTION

- In your Crock Pot, mix beans with onion, bacon, garlic, stock, mushrooms, salt, pepper and vinegar, stir, cover and cook on Low for 3 hours.
- Divide between plates and serve as a side dish.

PREPARATION	COOKING TIME	SERVINGS
15	3 hours	4

Beans and Red Peppers

NUTRITION Per Serving: Calories: 50, Total Fat: 0g, Fiber: 4g, Total Carbs: 8g, Protein: 2g

INGREDIENTS

- 2 cups green beans, halved
- 1 red bell pepper, cut into strips
- Salt and black pepper to the taste
- 1 tbsp. olive oil
- 1 and ½ tbsp. honey mustard

DIRECTION

- Add green beans; honey mustard, red bell pepper, oil, salt, and black to Crock Pot.
- Put on the cooker's lid on and set the cooking time to hours on High settings.
- Serve warm.

PREPARATION	COOKING TIME	SERVINGS
5	2 hours	2

Cabbage and Onion Mix

NUTRITION calories 211, fat 3, fiber 3, carbs 6, protein 8

INGREDIENTS

- 1 and ½ cups green cabbage, shredded
- 1 cup red cabbage, shredded
- 1 tablespoon olive oil
- 1 red onion, sliced
- 2 spring onions, chopped
- ½ cup tomato paste
- ¼ cup veggie stock
- 2 tomatoes, chopped
- 2 jalapenos, chopped
- 1 tablespoon chili powder
- 1 tablespoon chives, chopped
- A pinch of salt and black pepper

DIRECTION

- Grease your Crock Pot with the oil and mix the cabbage with the onion, spring onions and the other Ingredients: inside.
- Toss, put the lid on and cook on High for hours.
- Divide between plates and serve as a side dish.

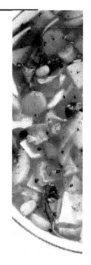

PREPARATION	COOKING TIME	SERVINGS
15	2 hours	2

Cauliflower and Potatoes Mix

NUTRITION calories 135, fat 5, fiber 1, carbs 7, protein 3

INGREDIENTS

- 1 cup cauliflower florets
- ½ pound sweet potatoes, peeled and cubed
- 1 cup veggie stock
- ½ cup tomato sauce
- 1 tablespoon chives, chopped
- Salt and black pepper to the taste
- 1 teaspoon sweet paprika

DIRECTION

- In your Crock Pot, mix the cauliflower with the potatoes, stock and the other Ingredients, toss, put the lid on and cook on High for 4 hours.
- Divide between plates and serve as a side dish.

PREPARATION	COOKING TIME	SERVINGS
15	4 hours	2

Broccoli Mix

NUTRITION calories 159, fat 11, fiber 1, carbs 11, protein 6

INGREDIENTS

- *6 cups broccoli florets*
- *1 and ½ cups cheddar cheese, shredded*
- *10 ounces canned cream of celery soup*
- *½ teaspoon Worcestershire sauce*
- *¼ cup yellow onion, chopped*
- *Salt and black pepper to the taste*
- *1 cup crackers, crushed*
- *2 tablespoons soft butter*

DIRECTION

- In a bowl, mix broccoli with cream of celery soup, cheese, salt, pepper, onion and Worcestershire sauce, toss and transfer to your Crock Pot.
- Add butter, toss again, sprinkle crackers, cover and cook on High for hours.
- Serve as a side dish.

PREPARATION	COOKING TIME	SERVINGS
15	2 *hours*	10

Roasted Beets

NUTRITION calories 100, fat 2, fiber 2, carbs 4, protein 5

INGREDIENTS

- *10 small beets*
- *5 teaspoons olive oil*
- *A pinch of salt and black pepper*

DIRECTION

- Divide each beet on a tin foil piece, drizzle oil, season them with salt and pepper, rub well, wrap beets, place them in your Crock Pot, cover and cook on High for 4 hours.
- Unwrap beets, cool them down a bit, peel, and slice and serve them as a side dish.

PREPARATION	COOKING TIME	SERVINGS
5	4 *hours*	5

Lemony Pumpkin Wedges

NUTRITION Per Serving: Calories: 35, Total Fat: 0.1g, Fiber: 1g, Total Carbs: 8.91g, Protein: 1g

INGREDIENTS

- 15 oz. pumpkin, peeled and cut into wedges
- 1 tbsp. lemon juice
- 1 tsp. salt
- 1 tsp. honey
- ½ tsp. ground cardamom
- 1 tsp. lime juice

DIRECTION

- Add pumpkin, lemon juice, honey, lime juice, cardamom, and salt to the Crock Pot.
- Put the slow cooker's lid on and set the cooking time to 6 hours on Low settings.
- Serve fresh.

PREPARATION	COOKING TIME	SERVINGS
15	6 *hours*	4

Thai Side Salad

NUTRITION calories 69, fat 2, fiber 2, carbs 8, protein 2

INGREDIENTS

- 8 ounces yellow summer squash, peeled and roughly chopped
- 12 ounces zucchini, halved and sliced
- 2 cups button mushrooms, quartered
- 1 red sweet potatoes, chopped
- 2 leeks, sliced
- 2 tablespoons veggie stock
- 2 garlic cloves, minced
- 2 tablespoon Thai red curry paste
- 1 tablespoon ginger, grated
- 1/3 cup coconut milk
- ¼ cup basil, chopped

DIRECTION

- In your Crock Pot, mix zucchini with summer squash, mushrooms, red pepper, leeks, garlic, stock, curry paste, ginger, coconut milk and basil, toss, cover and cook on Low for 3 hours.
- Stir your Thai mix one more time, divide between plates and serve as a side dish.

PREPARATION	COOKING TIME	SERVINGS
15	3 *hours*	8

Eggplants with Mayo Sauce

NUTRITION Per Serving: Calories: 40, Total Fat: 1.1g, Fiber: 3g, Total Carbs: 7.5g, Protein: 1g

INGREDIENTS

- 2 tbsp. minced garlic
- 1 chili pepper, chopped
- 1 sweet pepper, chopped
- 4 tbsp. mayo
- 1 tsp. olive oil
- 1 tsp. salt
- ½ tsp. ground black pepper
- 18 oz. eggplants, peeled and diced
- 2 tbsp. sour cream

DIRECTION

- Blend chili pepper, sweet peppers, salt, garlic, and black pepper in a blender until smooth.
- Add eggplant and this chili mixture to the Crock Pot then toss them well.
- Now mix mayo with sour cream and spread on top of eggplants.
- Put the cooker's lid on and set the cooking time to 5 hours on High settings.
- Serve warm

PREPARATION	COOKING TIME	SERVINGS
15	5 hours	8

Summer Squash Medley

NUTRITION Per Serving: Calories: 179, Total Fat: 13g, Fiber: 2g, Total Carbs: 10g, Protein: 4g

INGREDIENTS

- ¼ cup olive oil
- 2 tbsp. basil, chopped
- 2 tbsp. balsamic vinegar
- 2 garlic cloves, minced
- 2 tsp. mustard
- Salt and black pepper to the taste
- 3 summer squash, sliced
- 2 zucchinis, sliced

DIRECTION

- Add squash, zucchinis, and all other Ingredients: to the Crock Pot.
- Put the cooker's lid on and set the cooking time to hours on High settings.
- Serve.

PREPARATION	COOKING TIME	SERVINGS
15	2 hours	4

Garlic Butter Green Beans

NUTRITION calories 60, fat 4, fiber 1, carbs 3, protein 1

INGREDIENTS

- 22 ounces green beans
- 2 garlic cloves, minced
- ¼ cup butter, soft
- 2 tablespoons parmesan, grated

DIRECTION

- In your Crock Pot, mix green beans with garlic, butter and parmesan, toss, cover and cook on High for 2 hours.
- Divide between plates, sprinkle parmesan all over and serve as a side dish.

PREPARATION	COOKING TIME	SERVINGS
15	2 *hours*	6

Green Beans and Red Peppers

NUTRITION calories 50, fat 0, fiber 4, carbs 8, protein 2

INGREDIENTS

- 2 cups green beans, halved
- 1 red bell pepper, cut into strips
- Salt and black pepper to the taste
- 1 tablespoon olive oil
- 1 and ½ tablespoon honey mustard

DIRECTION

- In your Crock Pot, mix green beans with bell pepper, salt, pepper, oil and honey mustard, toss, cover and cook on High for 2 hours.
- Divide between plates and serve as a side dish.

PREPARATION	COOKING TIME	SERVINGS
15	2 *hours*	2

Cauliflower Carrot Gratin

NUTRITION Net Carbs: 3g; Calories: 579; Total Fat: 51g; Saturated Fat: 12g; Protein: 28g; Carbs: 4g; Fiber: 1g; Sugar: 0.1g

INGREDIENTS

- 16 oz. baby carrots
- 6 tbsp. butter, soft
- 1 cauliflower head, florets separated
- Salt and black pepper to the taste
- 1 yellow onion, chopped
- 1 tsp. mustard powder
- 1 and ½ cups of milk
- 6 oz. cheddar cheese, grated
- ½ cup breadcrumbs

DIRECTION

- Place pork in a 6-quart slow cooker, season with salt and thyme, add peppercorns and bay leaf and then pour in water.
- Plug in the slow cooker, then shut with its lid and cook for 8 hours at low heat setting or 4 hours at high heat setting.
- When done, transfer pork to a baking dish and reserve cooking sauce in a saucepan.
- Set oven to 450 degrees F and let preheat.
- In the meantime, stir together remaining Ingredients: in a small bowl until combined and then brush mixture all over pork.
- Place the baking sheet into the oven to bake pork for 10 to 15 minutes or until roasted.
- Cut roasted pork into thin slices and serve with reserved cooking sauce.

PREPARATION	COOKING TIME	SERVINGS
15	7 *hours*	12

Minty Peas and Tomatoes

NUTRITION calories 70, fat 1, fiber 1, carbs 4, protein 6

INGREDIENTS

- 1 pound okra, sliced
- ½ pound tomatoes, cut into wedges
- 1 tablespoon olive oil
- ½ cup veggie stock
- ½ teaspoon chili powder
- Salt and black pepper to the taste
- 1 tablespoon mint, chopped
- 3 green onions, chopped
- 1 tablespoon chives, chopped

DIRECTION

- Grease your Crock Pot with the oil, and mix the okra with the tomatoes and the other Ingredients: inside.
- Put the lid on, cook on Low for 3 hours, divide between plates and serve as a side dish.

PREPARATION	COOKING TIME	SERVINGS
15	3 *hours*	2

Lemon Artichokes

NUTRITION calories 100, fat 2, fiber 5, carbs 10, protein 4

INGREDIENTS

- 1 cup veggie stock
- 2 medium artichokes, trimmed
- 1 tablespoon lemon juice
- 1 tablespoon lemon zest, grated
- Salt to the taste

DIRECTION

- In your Crock Pot, mix the artichokes with the stock and the other Ingredients, and then toss it, put the lid on and cook on Low for 3 hours.
- Divide artichokes between plates and serve as a side dish.

PREPARATION	COOKING TIME	SERVINGS
15	3 hours	2

Mashed Potatoes

NUTRITION calories 135, fat 4, fiber 2, carbs 10, protein 4

INGREDIENTS

- 1 pound gold potatoes, peeled and cubed
- 2 garlic cloves, chopped
- 1 cup milk
- 1 cup water
- 2 tablespoons butter
- A pinch of salt and white pepper

DIRECTION

- In your Crock Pot, mix the potatoes with the water, salt and pepper, put the lid on and cook on Low for 6 hours.
- Mash the potatoes; add the rest of the Ingredients, whisk and serve.

PREPARATION	COOKING TIME	SERVINGS
15	6 hours	2

Jalapeno Meal

NUTRITION *Per Serving: Calories: 67, Total Fat: 4.7g, Fiber: 2g, Total Carbs: 6.02g, Protein: 1g*

PREPARATION	COOKING TIME	SERVINGS
15	6 *hours*	6

DIRECTION

- Place the jalapeno peppers in the Crock Pot.
- Top the pepper with olive oil, balsamic vinegar, onion, garlic, coriander, and water.
- Put the cooker's lid on and set the cooking time to 6 hours on Low settings.
- Serve warm.

INGREDIENTS

- 12 oz. jalapeno pepper, cut in half and deseeded
- 2 tbsp. olive oil
- 1 tbsp. balsamic vinegar
- 1 onion, sliced
- 1 garlic clove, sliced
- 1 tsp. ground coriander
- 4 tbsp. water

Blueberry Spinach Salad

NUTRITION *Per Serving: Calories: 140, Total Fat: 4g, Fiber: 3g, Total Carbs: 10g, Protein: 3g*

PREPARATION	COOKING TIME	SERVINGS
15	1 *hours*	3

DIRECTION

- Add pecans, maple syrup, and rest of the Ingredients: to the Crock Pot.
- Put the cooker's lid on and set the cooking time to 1 hour on High settings.
- Serve warm.

INGREDIENTS

- ¼ cup pecans, chopped
- ½ tsp. sugar
- 2 tsp. maple syrup
- 1 tbsp. white vinegar
- 2 tbsp. orange juice
- 1 tbsp. olive oil
- 4 cups spinach
- 2 oranges, peeled and cut into segments
- 1 cup blueberries

Dill Mixed Fennel

NUTRITION Per Serving: Calories: 53, Total Fat: 4.1g, Fiber: 2g, Total Carbs: 4g, Protein: 1g

PREPARATION	COOKING TIME	SERVINGS
15	3 hours 10 mins	6

INGREDIENTS

- 10 oz. fennel bulbs, diced
- 2 tbsp. olive oil
- 1 tsp. ground black pepper
- 1 tsp. paprika
- 1 tsp. cilantro
- 1 tsp. oregano
- 1 tsp. basil
- 3 tbsp. white wine
- 1 tsp. salt
- 2 garlic cloves
- 1 tsp. dried dill

DIRECTION

- Add fennel bulbs and all other Ingredients: to the Crock Pot.
- Put the cooker's lid on and set the cooking time to 3.5 hours on High settings.
- Serve warm.

Okra and Corn

NUTRITION calories 182, fat 3, fiber 6, carbs 8, protein 5

PREPARATION	COOKING TIME	SERVINGS
15	8 hours	4

DIRECTION

- In your Crock Pot, mix garlic with bell pepper, onion, water, okra, corn, paprika, tomatoes, oregano, thyme, marjoram, cayenne, salt and pepper, cover, cook on Low for 8 hours, divide between plates and serve as a side dish.

INGREDIENTS

- 3 garlic cloves, minced
- 1 small green bell pepper, chopped
- 1 small yellow onion, chopped
- 1 cup water
- 16 ounces okra, sliced
- 2 cups corn
- 1 and ½ teaspoon smoked paprika
- 28 ounces canned tomatoes, crushed
- 1 teaspoon oregano, dried
- 1 teaspoon thyme, dried
- 1 teaspoon marjoram, dried
- A pinch of cayenne pepper
- Salt and black pepper to the taste

Savoy Cabbage Mix

NUTRITION calories 100, fat 3, fiber 4, carbs 5, protein 2

PREPARATION	COOKING TIME	SERVINGS
15	2 _hours_	2

INGREDIENTS

- 1 pound Savoy cabbage, shredded
- 1 red onion, sliced
- 1 tablespoon olive oil
- ½ cup veggie stock
- A pinch of salt and black pepper
- 1 carrot, grated
- ½ cup tomatoes, cubed
- ½ teaspoon sweet paprika
- ½ inch ginger, grated

DIRECTION

- In your Crock Pot, mix the cabbage with the onion, oil and the other Ingredients, toss, put the lid on and cook it on High for two hours.
- Divide the mix between plates and serve as a side dish.

Balsamic-glazed Beets

NUTRITION Per Serving: Calories: 189, Total Fat: 11.3g, Fiber: 2g, Total Carbs: 12g, Protein: 10g

PREPARATION	COOKING TIME	SERVINGS
15	9 _hours_	2

INGREDIENTS

- 1 lb. beets, sliced
- 5 oz. orange juice
- 3 oz. balsamic vinegar
- 3 tbsp. almonds
- 6 oz. goat cheese
- 1 tsp. minced garlic
- 1 tsp. olive oil

DIRECTION

- Toss the beets with balsamic vinegar, orange juice, and olive oil in the insert of Crock Pot.
- Put the slow cooker's lid on and set the cooking time to 7 hours on Low settings.
- Toss goat cheese with minced garlic and almonds in a bowl.
- Spread this cheese garlic mixture over the beets.
- Put the cooker's lid on and set the cooking time to 10 minutes on High settings.
- Serve warm.

Cauliflower Rice and Spinach

NUTRITION *calories 200, fat 4, fibre 4, carbs 8, protein 2*

PREPARATION	COOKING TIME	SERVINGS
15	3 *hours*	8

DIRECTION

- Heat up a pan with the butter over medium heat, add onion, stir and cook for 4 minutes.
- Add garlic, thyme and stock, stir, cook for 1 minute more and transfer to your Crock Pot.
- Add spinach, coconut cream, cauliflower rice, salt and pepper, stir a bit, cover and cook on High for hours.
- Divide between plates and serve as a side dish.

INGREDIENTS

- 2 garlic cloves, minced
- 2 tablespoons butter, melted
- 1 yellow onion, chopped
- ¼ teaspoon thyme, dried
- 3 cups veggie stock
- 20 ounces spinach, chopped
- 6 ounces coconut cream
- Salt and black pepper to the taste
- 2 cups cauliflower rice

Cumin Quinoa Pilaf

NUTRITION *calories 152, fat 3, fiber 6, carbs 8, protein 4*

PREPARATION	COOKING TIME	SERVINGS
15	2 *hours*	2

DIRECTION

- Grease your Crock Pot with the butter, add the quinoa and the other Ingredients:, toss, put the lid on and then cook on High for about 2 hours
- Divide between plates and serve as a side dish.

INGREDIENTS

- 1 cup quinoa
- 2 teaspoons butter, melted
- Salt and black pepper to the taste
- 1 teaspoon turmeric powder
- 2 cups chicken stock
- 1 teaspoon cumin, ground

Balsamic Okra Mix

NUTRITION *calories 233, fat 12, fiber 4, carbs 8, protein 4*

PREPARATION	COOKING TIME	SERVINGS
15	2 *hours*	4

INGREDIENTS

- 2 cups okra, sliced
- 1 cup cherry tomatoes, halved
- 1 tablespoon olive oil
- ½ teaspoon turmeric powder
- ½ cup canned tomatoes, crushed
- 2 tablespoons balsamic vinegar
- 2 tablespoons basil, chopped
- 1 tablespoon thyme, chopped

DIRECTION

- In your Crock Pot, mix the okra with the tomatoes, crushed tomatoes and the other Ingredients, toss, put the lid on and cook on High for 2 hours.
- Divide between plates and serve as a side dish.

Asparagus Mix

NUTRITION *calories 241, fat 5, fiber 4, carbs 5, protein 12*

PREPARATION	COOKING TIME	SERVINGS
15	6 *hours*	4

DIRECTION

- Grease your Crock Pot with the oil, add cream of celery and cheese to the Crock Pot and stir.
- Add asparagus and eggs, cover and cook on Low for 6 hours.
- Divide between plates and serve as a side dish.

INGREDIENTS

- 10 ounces cream of celery
- 12 ounces asparagus, chopped
- 2 eggs, hard-boiled, peeled and sliced
- 1 cup cheddar cheese, shredded
- 1 teaspoon olive oil

Tarragon Sweet Potatoes

NUTRITION *calories 80, fat 4, fiber 4, carbs 8, protein 4*

PREPARATION	COOKING TIME	SERVINGS
15	3 *hours*	4

INGREDIENTS

- 1 pound sweet potatoes, peeled and cut into wedges
- 1 cup veggie stock
- ½ teaspoon chili powder
- ½ teaspoon cumin, ground
- Salt and black pepper to the taste
- 1 tablespoon olive oil
- 1 tablespoon tarragon, dried
- 2 tablespoons balsamic vinegar

DIRECTION

- In your Crock Pot, mix the sweet potatoes with the stock, chili powder and the other Ingredients, toss, put the lid on and cook on High for 3 hours.
- Divide the mix between plates and serve as a side dish.

Classic Veggies Mix

NUTRITION *calories 150, fat 2, fiber 2, carbs 6, protein 5*

PREPARATION	COOKING TIME	SERVINGS
15	3 *hours*	4

DIRECTION

- In your Crock Pot, mix onion pieces with tomatoes, zucchini, bell pepper, mushrooms, basil, thyme, oil and vinegar, toss to coat everything, cover and cook on High for 3 hours.
- Divide between plates and serve as a side dish.

INGREDIENTS

- 1 and ½ cups red onion, cut into medium chunks
- 1 cup cherry tomatoes, halved
- 2 and ½ cups zucchini, sliced
- 2 cups yellow bell pepper, chopped
- 1 cup mushrooms, sliced
- 2 tablespoons basil, chopped
- 1 tablespoon thyme, chopped
- ½ cup olive oil
- ½ cup balsamic vinegar

Mint Farro Pilaf

NUTRITION   *calories 162, fat 3, fiber 6, carbs 9, protein 4*

PREPARATION	COOKING TIME	SERVINGS
15	**4** hours	2

INGREDIENTS

- ½ tablespoon balsamic vinegar
- ½ cup whole grain farro
- A pinch of salt and black pepper
- 1 cup chicken stock
- ½ tablespoon olive oil
- 1 tablespoon green onions, chopped
- 1 tablespoon mint, chopped

DIRECTION

- In your Crock Pot, mix the farro with the vinegar and the other Ingredients, toss, put the lid on and cook on Low for 4 hours.
- Divide between plates and serve.

Chapter 17. Dessert Recipes

Almond Pie

NUTRITION *calories 90, fat 9.1, fiber 0.9, carbs 2.6, protein 1.2*

PREPARATION	COOKING TIME	SERVINGS
15	41 *mins*	6

INGREDIENTS

- 1 cup almond flour
- ½ cup of coconut milk
- 1 teaspoon vanilla extract
- 2 tablespoons butter, softened
- 1 tablespoon Truvia
- ¼ cup coconut, shredded
- 1 cup water, for cooking

DIRECTION

- In the mixing bowl, mix up almond flour, coconut milk, vanilla extract, butter, Truvia, and shredded coconut.
- When the mixture is smooth, transfer it in the baking pan and flatten.
- Pour water and insert the steamer rack in the instant pot.
- Put the baking pan with cake on the rack. Close and seal the lid.
- Cook the dessert on manual mode (high pressure) for 41 minutes. Allow the natural pressure release for 10 minutes.

Coconut Cupcakes

NUTRITION *calories 86, fat 5.8, fiber 2.2, carbs 9.2, protein 4.6*

PREPARATION	COOKING TIME	SERVINGS
15	1.5 *hours*	3

DIRECTION

- In the mixing bowl, mix up eggs, coconut milk, coconut flour, vanilla extract, Erythritol, and baking powder.
- Then pour the batter in the cupcake molds.
- Pour water and insert the steamer rack in the instant pot.
- Place the cupcakes on the rack. Close and seal the lid.
- Cook the cupcakes for 10 minutes on manual mode (high pressure).
- Then allow the natural pressure release for 5 minutes.

INGREDIENTS

- 4 eggs, beaten
- 4 tablespoons coconut milk
- 4 tablespoons coconut flour
- ½ teaspoon vanilla extract
- 2 tablespoons Erythritol
- 1 teaspoon baking powder
- 1 cup water, for cooking

Anise Hot Chocolate

NUTRITION *calories 131, fat 13.5, fiber 1.4, carbs 8.5, protein 1.5*

PREPARATION	COOKING TIME	SERVINGS
5	2 *hours*	3

INGREDIENTS

- 1 tablespoon cocoa powder
- 1 tablespoon Erythritol
- ¼ cup heavy cream
- ½ cup of coconut milk
- ½ teaspoon ground anise

DIRECTION

- Put all Ingredients in the instant pot bowl. Stir them well until you get a smooth liquid.
- Close and seal the lid.
- Cook the hot chocolate on manual (high pressure) for 2 minutes. Then allow the natural pressure release for 5 minutes.

Chocolate Mousse

NUTRITION *calories 162, fat 15.4, fiber 1.2, carbs 3.5, protein 4.5*

PREPARATION	COOKING TIME	SERVINGS
10	4 *hours*	1

DIRECTION

- Pour water and insert the steamer rack in the instant pot.
- Then whisk the egg yolk with Erythritol.
- When the mixture turns into lemon color, add coconut milk, cream cheese, and cocoa powder. Whisk the mixture until smooth.
- Then pour it in the glass jar and place it on the steamer rack.
- Close and seal the lid.
- Cook the dessert on manual (high pressure) for 4 minutes. Make a quick pressure release.

INGREDIENTS

- 1 egg yolk
- 1 teaspoon Erythritol
- 1 teaspoon of cocoa powder
- 2 tablespoons coconut milk
- 1 tablespoon cream cheese
- 1 cup water, for cooking

Lime Muffins

NUTRITION calories 153, fat 12.2, fiber 2.1, carbs 5.1, protein 6

PREPARATION	COOKING TIME	SERVINGS
10	15 mins	6

INGREDIENTS

- 1 teaspoon lime zest
- 1 tablespoon lemon juice
- 1 teaspoon baking powder
- 1 cup almond flour
- 2 eggs, beaten
- 1 tablespoon swerve
- ¼ cup heavy cream
- 1 cup water, for cooking

DIRECTION

- In the mixing bowl, mix up lemon juice, baking powder, almond flour, eggs, swerve, and heavy cream.
- When the muffin batter is smooth, add lime zest and mix it up.
- Fill the muffin molds with batter.
- Then pour water and insert the rack in the instant pot.
- Place the muffins on the rack. Close and seal the lid.
- Cook the muffins on manual (high pressure) for 15 minutes.
- Then allow the natural pressure release.

Blueberry Muffins

NUTRITION calories 95, fat 4.5, fiber 6.1, carbs 14.6, protein 3.4

PREPARATION	COOKING TIME	SERVINGS
15	14 mins	3

DIRECTION

- In the mixing bowl, mix up baking powder, apple cider vinegar, butter, eggs, coconut flour, and Erythritol.
- When the batter is smooth, add blueberries. Stir well.
- Put the muffin batter in the muffin molds.
- After this, pour water and insert the steamer rack in the instant pot.
- Then place the muffins on the rack. Close and seal the lid.
- Cook the muffins on manual mode (high pressure) for 14 minutes.
- When the time is finished, allow the natural pressure release for 6 minutes.

INGREDIENTS

- ¼ cup blueberries
- ¼ teaspoon baking powder
- 1 teaspoon apple cider vinegar
- 4 teaspoons butter, melted
- 2 eggs, beaten
- 1 cup coconut flour
- 2 tablespoons Erythritol
- 1 cup water, for cooking

Low Carb Brownie

NUTRITION *calories 146, fat 11, fiber 6.2, carbs 12.6, protein 2.2*

PREPARATION	COOKING TIME	SERVINGS
15	18 mins	8

INGREDIENTS

- 1 cup coconut flour
- 1 tablespoon cocoa powder
- 1 tablespoon coconut oil
- 1 teaspoon vanilla extract
- 1 teaspoon baking powder
- 1 teaspoon apple cider vinegar
- 1/3 cup butter, melted
- 1 tablespoon Erythritol
- 1 cup water, for cooking

DIRECTION

- In the mixing bowl, mix up Erythritol, melted butter, apple cider vinegar, baking powder, vanilla extract, coconut oil, cocoa powder, and coconut flour.
- Whisk the mixture until smooth and pour it in the baking pan. Flatten the surface of the batter.
- Pour water and insert the steamer rack in the instant pot.
- Put the pan with brownie batter on the rack. Close and seal the lid.
- Cook the brownie on manual mode (high pressure) for 15 minutes.
- Then allow the natural pressure release for 5 minutes.
- Cut the cooked brownies into the bars.

Pecan Pie

NUTRITION *calories 257, fat 26.1, fiber 3, carbs 8.5, protein 3.3*

PREPARATION	COOKING TIME	SERVINGS
20	25 mins	4

DIRECTION

- Make the pie crust: mix up coconut oil and almond flour in the bowl.
- Then knead the dough and put it in the baking pan. Flatten the dough in the shape of the pie crust.
- Then melt Erythritol, butter, and coconut flour.
- When the mixture is liquid, add chopped pecans.
- Pour water in the instant pot and insert the steamer rack.
- Pour the butter-pecan mixture over the pie crust, flatten it and transfer on the steamer rack.
- Cook the pecan pie on manual mode (high pressure) for 25 minutes.
- Allow the natural pressure release for 10 minutes and cool the cooked pie well.

INGREDIENTS

- 2 tablespoons coconut oil
- 4 tablespoons almond flour
- 4 pecans, chopped
- 1 tablespoon Erythritol
- 2 tablespoons butter
- 1 tablespoon coconut flour
- 1 cup water, for cooking

Vanilla Flan

NUTRITION calories 269, fat 25.8, fiber 0, carbs 2.3, protein 7.4

PREPARATION	COOKING TIME	SERVINGS
10	8 mins	4

INGREDIENTS

- 4 egg whites
- 4 egg yolks
- ½ cup Erythritol
- 7 oz. heavy cream, whipped
- 3 tablespoons water
- 1 tablespoon butter
- ½ teaspoon vanilla extract
- 1 cup water, for cooking

DIRECTION

- In the mixing bowl, mix up coconut flour, Erythritol, vanilla extract, eggs, and heavy cream.
- Grease the baking pan with melted butter.
- Pour the coconut mixture in the baking pan.
- Pour water and insert the steamer rack in the instant pot.
- Place the pie on the rack. Close and seal the lid.
- Cook the pie on manual mode (high pressure) for 35 minutes.
- Allow the natural pressure release for 10 minutes.

Vanilla Pie

NUTRITION calories 100, fat 6.8, fiber 4, carbs 12.1, protein 2.9

PREPARATION	COOKING TIME	SERVINGS
20	35 mins	12

DIRECTION

- In a slow cooker, place Velveeta cheese cubes.
- Cook on low and cook, covered, for about 30–60 minutes, stirring occasionally.
- Uncover the slow cooker and stir in tomatoes and taco seasoning. Cook, covered, for about 30 minutes
- Serve hot.

INGREDIENTS

- 1 cup heavy cream
- 3 eggs, beaten
- 1 teaspoon vanilla extract
- ¼ cup Erythritol
- 1 cup coconut flour
- 1 tablespoon butter, melted
- 1 cup water, for cooking

Custard

NUTRITION *calories 209, fat 17.9, fiber 0.8, carbs 10.3, protein 9.2*

PREPARATION	COOKING TIME	SERVINGS
10	7 mins	4

INGREDIENTS

- 6 eggs, beaten
- 1 cup heavy cream
- 1 teaspoon vanilla extract
- ¼ teaspoon ground nutmeg
- 2 tablespoons Erythritol
- 1 tablespoon coconut flour
- 1 cup water, for cooking

DIRECTION

- Whisk the eggs and Erythritol until smooth.
- Then add heavy cream, vanilla extract, ground nutmeg, and coconut flour.
- Whisk the mixture well again.
- Then pour it in the custard ramekins and cover with foil.
- Pour water and insert the steamer rack in the instant pot.
- Place the ramekins with custard on the rack. Close and seal the lid.
- Cook the meal on manual (high pressure) for 7 minutes. Make a quick pressure release.

Crème Brule

NUTRITION *calories 347, fat 33.5, fiber 0, carbs 5.2, protein 8*

PREPARATION	COOKING TIME	SERVINGS
10	25 mins	2

INGREDIENTS

- 1 cup heavy cream
- 5 egg yolks
- 2 tablespoons swerve
- 1 cup water, for cooking

DIRECTION

- Whisk the egg yolks and swerve together.
- Then add heavy cream and stir the mixture carefully.
- Pour the mixture in ramekins and place them on the steamer rack.
- Pour water in the instant pot. Add steamer rack with ramekins.
- Close and seal the lid.
- Cook crème Brule for 10 minutes – High pressure. Allow the natural pressure release for 15 minutes.

Lava Cake

NUTRITION *calories 218, fat 19.2, fiber 5.9, carbs 14.2, protein 3.4*

PREPARATION	COOKING TIME	SERVINGS
15	8 mins	4

DIRECTION

- Whisk together baking powder, cocoa powder, coconut cream, coconut flour, almond flour, Erythritol, and butter.
- Then pour the chocolate mixture in the baking cups.
- Pour water in the instant pot. Insert the steamer rack.
- Place the cups with cake mixture on the rack. Close and seal the lid.
- Cook the lava cakes on manual (high pressure) for 4 minutes. Allow the natural pressure release for 5 minutes.

INGREDIENTS

- 1 teaspoon baking powder
- 1 tablespoon cocoa powder
- 1 cup coconut cream
- 1/3 cup coconut flour
- 1 tablespoon almond flour
- 2 teaspoons Erythritol
- 1 tablespoon butter, melted
- 1 cup water, for cooking

Lemon Cake

NUTRITION *Calories: 142 , Carbs: 0g , Fat: 8g , Protein: 0g*

PREPARATION	COOKING TIME	SERVINGS
15	1.5 hours	3

DIRECTION

- In a bowl, combine the almonds, coconut, sweetener, baking powder. Whisk until combined.
- In a separate bowl, blend coconut oil, cream, juice, and eggs.
- Add the egg mixture to the dry fixing, mix.
- Line the crockpot with aluminum foil, pour in the batter.
- In a bowl, mix the topping. Pour it over the cake batter.
- Cover it with paper towels to absorb the water.
- Cover, cook on high for 3 hours. Serve warm.

INGREDIENTS

- 1 ½ cup ground almonds
- ½ cup coconut flakes
- 6 Tablespoons sweetener like Swerve (Erythritol, or a suitable substitute)
- 2 teaspoons baking powder
- Pinch of salt
- ½ cup softened coconut oil
- ½ cup cooking cream
- 2 Tablespoons lemon juice
- Zest from two lemons
- 2 eggs
- Topping:
- 3 tablespoons Swerve (or a suitable substitute)
- ½ cup boiling water
- 2 Tablespoons lemon juice
- 2 Tablespoons softened coconut oil

Raspberry & Coconut Cake

NUTRITION *Calories: 201 , Carbs: 24g, Fat: 10g, Protein: 0g*

PREPARATION	COOKING TIME	SERVINGS
15	3 hours	10

INGREDIENTS

- 2 cups ground almonds
- 1 cup shredded coconut
- ¾ cup sweetener, Swerve (or a suitable substitute)
- 2 teaspoon baking soda
- ¼ teaspoon salt
- 4 large eggs
- ½ cup melted coconut oil
- ¾ cup of coconut milk
- 1 cup raspberries, fresh or frozen
- ½ cup sugarless dark chocolate chips

DIRECTION

- Butter the crockpot.
- In a bowl, mix the dry ingredients.
- Beat in the eggs, melted coconut oil, and coconut milk. Mix in the raspberries plus chocolate chips.
- Combine the cocoa, almonds, and salt in a bowl.
- Pour the batter into the buttered crockpot.
- Cover the crockpot with a paper towel to absorb the water.
- Cover, cook on low for 3 hours. Let the cake cool in the pot.

Chocolate Cheesecake

NUTRITION *Calories: 330, Carbs: 34g , Fat: 19g , Protein: 6g*

PREPARATION	COOKING TIME	SERVINGS
15	2.5 hours	8

DIRECTION

- Whisk the cream cheese, sweetener, and salt in a bowl.
- Add the eggs one at a time. Combine thoroughly.
- Spread the cheesecake in a cake pan, which fits in the crockpot you are using.
- Dissolved the chocolate chips in a small pot and pour over the batter. Using a knife, swirl the chocolate through the batter.
- Put 2 cups of water inside the crockpot and set the cake pan inside. Cover it with a paper towel to absorb the water, then cook on high for 2.5 hours. Remove from the crockpot and let it cool in the pan for 1 hour. Refrigerate.

INGREDIENTS

- 3 cups cream cheese
- Pinch of salt
- 3 eggs
- 1 cup powder sweetener of your choice, Swerve (or a suitable substitute)
- 1 teaspoon vanilla extract
- ½ cup sugarless dark chocolate chips

Crème Brule

NUTRITION Calories: 120 , Carbs: 18g , Fat: 4g , Protein: 3g

PREPARATION	COOKING TIME	SERVINGS
15	2 hours	6

INGREDIENTS

- 5 large egg yolks
- 6 Tablespoons sweetener, Erythritol
- 2 cups double cream
- 1 Bourbon vanilla pod, scraped
- Pinch of salt

DIRECTION

- In a bowl, beat the eggs and sweetener together.
- Add the cream and vanilla. Whisk together.
- Put it in one big dish.
- Set it in the crockpot and pour hot water around- so the water reaches halfway up the dish.
- Cover, cook on high for 2 hours.
- Take the dishes out, let them cool. Refrigerate for 6-8 hours.

Peanut Butter & Chocolate Cake

NUTRITION Calories: 270 , Carbs: 39g , Fat: 11g , Protein: 5g

PREPARATION	COOKING TIME	SERVINGS
15	4 hours	12

DIRECTION

- Grease the crockpot well.
- In a bowl, mix the dry ingredients. Stir in the wet ingredients one at a time.
- Spread about 2/3 of batter in the crockpot, add half the chocolate. Swirl with a fork. Top up with the remaining batter and chocolate. Swirl again.
- Cook on low for 4 hours. Switch off. Let it sit covered for 30 minutes.

INGREDIENTS

- 1 Tablespoon butter for greasing the crockpot
- 2 cups almond flour
- ¾ cup sweetener of your choice
- ¼ cup coconut flakes
- ¼ cup whey protein powder
- 1 teaspoon baking powder
- ¼ teaspoon salt
- ¾ cup peanut butter, melted
- 4 large eggs
- 1 teaspoon vanilla extract
- ½ cup of water
- 3 Tablespoons sugarless dark chocolate, melted

Berry & Coconut Cake

NUTRITION Calories: 263 , Carbs: 9g , Fat: 22g , Protein: 5g

PREPARATION	COOKING TIME	SERVINGS
15	2 hours	8

DIRECTION

- Butter the crockpot well.
- In a bowl, whisk the egg, coconut milk, and oil together.
- Mix the dry ingredients. Slowly stir in the wet ingredients. Do not over mix.
- Pour the batter in the crockpot, spread evenly.
- Spread the berries on top.
- Cover, cook on high for 2 hours. Cool in the crock for 1-2 hours.

INGREDIENTS

- 1 Tablespoon butter for greasing the crock
- 1 cup almond flour
- ¾ cup sweetener of your choice
- 1 teaspoon baking soda
- ¼ teaspoon salt
- 1 large egg, beaten with a fork
- ¼ cup coconut flour
- ¼ cup of coconut milk
- 2 Tablespoons coconut oil
- 4 cups fresh or frozen blueberries and raspberries

Cocoa Pudding Cake

NUTRITION Calories: 250 , Carbs: 29g , Fat: 5g , Protein: 22g

PREPARATION	COOKING TIME	SERVINGS
15	3 hours	10

DIRECTION

- Butter the crockpot thoroughly.
- Whisk the dry fixing in a bowl.
- Stir in the melted butter, eggs, cream, and vanilla. Mix well.
- Pour the batter into the crockpot and spread evenly.
- Cook within 2½ to 3 hours, low. If preferred – more like pudding, cook cake shorter; more dry cake, cook longer.
- Cool in the crockpot for 30 minutes. Cut and serve.

INGREDIENTS

- 1 Tablespoon butter for greasing the crockpot
- 1 ½ cups ground almonds
- ¾ cup sweetener, Swerve (or a suitable substitute)
- ¾ cup cocoa powder
- ¼ cup whey protein
- 2 teaspoons baking powder
- ¼ teaspoon salt
- 4 large eggs
- ½ cup butter, melted
- ¾ cup full-fat cream
- 1 teaspoon vanilla extract

Keto Coconut Hot Chocolate

NUTRITION Calories: 135, Carbs: 5g , Fat: 11g , Protein: 5g

PREPARATION	COOKING TIME	SERVINGS
15	4 *hours*	8

INGREDIENTS

- 5 cups full-fat coconut milk
- 2 cups heavy cream
- 1 tsp vanilla extract
- 1/3 cup cocoa powder
- 3 ounces dark chocolate, roughly chopped
- ½ tsp cinnamon
- Few drops of stevia to taste

DIRECTION

- Add the coconut milk, cream, vanilla extract, cocoa powder, chocolate, cinnamon, and stevia to the crockpot and stir to combine.
- Cook for 4 hours, high, whisking every 45 minutes.
- Taste the hot chocolate and if you prefer more sweetness, add a few more drops of stevia.

Ambrosia

NUTRITION Calories: 57, Carbs: 11g , Fat: 1g , Protein: 1g

PREPARATION	COOKING TIME	SERVINGS
15	3 *hours*	10

DIRECTION

- Place the shredded coconut, slivered almonds, dark chocolate, pumpkin seeds, butter, and cinnamon into the crockpot.
- Cook for 3 hours, high, stirring every 45 minutes to combine the chocolate and butter as it melts.
- Remove the mixture from the crockpot, place in a bowl, and leave to cool.
- In a large bowl, whip the cream until softly whipped.
- Stir the yogurt through the cream.
- Slice the strawberries into pieces, then put it to the cream mixture, along with the other berries you are using, fold through.
- Sprinkle the cooled coconut mixture over the cream mixture.

INGREDIENTS

- 1 cup unsweetened shredded coconut
- ¾ cup slivered almonds
- 3 ounces dark chocolate (high cocoa percentage), roughly chopped
- 1/3 cup pumpkin seeds
- 2 ounces salted butter
- 1 tsp cinnamon
- 2 cups heavy cream
- 2 cups full-fat Greek yogurt
- 1 cup fresh berries – strawberries and raspberries are best

Dark Chocolate and Peppermint Pots

NUTRITION Calories: 125 , Carbs: 15g , Fat: 6g , Protein: 1g

PREPARATION   COOKING TIME   SERVINGS

15   2   6

hours

INGREDIENTS

- 2 ½ cups heavy cream
- 3 ounces dark chocolate, melted in the microwave
- 4 egg yolks, lightly beaten with a fork
- Few drops of stevia
- Few drops of peppermint essence to taste

DIRECTION

- Mix the beaten egg yolks, cream, stevia, melted chocolate, and peppermint essence in a medium-sized bowl.
- Prepare the pots by greasing 6 ramekins with butter.
- Pour the chocolate mixture into the pots evenly.
- Put the pots inside the slow cooker and put hot water below halfway up.
- Cook for 2 hours, high. Take the pots out of the slow cooker and leave to cool and set.
- Serve with a fresh mint leaf and whipped cream.

Creamy Vanilla Custard

NUTRITION Calories: 206, Carbs: 30g , Fat: 7g , Protein: 6g

PREPARATION COOKING TIME   SERVINGS

15   3   8

hours

DIRECTION

- Mix the cream, egg yolks, vanilla extract, and stevia in a medium-sized bowl.
- Pour the mixture into a heat-proof dish. Place the dish into the slow cooker.
- Put hot water into the pot, around the dish, halfway up. Set the temperature to high.
- Cook for 3 hours. Serve hot or cold!

INGREDIENTS

- 3 cups full-fat cream
- 4 egg yolks, lightly beaten
- 2 tsp vanilla extract
- Few drops of stevia

Coconut, Chocolate, and Almond Truffle Bake

NUTRITION Calories: 115 , Carbs: 8g , Fat: 10g , Protein: 2g

PREPARATION   COOKING TIME   SERVINGS
15   4   8
              hours

INGREDIENTS

- 3 ounces butter, melted
- 3 ounces dark chocolate, melted
- 1 cup ground almonds
- 1 cup desiccated coconut
- 3 tbsp. unsweetened cocoa powder
- 2 tsp vanilla extract
- 1 cup heavy cream
- A few extra squares of dark chocolate, grated
- ¼ cup toasted almonds, chopped

DIRECTION

- In a large bowl, mix the melted butter, chocolate, ground almonds, coconut, cocoa powder, and vanilla extract.
- Roll the mixture into balls. Grease a heat-proof dish.
- Place the balls into the dish—Cook for 4 hours, low setting.
- Leave the truffle dish to cool until warm. Mix the cream until soft peak.
- Spread the cream over the truffle dish and sprinkle the grated chocolate and chopped toasted almonds over the top. Serve immediately!

Peanut Butter, Chocolate, and Pecan Cupcakes

NUTRITION Calories: 145 , Carbs: 20g , Fat: 3g , Protein: 4g

PREPARATION   COOKING TIME   SERVINGS
15   4   14
              hours

DIRECTION

- Dissolve the dark chocolate plus coconut oil in the microwave, stir to combine, and set aside.
- Place the peanut butter and butter into a medium-sized bowl, microwave for 30 seconds at a time until the butter has just melted.
- Mix the peanut butter plus butter until combined and smooth.
- Stir the vanilla extract into the peanut butter mixture.
- Mix the ground almonds, eggs, baking powder, and cinnamon in a small bowl.
- Pour the melted chocolate and coconut oil evenly into the 14 paper cases.
- Spoon half of the almond/egg mixture evenly into the cases, on top of the chocolate and press down slightly.
- Spoon the peanut butter mixture into the cases, on top of the almond/egg mixture.
- Spoon the remaining almond/egg mixture into the cases.
- Put the pecans on top of each cupcake.
- Put the filled cases into the slow cooker—Cook for 4 hours, high setting.

INGREDIENTS

- 14 paper cupcake cases
- 1 cup smooth peanut butter
- 2 ounces butter
- 2 tsp vanilla extract
- 5 ounces dark chocolate
- 2 tbsp. coconut oil
- 2 eggs, lightly beaten
- 1 cup ground almonds
- 1 tsp baking powder
- 1 tsp cinnamon
- 10 pecan nuts, toasted and finely chopped

Vanilla and Strawberry Cheesecake

NUTRITION Calories: 156 , Carbs: 4g , Fat: 7g , Protein: 15g

INGREDIENTS

- Base:
- 2 ounces butter, melted
- 1 cup ground hazelnuts
- ½ cup desiccated coconut
- 2 tsp vanilla extract
- 1 tsp cinnamon
- Filling:
- 2 cups cream cheese
- 2 eggs, lightly beaten
- 1 cup sour cream
- 2 tsp vanilla extract
- 8 large strawberries, chopped

DIRECTION

- Mix the melted butter, hazelnuts, coconut, vanilla, and cinnamon in a medium-sized bowl.
- Press the base into a greased heat-proof dish.
- Mix the cream cheese, eggs, sour cream, and vanilla extract, beat with electric egg beaters in a large bowl until thick and combined.
- Fold the strawberries through the cream cheese mixture.
- Put the cream cheese batter into the dish, on top of the base, spread out until smooth.
- Put it in the slow cooker and put hot water around the dish until halfway up.
- Cook for 6 hours, low setting until just set but slightly wobbly.
- Chill before serving.

PREPARATION	COOKING TIME	SERVINGS
15	6 *hours*	8

Coffee Creams with Toasted Seed Crumble Topping

NUTRITION Calories: 35 , Carbs: 4g , Fat: 2g , Protein: 1g

INGREDIENTS

- 2 cups heavy cream
- 3 egg yolks, lightly beaten
- 1 tsp vanilla extract
- 3 tbsp. strong espresso coffee (or 3tsp instant coffee dissolved in 3tbsp boiling water)
- ½ cup mixed seeds – sesame seeds, pumpkin seeds, chia seeds, sunflower seeds,
- 1 tsp cinnamon
- 1 tbsp. coconut oil

DIRECTION

- Heat-up the coconut oil in a small frypan until melted.
- Add the mixed seeds, cinnamon, and a pinch of salt, toss in the oil and heat until toasted and golden, place into a small bowl and set aside.
- Mix the cream, egg yolks, vanilla, and coffee in a medium-sized bowl.
- Pour the cream/coffee mixture into the ramekins.
- Place the ramekins into the slow cooker. Put hot water inside until halfway.
- Cook on low setting for 4 hours.
- Remove, then leave to cool slightly on the bench.
- Sprinkle the seed mixture over the top of each custard before serving.

PREPARATION	COOKING TIME	SERVINGS
15	4 *hours*	6

Lemon Cheesecake

NUTRITION Calories: 271 , Carbs: 33g , Fat: 15g , Protein: 2g

INGREDIENTS

- 2 ounces butter, melted
- 1 cup pecans, finely ground in the food processor
- 1 tsp cinnamon
- 2 cups cream cheese
- 1 cup sour cream
- 2 eggs, lightly beaten
- 1 lemon
- Few drops of stevia
- 1 cup heavy cream

DIRECTION

- Mix the melted butter, ground pecans, and cinnamon until it forms a wet, sand-like texture.
- Press the butter/pecan mixture into a greased, heat-proof dish and set aside.
- Place the cream cheese, eggs, sour cream, stevia, zest, and juice of one lemon into a large bowl, beat with electric egg beaters until combined and smooth.
- Put the cream cheese batter into the dish, on top of the base.
- Place the dish inside the slow cooker, then put warm water in halfway up.
- Cook within 6 hours, low setting.
- Set the cheesecake on the bench to cool and set.
- Whip the cream until soft peak, and spread over the cheesecake before serving.

PREPARATION	COOKING TIME	SERVINGS
15	6 *hours*	*10*

Macadamia Fudge Truffles

NUTRITION Calories: 150 , Carbs: 19g , Fat: 6g , Protein: 6g

INGREDIENTS

- 1 cup roasted macadamia nuts, finely chopped
- ½ cup ground almonds
- 2 ounces butter, melted
- 5 ounces dark chocolate, melted
- 1 tsp vanilla extract
- 1 egg, lightly beaten

DIRECTION

- Place the macadamia nuts, almonds, melted butter, melted chocolate, vanilla, and egg into a large bowl, stir until combined.
- Grease the bottom of the crockpot by rubbing with butter. Place the mixture into the crockpot and press down.
- Set to cook low setting within 4 hours.
- Allow the batter to cool until just warm. Take a teaspoon, scoop the mixture out, and roll into balls.
- Refrigerate to harden slightly. Store the truffle balls in the fridge.

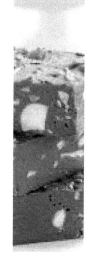

PREPARATION	COOKING TIME	SERVINGS
15	4 *hours*	*8*

Chocolate Covered Bacon Cupcakes

NUTRITION Calories: 185 , Carbs: 27g , Fat: 8g , Protein: 4g

INGREDIENTS

- 10 paper cupcake cases
- 5 slices streaky bacon, cut into small pieces, fried in a pan until crispy
- 5 ounces dark chocolate, melted
- 1 cup ground hazelnuts
- 1 tsp baking powder
- 2 eggs, lightly beaten
- ½ cup full-fat Greek yogurt
- 1 tsp vanilla extract

DIRECTION

- Mix the fried bacon pieces and melted chocolate in a bowl, set aside.
- Mix the ground hazelnuts, baking powder, eggs, yogurt, vanilla, and a pinch of salt in a medium-sized bowl.
- Spoon the hazelnut mixture into the cupcake cases.
- Spoon the chocolate and bacon mixture on top of the hazelnut mixture.
- Place the cupcake cases into the crock-pot. Cook for 3 hours, high setting.
- Remove the cupcakes from the pot and leave to cool on the bench before storing serving. Serve with whipped cream!

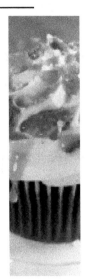

PREPARATION	COOKING TIME	SERVINGS
15	3 *hours*	*10*

Chocolate, Berry, And Macadamia Layered Jars

NUTRITION Calories: 150 , Carbs: 25g , Fat: 15g , Protein: 3g

INGREDIENTS

- 5 ounces dark chocolate, melted
- ½ cup mixed berries, (fresh) – any berries you like
- 3/4 cup toasted macadamia nuts, chopped
- 7 ounces cream cheese
- ½ cup heavy cream
- 1 tsp vanilla extract

DIRECTION

- Whisk the cream cheese, cream, and vanilla extract in a medium-sized bowl.
- Scoop a small amount of melted chocolate, put it into each jar or ramekin.
- Place a few berries on top of the chocolate.
- Sprinkle some toasted macadamias onto the berries. Scoop the cream cheese mixture into the ramekin.
- Place another layer of chocolate, berries, and macadamia nuts on top of the cream cheese mixture.
- Put the jars inside the slow cooker and put the hot water until it reaches halfway up.
- Set to low, then cook for 6 hours.
- Remove the jars and leave them to cool and set on the bench for about 2 hours before serving.

PREPARATION	COOKING TIME	SERVINGS
15	6 *hours*	6

Salty-Sweet Almond Butter and Chocolate Sauce

NUTRITION Calories: 200 , Carbs: 21g, Fat: 7g, Protein: 15g

INGREDIENTS

- *1 cup almond butter*
- *2 ounces salted butter*
- *1-ounce dark chocolate*
- *½ tsp sea salt*
- *Few drops of stevia*

DIRECTION

- Place the almond butter, butter, dark chocolate, sea salt, and stevia to the crockpot.
- Cook for 4 hours, high, stirring every 30 minutes to combine the butter and chocolate as they melt. Serve or store in a fridge.

PREPARATION	COOKING TIME	SERVINGS
15	4 *hours*	1

Coconut Squares with Blueberry Glaze

NUTRITION Calories: 115, Carbs: 20g, Fat: 3g, Protein: 3g

INGREDIENTS

- *2 cups desiccated coconut*
- *1-ounce butter, melted*
- *3 ounces cream cheese*
- *1 egg, lightly beaten*
- *½ tsp baking powder*
- *2 tsp vanilla extract*
- *1 cup of frozen berries*

DIRECTION

- Beat the coconut, butter, cream cheese, egg, baking powder, and vanilla extract, using a wooden spoon in a bowl until combined and smooth.
- Grease a heat-proof dish with butter. Spread the coconut mixture into the dish.
- Defrost the blueberries in the microwave until they resemble a thick sauce. Spread the blueberries over the coconut mixture.
- Put the dish into the slow cooker, then put hot water until it reaches halfway up the dish.
- Cook for 3 hours, high. Remove the dish from the pot and leave to cool on the bench before slicing into small squares.

PREPARATION	COOKING TIME	SERVINGS
15	3 *hours*	20

Chocolate and Blackberry Cheesecake Sauce

NUTRITION Calories: 200, Carbs: 18g, Fat: 13g, Protein: 3g

INGREDIENTS

- *¾ lb. cream cheese*
- *½ cup heavy cream*
- *1 ½ ounces butter*
- *3 ounces dark chocolate*
- *½ cup fresh blackberries, chopped*
- *1 tsp vanilla extract*
- *Few drops of stevia*

DIRECTION

- Place the cream cheese, cream, butter, dark chocolate, blackberries, vanilla, and stevia into the slow cooker.
- Place the lid onto the pot and set the temperature to low.
- Cook for 6 hours, stirring every 30 minutes to combine the butter and chocolate as it melts. Serve, or store in a fridge.

PREPARATION	COOKING TIME	SERVINGS
15	6 *hours*	1

Hot Fudge Cake

NUTRITION Calories 252, Fat 13 , Sodium 177 mg, Carbs 28 , Sugar 25 , Protein 3 g

INGREDIENTS

- *1¼ cup Sukrin Gold, divided*
- *1 cup almond flour*
- *¼ cup plus 3 Tbsp. unsweetened cocoa powder, divided*
- *2 tsp baking powder*
- *½ tsp. salt*
- *½ cup heavy cream*
- *2 Tbsp. melted butter*
- *½ tsp. vanilla extract*
- *1¾ cups boiling water*

DIRECTION

- *Mix ¾ cup Sukrin Gold, almond flour, cocoa, baking powder, and salt. Stir in heavy cream, butter, and vanilla. Put it inside the slow cooker.*
- *Mix ½ cup Sukrin Gold and ¼ cup cocoa, then sprinkle over the mixture in the slow cooker. Pour in boiling water. Do not stir.*
- *Cook 2–3 hours, high. Serve.*

PREPARATION	COOKING TIME	SERVINGS
25	3 *hours*	10

Fudgy Secret Brownies

NUTRITION Calories 421, Fat 38 , Sodium 113 m, Carbs 15 , Sugar 1 , Protein 8 g

INGREDIENTS

- 4 oz. unsweetened chocolate
- ¾ cup of coconut oil
- ¾ cup frozen diced okra, partially thawed
- 3 large eggs
- 36 stevia packets
- 1 teaspoon pure vanilla extract
- ¼ tsp. mineral salt
- ¾ cup coconut flour
- ½–¾ cup coarsely chopped walnuts or pecans, optional

DIRECTION

- Melt chocolate and coconut oil in a small saucepan. Put okra and eggs in a blender. Blend until smooth.
- Measure all other Ingredients: in the mixing bowl.
- Pour melted chocolate and okra over the dry Ingredients: and stir with a fork just until mixed.
- Pour into the greased slow cooker—cover and cook on high for 1½–2 hours.

PREPARATION	COOKING TIME	SERVINGS
10	2 *hours*	8

Black and Blue Cobbler

NUTRITION Calories 224, Fat 16 , Sodium 174 m, Carbs 21 , Sugar 8 g, Protein 7 g

INGREDIENTS

- 1 cup almond flour
- 36 packets stevia, divided
- 1 tsp baking powder
- ¼ tsp salt
- ¼ tsp ground cinnamon
- ¼ tsp ground nutmeg
- 2 eggs, beaten
- 2 Tbsp. whole milk
- 2 Tbsp. coconut oil, melted
- 2 cups fresh or frozen blueberries
- 2 cups fresh or frozen blackberries
- ¾ cup of water
- 1 tsp. grated orange peel

DIRECTION

- Combine almond flour, 18 packets stevia, baking powder, salt, cinnamon, and nutmeg.
- Combine eggs, milk, and oil. Stir into dry fixing. Put it inside the greased slow cooker.
- Mix the berries, water, orange peel, and remaining 18 packets stevia in a saucepan. Bring to boil. Remove from heat and pour over batter. Cook on 2–2½ hours, high. Let it cool within 30 minutes. Serve.

PREPARATION	COOKING TIME	SERVINGS
10	20 *hours*	6

Baked Custard

NUTRITION Calories 254, Fat 3 , Sodium 6 , Carbs 52 , Sugar 11 , Protein 4 g

INGREDIENTS

- 2 cups whole milk
- 3 eggs, slightly beaten
- 2½ Tsp., plus ¼ tsp., erythritol, divided
- 1 tsp. vanilla extract
- ¼ tsp. cinnamon

DIRECTION

- Heat milk in a small uncovered saucepan until a skin forms on top. Remove from heat and let cool slightly.
- Mix the eggs, 2½ tbsp. erythritol, and vanilla in a large bowl. Slowly stir cooled milk into the egg-erythritol mixture.
- Pour into a greased 1-qt baking dish which will fit into your slow cooker, or into a baking insert designed for your slow cooker.
- Mix cinnamon and 1/2 tsp reserved erythritol in a small bowl. Sprinkle over custard mixture.
- Cover baking dish or insert with foil—set the container on a metal rack or trivet in the slow cooker. Pour warm water around the dish to a depth of 1 inch.
- Cover cooker. Cook on High 2–3 hours, or until custard is set. Serve warm from baking dish or insert.

PREPARATION	COOKING TIME	SERVINGS
15	3 _hours_	6

Maple Pot de Crème

NUTRITION Calories 102, Fat 18 , Sodium 46 , Carbs 12 , Sugar 2 , Protein 5 g

INGREDIENTS

- 2 egg yolks
- 2 eggs
- 1 cup heavy cream
- ½ cup whole milk
- ½ cup plus 1 Tbsp. Sukrin Gold
- Pinch salt
- 1 tsp. vanilla extract
- ¼ tsp. ground nutmeg
- Whipped cream, for garnish, optional

DIRECTION

- Whisk the egg yolks plus eggs in a bowl until light and frothy.
- Add cream, milk, 1 tbsp. Sukrin Gold, salt, vanilla, and nutmeg. Mix well.
- Pour mixture in a baking dish and set it in a slow cooker. Carefully pour water around the baking dish until the water comes halfway up the sides.
- Cover cooker. Cook on high for 2–3 hours, until Pot de Crème is set but still a little bit jiggly in the middle.
- Wearing oven mitts to protect your knuckles, carefully remove the hot dish from the cooker. Set on a wire rack to cool to room temperature.
- Chill within 2 hours before you serve. Garnish with whipped cream if you wish.

PREPARATION	COOKING TIME	SERVINGS
15	3 _hours_	6

Slow-Cooker Pumpkin Pie Pudding

NUTRITION Calories 168, Fat 15 , Sodium 91 g, Carbs 22 g, Sugar 3 g, Protein 9 g

INGREDIENTS

- 15-oz. can solid pack pumpkin
- 12-oz. can evaporate milk
- ¼ cup plus 2 Tbsp. erythritol
- ½ cup keto-friendly baking mix
- 2 eggs, beaten
- 2 Tbsp. melted butter
- 1 Tbsp. pumpkin pie spice
- 2 tsp. vanilla extract

DIRECTION

- 1. Mix all Ingredients. Pour into the greased slow cooker.
- 2. Cook within 6–7 hours, high. Serve.

PREPARATION	COOKING TIME	SERVINGS
7	7 *hours*	6

Choco-peanut Cake

NUTRITION Calories: 60, Carbohydrates: 57g, Protein: 13g, Fat: 39g, Saturated Fat: 13g

INGREDIENTS

- 15.25 oz. devil's food cake mix
- 1 cup of water
- 1/2 cup salted butter, melted
- 3 eggs
- 8 oz. pkg. mini Reese's peanut butter cups
- For the topping
- 1 cup creamy peanut butter
- 3 Tbsp. powdered sugar
- Ten bite-size Reese's peanut butter cups

DIRECTION

- Mix the cake mixture, ice, butter, and eggs in a large bowl until smooth. Some lumps are all right, that's all right. Cut the cups of the mini peanut butter.
- Cleaner non-stick spray on the slow cooker. Add the butter slowly and spread over an even layer.
- Cover and cook on high during the cooking time for 2 hours without opening the lid.
- Melt the peanut butter over medium heat in a pan. Stir until melted and smooth; observe as it burns hard. To smooth, add the powdered sugar and whisk.
- Pour over the butter of the sweetened peanut in the cake, then serve.

PREPARATION	COOKING TIME	SERVINGS
15	2 *hours*	10

Crockpot Apple Pudding Cake

NUTRITION Calories 405, Fat 9g, Saturated Fat 3g, Carbohydrates 79g, Fiber 2g, Sugar 63g, Protein 3g

INGREDIENTS

- 2 cups all-purpose flour
- 2/3 plus 1/4 cup sugar, divided
- 3 tsp baking powder
- 1 tsp salt
- 1/2 cup butter cold
- 1 cup milk
- 4 apples, diced
- 1 1& /2 cups orange juice
- 1/2 cup honey
- 2 tbsp. butter melted
- 1 tsp cinnamon

DIRECTION

- Mix the flour, 2/3 cup sugar, baking powder, and salt. Slice the butter until you have coarse crumbs in the mixture.
- Remove the milk from the crumbs until moistened.
- Grease a 4 or 5 qtr. crockpot's bottom and sides. Spoon the batter into the crockpot's bottom and spread evenly. Place the diced apples evenly over the mixture.
- Whisk together the orange juice, honey, butter, remaining sugar, and cinnamon in a medium-sized pan. Garnish the apples.
- Place the crockpot opening with a clean kitchen towel, place the lid on, it prevents condensation from reaching the crockpot from the cover.
- Place the crockpot on top and cook until apples are tender for 2 to 3 hours. Serve hot.

PREPARATION	COOKING TIME	SERVINGS
15	3 *hours*	10

Crockpot Brownie Cookies

NUTRITION Calories 452, Fat 21, Saturated Fat 7, Carbohydrates 59, Sugar 38, Protein 5g

INGREDIENTS

- One box brownie mix
- Two eggs
- 1/4 c butter melted
- 1/2 c mini chocolate chips
- 1/2 c chopped walnuts optional
- 8 slices cookie dough slices

DIRECTION

- *Combine your brownie mixture with butter, eggs, chocolate chips, and nuts.*
- *Sprinkle with non-stick spray the inside of your crockpot. Place eight slices of ready-made cookie dough or pile tbsp. of it on the bottom.*
- *In your slow cooker, pour brownie mixture on top and smooth out evenly. Put on the lid and cook on top for 2 hours.*
- *To get both textures in your meal, scoop from the middle out to the edge for each serving. If desired, serve warm for best results, top with ice cream.*

PREPARATION	COOKING TIME	SERVINGS
15	2 *hours*	10

Crockpot Chocolate Caramel Monkey Bread

NUTRITION Calories: 337, Fat: 16g, Saturated Fat: 4g, Carbohydrates: 44g, Fiber: 1g, Sugar: 12g , Protein: 5g

INGREDIENTS

- 1/2 tbsp. sugar
- 1/4 tsp ground cinnamon
- 15 oz. buttermilk biscuits
- 20 milk chocolate-covered caramels
- Caramel sauce for topping (optional)
- Chocolate sauce for topping (optional)

DIRECTION

- Mix sugar and cinnamon and set aside. Fill a parchment paper crockpot, cover up to the bottom.
- Wrap 1 buttermilk biscuit dough around one chocolate candy to cover the candy completely, pinching the seam closed.
- Place the biscuit-wrapped candy in the crockpot bottom, start in the middle of the crockpot and work your way to the sides.
- Continue to wrap candy and put it in the crockpot, leaving roughly 1/2 inch between each. Repeat these steps with sweets wrapped in the second layer of biscuit.
- Sprinkle the remaining cinnamon-sugar mixture on top when using all the dough and confectionery.
- Cover the crockpot and cook for 1 1/2 hours on the lower side. Once cooked, remove the lid and let cool slightly.
- Use the edges of the parchment paper to lift the monkey bread out of the crockpot. Allow cooling for at least 10-15 minutes.
- Cut off any excess parchment paper around the edge when ready to serve. In a shallow bread or bowl, put monkey bread and drizzle with chocolate and caramel sauces.

PREPARATION	COOKING TIME	SERVINGS
15	1 30	6
	hours mins	

Slow Cooker Coffee Cake

NUTRITION Calories: 41, Carbohydrates: 56g, Protein: 6g, Fat: 19g, Saturated Fat: 3g, Fiber: 2g, Sugar: 33g

INGREDIENTS

- 2 1/2 cups of all-purpose flour
- 1 & 1/2 cups of brown sugar
- 2/3 cup vegetable oil
- 1 1/3 cups almond milk
- Two teaspoons baking powder
- 1/2 teaspoon baking soda
- One teaspoon ground cinnamon
- One teaspoon white vinegar
- One teaspoon salt
- Two eggs
- 1/2 cup chopped nuts optional

DIRECTION

- In a large bowl, whisk in flour, brown sugar, and salt. Remove the oil until it is crumbly mixed.
- In the flour mixture, combine the baking powder, baking soda, and cinnamon with a wooden spoon or spatula. In a measuring cup, place milk, oil, eggs, and vinegar and whisk until the eggs are pounded, then add to the flour mixture and stir until mixed.
- Spray a non-stick cooking spray 5-7Qt slow cooker or line with a slow cooker liner. Pour into the crockpot with the batter.
- Sprinkle the cake batter's nuts over the end. Put a paper towel over the crockpot insert and place the lid on top of it.
- Cook within 1 hour and 30 minutes, high s or 2 hours, and 30 minutes.
- Serve warm directly from the crockpot or store for up to 3 days in an airtight container.

PREPARATION	COOKING TIME	SERVINGS
15	2.5	12
	hours	

Slow Cooker Apple Pear Crisp

NUTRITION Calories: 267, Carbohydrates: 27g, Protein: 3g, Fat: 17g, Saturated Fat: 7g , Fiber: 4g, Sugar: 16g.

INGREDIENTS

- Four apples, peeled and cut into 1/2-inch slices
- 3 Bosc pears, peeled and cut into 1/2-inch slices
- 1/3 cup light brown sugar
- One tablespoon all-purpose flour
- One tablespoon lemon juice
- 1/2 teaspoon ground cinnamon
- 1/4 teaspoon kosher salt
- Pinch of ground nutmeg
- For the Topping:
- 3/4 cup all-purpose flour
- 3/4 cup old fashioned oats
- 1/2 cup chopped pecans
- 1/3 cup light brown sugar
- 1/2 teaspoon ground cinnamon
- 1/2 teaspoon kosher salt
- Eight tablespoons unsalted butter, cut into cubes

DIRECTION

- Combine flour, oats, pecans, sugar, cinnamon, and salt to make the topping. Press the butter into the dry fixing until it looks like coarse crumbs; set aside.
- Coat lightly with a non-stick spray inside a 4-qt slow cooker: put apples and pears in the slow cooker. Add brown sugar, flour, juice of lemon, cinnamon, salt, and nutmeg. Sprinkle with reserved topping, gently pressing the crumbs into the butter using your fingertips.
- Layer the slow cooker with a clean dishtowel. Cover and cook for 2-3 hours at low heat or 90 minutes at high temperature, remove the dishtowel and continue to cook, uncovered until the top is browned and apples are tender for about 1 hour. Serve cold.

PREPARATION	COOKING TIME	SERVINGS
15	4 hours	8

Key Lime Dump Cake Recipe

NUTRITION Calories: 28, Carbohydrates: 58g, Protein: 2g, Fat: 4g, Saturated Fat: 2g, Sugar: 41g

INGREDIENTS

- 15.25 oz. Betty Crocker French Vanilla Cake Mix box
- 44 oz. Key Lime Pie Filling
- 8 tbsp. or 1/2 cup butter melted

DIRECTION

- Spray inside the Crock-Pot with a non-stick cooking spray. Empty key lime pie cans filling in the Crock-Pot bottom and then spread evenly.
- Mix the dry vanilla cake mix with the dissolved butter in a bowl.
- Pour the crumble cake/butter mixture over the crockpot, spread evenly, and cover the crockpot with the lid.
- Cook for 2 hours at high or 4 hours at low. Serve with ice cream or whip cream.

PREPARATION	COOKING TIME	SERVINGS
15	2 hours	8

Crockpot Cherry Dump Cake Recipe

NUTRITION Calories 56, Fat 17g, Saturated Fat 11g, Carbohydrates 98g, Fiber 1g, Sugar 37g, Protein 3g

INGREDIENTS

- 15.25 oz. Betty Crocker Devil's Food Cake Mix
- 42 oz. Cherry Pie Filling
- 1/2 cup butter melted

DIRECTION

- Spray with a non-stick cooking spray inside the crockpot.
- Empty cherry pie filling cans into crockpot's bottom, then evenly spread out.
- Combine dry cake mix with butter in a medium bowl.
- Pour the crumble cake/butter mixture over the crockpot plus cherries, scatter
- Evenly, and cover the crockpot with a lid.
- Cook for 2 hours at high, or 4 hours at low. Use ice cream or whip cream to serve.

PREPARATION	COOKING TIME	SERVINGS
15	2 *hours*	8

Crockpot Pumpkin Spice Cake Recipe

NUTRITION Calories: 34, Fat: 30.38, Carbohydrate: 10.03, Fiber: 5.61g, Protein: 8.26g

INGREDIENTS

- 15.25 oz. Betty Crocker Spice Cake Mix
- 15 oz. Libby's Pure Pumpkin
- ½ cup Applesauce
- Three eggs
- 1 tsp. Pumpkin Pie Spice

DIRECTION

- Whisk all the fixing with a mixer for 1 minute. Spray with nonstick cooking spray inside the crockpot.
- Pour over and cover the mixture into the crockpot.
- Cook for 1.5 – 2 hours or until finished. Serve.

PREPARATION	COOKING TIME	SERVINGS
15	2 *hours*	8

Crockpot Blueberry Dump Cake Recipe

NUTRITION Calories: 34, Fat: 30.38, Carbohydrate: 10.03, Fiber: 5.61, Protein: 8.26g

INGREDIENTS

- 15.25 oz. Betty Crocker Lemon Cake Mix
- 42 oz. Blueberry Pie Filling
- 1/2 cup butter melted

DIRECTION

- Spray with non-stick cooking spray the crockpot. Put blueberry pie filling evenly into the bottom of the crockpot.
- In a mixing bowl, combine dry lemon cake mix with melted butter and stir until crumbly. Break some big chunks into the crumbles of a small spoon.
- Pour the crumble cake/butter mixture over the blueberry mixture into crockpot, spread evenly, and cover with a lid the crockpot.
- Cook at high for 2 hours, and at low for 4 hours. Serve.

PREPARATION	COOKING TIME	SERVINGS
15	2 *hours*	8

Crockpot Strawberry Dump Cake Recipe

NUTRITION Calories: 34, Fat: 30.38, Carbohydrate: 10.03g, Fiber: 5.61g, Protein: 8.26g

INGREDIENTS

- 15.25 oz. Betty Crocker Strawberry Cake Mix
- 42 oz. Strawberry Pie Filling
- 1/2 cup butter melted

DIRECTION

- Spray with a non-stick cooking spray inside the crockpot.
- Put the Strawberry Pie Filling into the crockpot's bottom and spread evenly.
- Combine strawberry dry cake mixture with the butter in a mixing bowl.
- Pour the cake/butter crumbled mixture into crockpot over strawberries and spread evenly, covering the crockpot with a lid.
- Cook for 2 hours at high, or 4 hours at low. Serve.

PREPARATION	COOKING TIME	SERVINGS
15	2 *hours*	8

Crockpot Baked Apples Recipe

NUTRITION Calories: 121, Fat 3, Carbohydrates 48, Fiber 5, Sugar 36, Protein 1g.

INGREDIENTS

- *Five medium Gala apples*
- *½ cup Quaker Old Fashioned Oats*
- *½ cup Brown Sugar*
- *3 tsp. Cinnamon*
- *1 tsp. Allspice*
- *1/4 cup butter*

DIRECTION

- Pour 1/4 cup of water at crockpot's edge.
- Use a sharp knife to carefully core apples.
- Mix the oats, cinnamon, brown sugar, and allspice. Fill a single apple with a mixture of oats, sugar, and spice.
- Use a butter pat to top each apple. Set in crockpot carefully and put the lid on crockpot.
- Cook for 3–4 hours or until finished.

PREPARATION	COOKING TIME	SERVINGS
15	4 *hours*	6

Sugar-Free Chocolate Molten Lava Cake

NUTRITION Calories 15, Fat 13, Carbs 10.5, Protein 3.9g

INGREDIENTS

- *1/2 cup hot water*
- *1-ounce chocolate chips, sugar-free*
- *1/4 teaspoon vanilla liquid stevia*
- *1/4 teaspoon vanilla extract*
- *1 egg yolk*
- *1 whole egg*
- *2 tablespoons butter melted, cooled*
- *1/4 teaspoon baking powder*
- *1/8 teaspoon salt*
- *3 ¾ teaspoons cocoa powder, unsweetened*
- *2 tablespoons almond flour*
- *6 tablespoons Swerve sweetener divided*

DIRECTION

- Grease the slow cooker, mix the flour, baking powder, 2 tablespoons cocoa powder, almond flour, and 4 tablespoons of Swerve in a bowl.
- In a separate bowl, stir in eggs with melted butter, liquid stevia, vanilla extract, egg yolks, and eggs.
- Mix the wet fixing to the dry ones and combine to incorporate fully. Pour the mixture into the slow cooker.
- Top the mixture with chocolate chips.
- Mix the remaining swerve with cocoa powder and hot water in a separate bowl, and pour this mixture over chocolate chips.
- Cook on low within 3 hours. Once done, let cool and then serve.

PREPARATION	COOKING TIME	SERVINGS
15	3 *hours*	3

Blueberry Lemon Custard Cake

NUTRITION Calories 14, Fat 9.2, Carbs 7.3, Protein 3.9g

INGREDIENTS

- 2 tablespoons fresh blueberries
- 1/2 cup light cream
- 1/8 teaspoon salt
- 2 tablespoons Swerve sweetener
- 1/4 teaspoon lemon liquid stevia
- 1 1/3 tablespoon lemon juice
- 1/2 teaspoon lemon zest
- 2 tablespoons coconut flour
- 1 ½ egg separated

DIRECTION

- Put egg whites into a stand mixture and whip to achieve stiff peaks consistency.
- Set the egg whites aside, whisk the yolks and the other Ingredients: apart from the blueberries.
- Mix the egg whites into the batter to thoroughly combine, and then grease the slow cooker.
- Put the batter into it, then top with the blueberries—Cook within 3 hours, low.
- Let cool when not covered for 1 hour, then keep it chilled for at least 2 hours or overnight.
- Serve the cake topped with unsweetened cream if you like.

PREPARATION	COOKING TIME	SERVINGS
15	7 *hours*	12

Slow-Cooked Pumpkin Custard

NUTRITION calories 70, fat 1, fiber 1, carbs 4, protein 6

INGREDIENTS

- 2 large eggs
- 2 tablespoons butter or coconut oil
- Dash sea salt
- 1/2 teaspoon pumpkin pie spice
- 1/4 cup superfine almond flour
- 1/2 teaspoon vanilla extract
- 1/2 cup pumpkin puree
- 1/4 cup granulated stevia

DIRECTION

- Grease a crockpot with butter or coconut oil and set aside. With a mixer, break the eggs into a mixing bowl, and blend until incorporated and thickened.
- Gently beat in the stevia, then add in vanilla extract and pumpkin puree. Then blend in pumpkin pie spice, salt, and almond flour.
- Once almost incorporated, stream in coconut oil, ghee, and melted butter. Mix until smooth, then move the mixture into a crockpot.
- Put a paper towel over the slow cooker to help absorb condensed moisture and prevent it from dripping on your pumpkin custard. Then cover with a lid.
- Now cook on low for 2 hours to 2 hours 45 minutes, and check the content after two hours elapse.
- Serve the custard with whipped cream sweetened with a little stevia and a sprinkle of nutmeg if you like.

PREPARATION	COOKING TIME	SERVINGS
15	2 45 *hours* *mins*	3

Almond Flour Mocha Fudge Cake

NUTRITION Calories 20, Carbs 5., Protein 6, Fat 18g

INGREDIENTS

- 1/8 teaspoon Celtic sea salt
- 1/3 teaspoon vanilla or chocolate extract
- 3 tablespoons hot coffee
- 1/3 teaspoon baking soda
- 6 tablespoons blanched almond flour
- 3 tablespoons sour cream
- 3/4 oz. unsweetened chocolate, melted
- 1 egg
- 1 tablespoon butter or coconut oil
- 6 tablespoons Swerve

DIRECTION

- Grease the crockpot with oil. Then beat coconut oil and natural sweetener in a bowl until fully incorporated.
- Beat in eggs, cream and chocolate. In a bowl, sift baking soda and almond flour and add in the chocolate mixture.
- Then beat in coffee, salt, and vanilla until well incorporated. Once done, pour the batter into the cooking pot of the slow cooker.
- Cook on low for 2 to 4 hours or until a toothpick inserted in the cake comes out clean.

PREPARATION	COOKING TIME	SERVINGS
15	4 *hours*	3

Slow Cooker Bread Pudding

NUTRITION Calories 18, Fat 2g, Carbs 11g, Protein 8g

INGREDIENTS

- 1 tablespoons raisin
- 1/2 teaspoon cinnamon
- 1 1/2 teaspoon vanilla extract
- 1/4 cup swerve
- 1 egg white
- 1 whole egg
- 1 1/2 cups almond milk
- 4 slices of pumpkin bread

DIRECTION

- Slice the pumpkin bread into pieces. Then mix all the rest of the fixing in the slow cooker.
- Cook within 4 to 5 hours, then serve.

PREPARATION	COOKING TIME	SERVINGS
15	6 *hours*	2

Tiramisu Bread Pudding

NUTRITION Calories 19, Fat 9, Protein 6.7, Carbs 9g

INGREDIENTS

- *3/4 teaspoons unsweetened cocoa*
- *1/3 teaspoon vanilla extract*
- *2 tablespoons mascarpone cheese*
- *Cooking spray*
- *3 1/4 cups Keto bread*
- *1 large egg, lightly beaten*
- *ounces of almond milk, divided*
- *3/4 tablespoons Kahlua (coffee-flavored liqueur)*
- *1 3/4 teaspoons instant espresso granules*
- *2 tablespoons coconut sugar*
- *1.6-ounce water*

DIRECTION

- Mix the water, coconut sugar, plus instant espresso granules in a saucepan.
- Boil while occasionally stirring for 1 minute, remove, then mix in the Kahlua liqueur.
- Whisk the eggs, then the almond milk in a large bowl. Mix in the espresso mixture into it.
- Put the Keto friendly bread into a greased casserole. Cook it inside the slow cooker within 2 hours, low.
- Mix vanilla, mascarpone cheese plus the remaining almond milk in a bowl.
- Garnish with cocoa and serve.

PREPARATION	COOKING TIME	SERVINGS
15	7 *hours*	*12*

Crock Pot Sugar-Free Dairy-Free Fudge

NUTRITION Calories 6, Fat 5g, Carbs 2g, Protein 1g

INGREDIENTS

- *A dash of salt*
- *Dash of pure vanilla extract*
- *½ tablespoon coconut milk*
- *4 tablespoons sugar-free chocolate chips*
- *1/4 teaspoons vanilla liquid stevia*

DIRECTION

- *Mix in coconut milk, stevia, vanilla, chocolate chips plus salt in a slow cooker.*
- *Cook within 2 hours, then let it sit within 30 minutes.*
- *Mix in within 5 minutes. Put the batter in a casserole dish with parchment paper.*
- *Chill, then serve.*

PREPARATION	COOKING TIME	SERVINGS
15	3 *hours*	2

Poppy Seed-Lemon Bread

NUTRITION Calories 295, Fat 24.3g, Carbs 17.9g, Protein 6.0g

INGREDIENTS

- 1/2 cups almond flour
- 1/4 tbsp. baking powder
- 1 tbsp. poppy seeds
- 1 egg
- 1/4 cup coconut sugar
- 1/8 tsp salt
- 2 tbsp. vegetable oil
- 3 tbsp. tofu (puree)
- 1/4 cup almond milk
- 3/4 cup plain Greek-style yogurt
- 1/4 cup lemon juice
- 3/4 tsp shredded lemon peel
- 1/4 tsp vanilla

DIRECTION

- Grease the slow cooker using a non-stick cooking spray.
- Mix the poppy seeds, flour, salt, and baking powder in a bowl, then put it aside.
- Mix the tofu puree, sugar, oil, milk, yogurt, lemon juice, lemon peel, and vanilla in a medium bowl.
- Put the sugar batter to the flour batter, then mix.
- Transfer it in the slow cooker, then cook on high for 1 and 30 minutes to 2 hours, or until set.
- Leave for 10-15 minutes to cool. then serve.

PREPARATION	COOKING TIME	SERVINGS
15	2 *hours*	3

Nutmeg-Infused Pumpkin Bread

NUTRITION Calories 159, Carbs 21g, Fat 65g, Protein 4g, Calories 147, Fat 12g, Carbs 4g, Protein 5g

INGREDIENTS

- 0.5 oz. unsalted pecan pieces, toasted
- 1/4 tablespoon pure vanilla extract
- 1 tablespoon safflower oil
- 1 egg white
- 2 tablespoons plain Greek yogurt
- 1/4 cup cooked and puréed pumpkin
- 1/8 teaspoon sea salt
- Dash ground allspice
- 1/4 teaspoon ground nutmeg
- Dash teaspoon baking soda
- 1/2 teaspoon baking powder
- 2 tablespoons coconut sugar
- 7 tablespoons almond flour
- 2 tablespoons dried apple cranberries, unsweetened
- 3 tablespoons 100% apple juice, plain
- Olive oil cooking spray

DIRECTION

- Lightly grease a non-stick loaf pan with cooking spray. Set aside.
- Mix cranberries and apple juice in a small saucepan, heat the mixture on high to boil.
- Remove, then let cool for around 10 minutes.
- Then mix nutmeg, baking soda, allspice, baking powder, salt, maple sugar flakes, and flour in a large bowl. Set aside.
- Now mix vanilla, oil, egg whites, yogurt, pumpkin, and the cranberry mixture in a medium bowl.
- To the flour mixture, add the pecans and cranberry-pumpkin mixture and stir to incorporate fully.
- Spoon the batter into the pan, and use a rubber spatula or back of a spoon to smooth the top.
- Arrange a rack inside a crockpot to elevate the pan, and then put the pan on top.
- Cook within 3 hours, high.
- Cool it down within 10 minutes, before slicing, then serve.

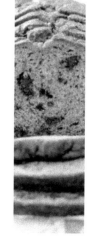

PREPARATION	COOKING TIME	SERVINGS
15	3 *hours*	4

Chapter 18. Other Recipes

Citrus Rich Cabbage

NUTRITION Calories 145, Total Fat 13.1 g, Saturated Fat 9.1 g, Cholesterol 96 mg , Sodium 35 mg , Total Carbs 4 g , Sugar 1.2 g, Fiber 1.5 g , Protein 3.5 g

INGREDIENTS

- 1 lb. green cabbage, shredded
- ½ cup of chicken stock
- A pinch of salt and black pepper
- 1 tablespoon of lemon juice
- 1 tablespoon of chives, diced
- 1 tablespoon of lemon zest (grated)

DIRECTION

- Start by throwing all the Ingredients: into the Crockpot.
- Cover its lid and cook for 3 hours on Low setting.
- Once done, remove its lid of the crockpot carefully.
- Mix well and garnish as desired.
- Serve warm.

PREPARATION	COOKING TIME	SERVINGS
10	3 *hours*	2

Herb Mixed Radish

NUTRITION Calories 266, Total Fat 26.9 g , Saturated Fat 15.8 g , Cholesterol 18 mg , Sodium 218 mg , Total Carbs 2.5 g , Sugar 0.4 g , Fiber 0.2 g , Protein 4.5 g

INGREDIENTS

- 3 cups of red radishes, halved
- ½ cup of vegetable broth
- 2 tablespoons of basil, diced
- 1 tablespoon of oregano, diced
- 1 tablespoon of chives, diced
- 1 tablespoon of green onion, diced
- A pinch of salt and black pepper

DIRECTION

- Start by throwing all the Ingredients: into the Crockpot.
- Cover its lid and cook for 3 hours on Low setting.
- Once done, remove its lid of the crockpot carefully.
- Mix well and garnish as desired.
- Serve warm.

PREPARATION	COOKING TIME	SERVINGS
10	3 *hours*	4

Creamy Mustard Asparagus

NUTRITION Calories 149, Total Fat 14.5 g , Saturated Fat 8.1 g, Cholesterol 56 mg, Sodium 56 mg, Total Carbs 10.6 g, Sugar 0.3 g, Fiber 0.2 g, Protein 2.6 g

INGREDIENTS

- 1 lb. asparagus, trimmed and halved
- 2 teaspoons of mustard
- ¼ cup of coconut cream
- 2 garlic cloves, minced
- 1 tablespoon of chives, diced
- Salt and black pepper- to taste

DIRECTION

- Start by throwing all the Ingredients: into the Crockpot.
- Cover its lid and cook for 3 hours on Low setting.
- Once done, remove its lid of the crockpot carefully.
- Mix well and garnish as desired.
- Serve warm.

PREPARATION	COOKING TIME	SERVINGS
10	3 *hours*	2

Savory Pine Nuts Cabbage

NUTRITION *Calories 145 , Total Fat 13.1 g , Saturated Fat 9.1 g , Cholesterol 96 mg , Sodium 35 mg , Total Carbs 4 g, Sugar 1.2 g , Fiber 1.5 g, Protein 3.5 g*

PREPARATION	COOKING TIME	SERVINGS
10	2 hours	2

INGREDIENTS

- 1 savoy cabbage, shredded
- 2 tablespoons of avocado oil
- 1 tablespoon of balsamic vinegar
- ¼ cup of pine nuts, toasted
- ½ cup of vegetable broth
- Salt and black pepper- to taste

DIRECTION

- Start by throwing all the Ingredients: into the Crockpot.
- Cover its lid and cook for 2 hours on Low setting.
- Once done, remove its lid of the crockpot carefully.
- Mix well and garnish as desired.
- Serve warm.

Nutmeg Fennel

NUTRITION *Calories 244, Total Fat 24.8 g, Saturated Fat 15.6 g, Cholesterol 32 mg, Sodium 204 mg, Total Carbs 2.1 g , Sugar 0.4 g, Fiber 0.1 g, Protein 24 g*

PREPARATION	COOKING TIME	SERVINGS
10	3 hours	2

DIRECTION

- Start by throwing all the Ingredients: into the Crockpot.
- Cover its lid and cook for 3 hours on Low setting.
- Once done, remove its lid of the crockpot carefully.
- Mix well and garnish as desired.
- Serve warm.

INGREDIENTS

- 2 fennel bulbs, sliced
- 2 tablespoon of olive oil
- 4 garlic cloves, diced
- 2 tablespoons of balsamic vinegar
- 2 and ½ cups of baby spinach
- ½ teaspoon of nutmeg, ground
- ¼ cup of vegetable broth

Herbed Cherry Tomatoes

NUTRITION Calories 145, Total Fat 13.1 g, Saturated Fat 9.1 g, Cholesterol 96 mg, Sodium 35 mg, Total Carbs 4 g, Sugar 1.2 g, Fiber 1.5 g, Protein 3.5 g

PREPARATION	COOKING TIME	SERVINGS
10	1 *hours*	2

INGREDIENTS

- 4 garlic cloves, minced
- A pinch of salt and black pepper
- 2 lbs. Cherry tomatoes halved
- 2 tablespoon of olive oil
- 1 tablespoon of dill, diced
- ½ cups of chicken stock
- ¼ cup of basil, diced

DIRECTION

- Start by throwing all the Ingredients: into the Crockpot.
- Cover its lid and cook for 1 hour on Low setting.
- Once done, remove its lid of the crockpot carefully.
- Mix well and garnish as desired.
- Serve warm.

Viennese Coffee

NUTRITION Calories 231, Total Fat 32.9 g , Saturated Fat 6.1 g, Cholesterol 10 mg, Sodium 18 mg, Total Carbs 9.1 g, Sugar 2.8 g, Fiber 0.8 g, Protein 4.4 g

PREPARATION	COOKING TIME	SERVINGS
10	2.5 *hours*	2

DIRECTION

- Start by throwing all the Ingredients: into the Crockpot.
- Cover its lid and cook for 2.5 hours on Low setting.
- Once done, remove its lid of the crockpot carefully.
- Garnish with whipped cream.
- Serve warm.

INGREDIENTS

- 3 cups of strong brewed coffee
- 3 tablespoons of sugar-free chocolate syrup
- 1 teaspoon of stevia
- 1/3 cup of heavy whipping cream
- 1/4 cup of crème de cacao
- Whipped cream, optional

Ginger Tea Drink

NUTRITION Calories 179, Total Fat 15.7 g, Saturated Fat 8 g , Cholesterol 0 mg, Sodium 43 mg, Total Carbs 4.8 g , Sugar 3.6 g, Fiber 0.8 g, Protein 5.6 g

PREPARATION	COOKING TIME	SERVINGS
10	2 hours	4

INGREDIENTS

- 4 cups of boiling water
- 15 individual green tea bags
- 4 cups of white grape juice
- 1 to 2 tablespoons of honey
- 1 tablespoon of minced fresh ginger root
- Crystallized ginger, optional

DIRECTION

- Start by throwing all the Ingredients: into the Crockpot.
- Cover its lid and cook for 2 hours on Low setting.
- Once done, remove its lid of the crockpot carefully.
- Strain the slow-cooked tea into the glasses.
- Serve warm.

Hot Spiced Wine

NUTRITION Calories 220, Total Fat 20.1 g, Saturated Fat 7.4 g , Cholesterol 132 mg , Sodium 157 mg, Total Carbs 3 g, Sugar 0.4 g , Fiber 2.4 g, Protein 6.1 g

PREPARATION	COOKING TIME	SERVINGS
10	3 hours	2

INGREDIENTS

- 2 cinnamon sticks (3 inches)
- 3 whole cloves
- 3 medium pears, peeled and sliced
- 1/2 cup of stevia
- 2 cups of sugar-free apple juice
- 1 teaspoon of lemon juice
- 2 bottles (750 ml) dry red wine

DIRECTION

- Start by tying the whole spices in cheesecloth.
- Now place the tied spices along with all the Ingredients: into the Crockpot.
- Cover its lid and cook for 3 hours on Low setting.
- Once done, remove its lid of the crockpot carefully.
- Strain the slow-cooked tea into the serving glass.
- Serve warm.

Sweet Kahlua Coffee

NUTRITION *Calories 213, Total Fat 28.4 g, Saturated Fat 12.1 g , Cholesterol 27 mg, Sodium 39 mg, Total Carbs 9.2 g , Sugar 3.1 g, Fiber 4.6 g, Protein 8.1 g*

PREPARATION	COOKING TIME	SERVINGS
10	4 hours	4

DIRECTION

- Start by throwing all the Ingredients: into the Crockpot.
- Cover its lid and cook for 4 hours on Low setting.
- Once done, remove its lid of the crockpot carefully.
- Garnish with whipping cream and chocolate chips.
- Serve warm.

INGREDIENTS

- 2 quarts hot water
- 1/2 cup of Kahlua (coffee liqueur)
- 1/4 cup of crème de cacao
- 3 tablespoons of instant coffee granules
- 2 cups of heavy whipping cream, to garnish
- 1/4 cup of stevia
- 1 teaspoon of vanilla extract
- 2 tablespoons of sugar-free chocolate chips, to garnish

Crockpot Milk Tea

NUTRITION *Calories 214, Total Fat 19 g, Saturated Fat 5.8 g , Cholesterol 15 mg, Sodium 123 mg, Total Carbs 6.5 g , Sugar 1.9 g Fiber 2.1 g, Protein 6.5 g*

PREPARATION	COOKING TIME	SERVINGS
10	8 hours	12

DIRECTION

- Start by tying all the whole spices in cheesecloth.
- Now place the tied spices along with all other Ingredients: into the Crockpot.
- Cover its lid and cook for 8 hours on Low setting.
- Once done, remove its lid of the crockpot carefully.
- Strain the slow-cooked tea into the serving glasses.
- Serve warm.

INGREDIENTS

- 15 slices fresh ginger root (about 3 oz.)
- 3 cinnamon sticks (3 inches)
- 25 whole cloves
- 15 cardamom pods, lightly crushed
- 3 whole peppercorns
- 31/2 quarts water
- 8 black tea bags
- 1 cup of evaporated milk
- 2 tablespoons of stevia

Spiced Lemon Drink

NUTRITION Calories 158, Total Fat 35.2 g, Saturated Fat 15.2 g , Cholesterol 69 mg, Sodium 178 mg, Total Carbs 7.4 g, Sugar 1.1 g, Fiber 3.5 g, Protein 5.5 g

PREPARATION	COOKING TIME	SERVINGS
10	3 *hours*	4

INGREDIENTS

- 2 1/2 quarts water
- 2 cups of stevia
- 1 1/2 cups of lime juice
- 1/2 cup of plus 2 tablespoons of lemon juice
- 1/4 cup of cranberry juice
- 1 cinnamon stick (3 inches)
- 1/2 teaspoon of whole cloves

DIRECTION

- Start by tying all the whole spices in cheesecloth.
- Now place the tied spices along with all other Ingredients into the Crockpot.
- Cover its lid and cook for 3 hours on Low setting.
- Once done, remove its lid of the crockpot carefully.
- Strain the slow-cooked tea into the serving glasses.
- Serve warm.

Wrapped Avocado Sticks

NUTRITION Calories 198, Fat 17.4, Fiber 2, Carbs 2.9, Protein 8.1

PREPARATION	COOKING TIME	SERVINGS
15	2 *hours*	7

DIRECTION

- Cut the avocado into the medium sticks.
- Sprinkle the avocado sticks with the paprika and salt.
- Wrap the avocado sticks in the sliced bacon.
- Place the avocado sticks in the slow cooker and add the butter.
- Close the lid and cook the snack for 2 hours on High.
- Cool the cooked avocado sticks to room temperature and serve!

INGREDIENTS

- 5 oz. bacon, sliced
- 1 avocado, pitted
- 1 teaspoon paprika
- ½ teaspoon salt
- 2 tablespoons butter

Appendix: Measurements & Conversions

Abbreviations

Table spoon--tbsp.
Tea spoon---tsp.
Pound---lb.
Ounce---oz.
Gallon--gal.

Conversions

¼ teaspoon = 1 ml
½ teaspoon = 2 ml
1 teaspoon = 5 ml
1 tablespoon = 15 ml
¼ cup = 59 ml
½ cup = 118 ml
½ ounce = 15 g
1 cup = 235 ml
1 ounce = 30 g
2 ounces = 60 g
4 ounces = 115 g
8 ounces = 225 g
12 ounces = 340 g
16 ounces or 1 lb. = 455 g

Conclusion

Now you can cook healthier meals for yourself, your family, and your friends to get your metabolism running at the peak of perfection and help you feel healthy, lose weight, and maintain a healthy balanced diet. A new diet isn't so bad when you have so many options from which to choose. You may miss your carbs, but with all these tasty recipes at your fingertips, you'll find them easily replaced with new favorites.

You will marvel at how much energy you have after sweating through the first week or so of almost no carbs. It can be a challenge, but you can do it! Pretty soon, you won't miss those things that bogged down your metabolism as well as your thinking and made you tired and cranky. You will feel like you can rule the world and do anything once your body is purged of heavy carbs, and you start eating things that rejuvenate your body. It is worth a few detox symptoms when you start enjoying the food you are eating.

A Keto diet isn't one that you can keep going on and off. It will take your body some time to get adjusted and for ketosis to set in. This process could take anywhere between two to seven days. It is dependent on the level of activity, your body type and the food that you are eating.

There are various mobile applications that you can make use of for tracking your carbohydrate intake. There are paid and free applications as well. These apps will help you in keeping track of your total carbohydrate and fiber intake. However, you won't be able to track your net carb intake. MyFitnessPal is one of the popular apps. You just need to open the app store on your smartphone, and you can select an app from the various apps that are available.

The amount of weight that you will lose will depend on you. If you add exercise to your daily routine, then the weight loss will be greater. If you cut down on foods that stall weight loss, then this will speed up the process. For instance, completely cutting out things like artificial sweeteners, dairy and wheat products and other related products will definitely help in speeding up your weight loss. During the first two weeks of the Keto diet, you will end up losing all the excess water weight. Ketosis has a diuretic effect on the body, and you might end up losing a couple of pounds within the first few days of this diet. After this, your body will adapt itself to burning fats for generating energy, instead of carbs.

You now have everything you need to break free from a dependence on highly processed foods, with all their dangerous additives that your body interprets as toxins. Today, when you want a sandwich for lunch, you'll roll the meat in Swiss cheese or a lettuce leaf and won't miss the bread at all, unless that is, you've made up the Keto bread recipe you discovered in this book! You can still enjoy your favorite pasta dishes, even taco salad, but without the grogginess in the afternoon that comes with all those unnecessary carbs.

So, energize your life and sustain a healthy body by applying what you've discovered. You don't have to change everything at once. Just start by adopting a new recipe each week that sounds interesting to you. Gradually, swap out less-than-healthy options for ingredients and recipes from this book that will promote your well-being.

Each time you make a healthy substitution or try a new ketogenic recipe, you can feel proud of yourself; you are actually taking good care of your mind and body. Even before you start to experience the benefits of a ketogenic lifestyle, you can feel good because you are choosing the best course for your life.
Thanks for reading.

CPSIA information can be obtained
at www.ICGtesting.com
Printed in the USA
LVHW051243140121
676458LV00019B/645

9 781801 472432